# The World Trade Organization

# CHATHAM HOUSE PAPERS

A International Economics Programme Publication
Programme Head: Dr Benn Steil

The Royal Institute of International Affairs, at Chatham House in London, has provided an impartial forum for discussion and debate on current international issues for over 75 years. Its resident research fellows, specialized information resources, and range of publications, conferences, and meetings span the fields of international politics, economics, and security. The Institute is independent of government.

Chatham House Papers are short monographs on current policy problems which have been commissioned by the RIIA. In preparing the papers, authors are advised by a study group of experts convened by the RIIA, and publication of a paper indicates that the Institute regards it as an authoritative contribution to the public debate. The Institute does not, however, hold opinions of its own; the views expressed in this publication are the responsibility of the author.

# The World Trade Organization

## Constitution and Jurisprudence

*John H. Jackson*

THE ROYAL INSTITUTE
OF INTERNATIONAL
AFFAIRS

**Pinter**
*A Cassell Imprint*
Wellington House, 125 Strand, London WC2R 0BB, United Kingdom
PO Box 605, Herndon, VA 20172, USA

First published in 1998

**British Library Cataloguing in Publication Data**
A CIP catalogue record for this book is available from the British Library

**Library of Congress Cataloging in Publication Data**
A CIP catalogue record for this book is available from the Library of Congress

ISBN 1-85567-553-3 (Paperback)
     1-85567-652-5 (Hardback)

Typeset by Koinonia Limited
Printed and bound in Great Britain by
Biddles Limited, Guildford and King's Lynn

# Contents

*Contents*

# Foreword

Over the past ten years, the International Economics Programme (IEP) at Chatham House has made the development of international trade policy its core area of study and debate. As the agenda and the issues have widened, we have endeavoured to remain at the forefront. With a fully developed research and seminar programme in financial services liberalization and environmental economics, IEP has extended the boundaries of its public policy analysis and contributed to a wider and deeper understanding of tomorrow's most critical trade issues.

The publication which served most to establish our abiding interest and reputation in the trade policy area was John Jackson's 1990 book, *Restructuring the GATT System*. Jackson's concise and erudite volume defined the Chatham House ideal: melding scholarship with a keen appreciation for the importance and methods of public policy development. Nowhere was this more evident than in the final chapter, which laid the foundations for his proposed 'World Trade Organization'. The wealth of high-level testimony to the importance of this book in the creation and development of the actual WTO is an outstanding tribute to Jackson's impact.

1998 represents the GATT's fiftieth anniversary, and it is with considerable pleasure and pride that we are able to mark it with the publication of this important sequel. Like its predecessor, this new volume is full of valuable information and insights, and will undoubtedly establish itself quickly as the definitive reference on the WTO's founding, role, powers and structure.

Benn Steil
Head of the International Economics Programme, RIIA

# Acknowledgments

I would like to thank many individuals who provided able assistance in the preparation of this book. A number of colleagues and other scholars, as well as practitioners, have kindly assisted me with information and by reviewing various parts of draft manuscript material. Among these, I particularly thank William Davey, Director of the Legal Affairs Division of the WTO, and Debra Steger, Director of the Appellate Body Secretariat. Also appreciation goes to others in these divisions, including Werner Zdouc, Peter Van den Bossche, Roberto Echandi. I also wish to thank Professors Ernst-Ulrich Petersmann, Meinhard Hilf, and Thomas Cottier.

During the course of preparing this book, I have been very fortunate to have the able assistance of Erika J. Hrabec, and the diligent and able research assistance of a number of very capable law students at the University of Michigan. I also want to acknowledge with thanks the extraordinary secretarial, and administrative and research assistance provided to me by the University of Michigan Law School, and particularly its William W. Cook research funds.

J.J.

# About the author

John H. Jackson has been Hessel E. Yntema Professor of Law at the University of Michigan since 1983 and has a worldwide reputation as a leading authority on international trade law. He joined the Faculty of Law at Georgetown University, in Washington, DC, in 1998.

# Abbreviations

| | |
|---|---|
| ASEAN | Association of South East Asian Nations |
| BISD | Basic Instruments and Selected Documents |
| CPs | Contracting Parties |
| CU | customs union |
| DISC | Domestic Internal Sales Corporation |
| DSB | Dispute Settlement Body |
| DSU | Dispute Settlement Understanding |
| ECOSOC | (United Nations) Economic and Social Council |
| FOGS | functioning of the GATT system |
| FTA | free trade association |
| GATS | General Agreement on Trade in Services |
| GATT | General Agreement on Tariffs and Trade |
| GNG | Group on Negotiating Goods |
| GNS | Group of Negotiations on Services |
| ICITO | Interim Commission for the International Trade Organization |
| ICJ | International Court of Justice |
| IGOs | international governmental organizations |
| IMF | International Monetary Fund |
| IP | intellectual property |
| ITO | International Trade Organization |
| MAI | Multilateral Agreement on Investment |
| MC | Ministerial Conference |
| MFN | most favoured nation |
| MTN | Multilateral Trade Negotiations |
| MTO | Multilateral Trade Organization |

| | |
|---|---|
| NAFTA | North American Free Trade Agreement |
| NGOs | non-governmental organizations |
| NTMs | non-tariff measures |
| OECD | Organization for Economic Cooperation and Development |
| OTC | Organization for Trade Cooperation |
| PPA | Protocol of Provisional Application |
| TPRM | Trade Policy Review Mechanisms |
| TRIPS | Agreement on Trade-Related Aspects of Intellectual Property Rights |
| UR | Uruguay Round |
| USTR | United States Trade Representative |
| WIPO | World Intellectual Property Organization |
| WTO | World Trade Organization |

# Prefatory remarks

**Warren Lavorel, current Deputy Director General of the World Trade Organization, and former US Ambassador to the GATT for the Uruguay Round Negotiations.**

The creation of the World Trade Organization has been hailed by some commentators as the completion of the third pillar of the world economic system, taking its place beside the International Monetary Fund and the World Bank. The rationale behind such statements is that a stable international economic order is viewed as an essential ingredient in maintaining peace and avoiding the mistakes of the past. Never has this been more true for trade relations than at present, when technology is shrinking borders and increasing the interaction among nations, many of which are undergoing a difficult transition to a market economy.

Even if the WTO is barely three years old, it is becoming the chosen forum for negotiating many of the rules and for resolving disputes related to this process of 'globalization'. Already its Members have successfully negotiated major agreements on telecommunications and information technology, and they have an ambitious program for negotiations stretching into the next century. Over 100 disputes have been brought to the WTO, witness to the desire of the Members to resolve problems through persuasion and the rule of law rather than by means of power. Yet, too little is known, and much is misunderstood, about the role and functioning of the WTO. Rather than an intergovernmental forum for economic progress and the peaceful resolution of disputes it is viewed in some quarters as a threat to state sovereignty and national agendas.

Professor Jackson's volume should facilitate a better understanding of the WTO as an organization and aid in convincing doubters of the important role that the WTO is playing in the evolving world economy. For no one has a better understanding of the evolution of world trade law and the WTO as an organization than does John Jackson. I first learned about the GATT, the precursor of the WTO from an earlier work by him. We in the WTO have sought his opinion on a range of matters related to the organization, particularly its Dispute Settlement procedures, and, as an advisor to the Canadian Government, he contributed to drawing up the blueprint for the WTO. While the negotiators in the Uruguay Round may have altered it somewhat, the final edifice contains many of Professor Jackson's ideas, and we are all indebted to him.

**Hugo Paemen, Ambassador for the European Union to the United States, and formally Chief Negotiator for the European Community in the Uruguay Round.**

This is, in my opinion, the most authoritative comment published until now on the institutional results of the Uruguay Round negotiations and the one which trade negotiators and practitioners have been looking for.

In his erudite and clear way Professor Jackson explains how the GATT was transformed and integrated in the structure of the new World Trade Organization. He devotes special attention to the most innovative features of the new trading system, which is the dispute settlement procedure. He had himself worked extensively on this issue and one can say that the final shape which resulted from the negotiations has been largely inspired by his own thoughts on the subject.

**Ambassador John M. Weekes, Government of Canada, Ambassador the World Trade Organization, and negotiator for Canada at the Uruguay Round.**

When Trade Minister John Crosbie put forward Canada's proposals for a World Trade Organization in 1990 he did so out of the conviction that world trade was too important to be left to a provisional organization and that the trade rules needed a surer foundation.

In Geneva, under the urging of Director General Arthur Dunkel negotiators were coming to the conclusion that the existing institutional structure was an inadequate framework for the emerging results of the

Uruguay Round. The result, a compromise between the Canadian vision and the practical requirements of the negotiating situation, was typical of 50 years of incremental construction of the multilateral trading system. However, the creation of the WTO was more than just another step in the evolution of the system. It represents a major mutation which has irrevocably changed intergovernmental cooperation in the trade field, most importantly through regular meetings of ministers in the Ministerial Council and a predictable and definitive dispute settlement system, unprecedented in international law. John Jackson's book provides invaluable information for those who want to understand the new WTO and the role it will play in the future. Indeed Mr Crosbie and his advisors benefited from the advice of Professor Jackson in developing the Canadian proposal for the WTO.

# Chapter 1

# The Uruguay Round and the WTO: The new organization and its antecedents

## 1.1 Introduction

On 1 January 1995 a new international economic organization came into being. Depending on one's perspective, the World Trade Organization (WTO) is either a modest enhancement of the General Agreement on Tariffs and Trade (GATT) that preceded it, or a watershed moment for the institutions of world economic relations reflected in the Bretton Woods system.[1] After more than three years of the WTO's existence, it now looks highly probable that the latter conclusion will prevail. All this suggests that it is particularly fitting in 1998, the fiftieth anniversary year of the founding of GATT, for Chatham House to publish this book, which will begin in a small way to explore the many significant aspects of this new institution for international economic relations.

The Uruguay Round (UR) Agreement of the GATT/WTO has been described as 'the most important event in recent world economic history'.[2] In addition, the WTO is already being described as the 'central international economic institution', and nations are becoming ever more engaged with the detailed processes of the WTO, especially its dispute settlement procedures, than had been contemplated at the time of signing. Indeed, the WTO Agreement, including all its elaborate Annexes, is probably fully understood by no nation that has accepted it, including some of the richest and most powerful trading nations that are members.[3]

For twelve years preceding 1995, over 120 nations of the world[4] participated in the largest and most complex negotiation in history concerning international economics. The Round was launched formally under GATT auspices in Punta del Este, Uruguay, in September 1986 (after some years of preparation), with a Ministerial Declaration setting forth the agenda (see Appendix G). The Uruguay Round negotiating results were formally signed at Marrakesh, Morocco, on 15 April 1994 and were ratified by a sufficient number of nations to bring those results into force on 1 January 1995. The results are embodied in a 'document' of some 26,000 pages! Most of these pages are detailed schedules of tariffs, services trade and other concessions, but the basic texts of the Agreement alone can approach 1,000 pages.[5]

From its beginning, a most important objective of this trade round was to extend a GATT-type treaty rule-oriented discipline to three new subject areas: trade in services, agriculture product trade, and intellectual property matters. Of these three, services and intellectual property were truly new for the GATT. Although the GATT had always formally applied to agriculture product trade, for a variety of reasons this sector had largely escaped GATT discipline. Attempts to bring it 'into the GATT fold' had failed in the two previous negotiating rounds (the Kennedy Round of 1962–67 and the Tokyo Round of 1973–79).[6]

In addition, the 1986 Punta declaration expressed priority for subsidy rules, changes in the dispute settlement procedures, new attention to the problems of textile trade and more elaboration of rules relating to product standards. A number of other measures were also targeted for attention.[7]

The Uruguay Round result is remarkably fulfilling of the original intentions, although with some gaps. A list of the important achievements of the Round includes:[8]

(1) *Services* The services agreement (GATS – General Agreement on Trade in Services) is a major new chapter in GATT history. Although in some ways flawed, it offers an overall 'umbrella' concept for trade in services that, it is hoped, will allow an ongoing negotiating process (probably lasting at least fifty years) for additional detail to occur. For more than a decade, various policy groups and interested enterprises had foreseen the need for some kind of international rule discipline for trade in services. The service 'sector' is extraordinarily complex, consisting of some 150 specific service sectors,[9] but in the aggregate services are beginning to represent a larger portion of gross domestic product of many of the Western industrialized countries than the production of goods. Service providers have begun to encounter government actions designed to restrict their commercial activity and presence, and so they have begun to urge an international cooperative mechanism that would develop rules against such protectionist activity. The Uruguay Round text must be deemed a worthy beginning.

(2) *Intellectual property* The TRIPS agreement (Trade Related Intellectual Property) is an excellent new achievement, bringing new international rule discipline to the level of protection for patents, copyrights, trade secrets and similar intellectual property subjects, even though some of the specialists or particular interest groups appear disappointed by certain gaps in the text.

(3) *Agriculture* The result in agriculture is in many respects meagre, certainly as measured against the 1986 Punta del Este (and US!) aspirations. Nevertheless, there is now some realistic expectation for trade rule discipline over agricultural trade (especially subsidies and border quantitative restrictions). Like many subjects of the Uruguay Round, further attention will be needed over the years ahead, but the Uruguay Round achieved an important beginning which is already impacting on national agricultural policies.

(4) *Subsidies/countervailing duties* Results include a new subsidies 'Code', again not without flaw, but with an overall conceptual approach that improves the Tokyo Round code. Worries about this text focus on the ambiguity of several 'exceptions' clauses which could lead to abuse.

(5) *Textiles* For decades, trade in textiles has escaped normal GATT discipline and has been governed by a byzantine fine set of embarrassing rules providing quantitative restrictions that are actually inconsistent with the normal GATT rules. The Uruguay Round provides a 'phase-out' agreement for the special textile regime, to be accomplished over a decade. Again, many feel the Textile Agreement is flawed – the phase-out is considered either too slow or too fast – but the direction seems right.

(6) *Standards* Trade rules for product standards have been further addressed, after the accomplishment of the Tokyo Round Code. It has become obvious that standards questions are much more complex than many thought, with some fundamental policy differences (such as the clash of environmentalist interests with trade policy goals, and questions about which government institutions should make decisions regarding difficult scientific evidence).

(7) *Safeguards* One of the major failures of the Tokyo Round in 1979 was its inability to achieve an agreement on safeguards and escape clause measures. Here the Uruguay Round succeeded where the Tokyo Round failed, and a very impressive and ambitious Safeguards Code is part of the UR results. This not only provides guidelines and criteria for normal escape clause use, but also establishes a rule against the use of voluntary export restraints of various kinds. If this agreement is satisfactorily implemented, it could be a needed addition to world trading discipline.

(8) *Market access* The Uruguay Round results include impressive advances in so-called 'market access', with a reduction in the use of quotas (and a shift from quotas to tariffs), as well as very substantial tariff-cutting (some say the most of any round). Some of the most substantial tariff-cutting has been accomplished by developing countries, but there have also been some important achievements in reducing tariffs of certain industry sectors to zero for important groups of countries.

(9) *Integration of developing countries and economies in transition* Developing countries are more fully integrated into the GATT/WTO system than before, with a requirement that all countries have tariff and service schedules, and with constraints on certain less developed country (LDC) exceptions. This measure could be one of the most important features of the Uruguay Round result, bringing a discipline at least to the 'newly industrializing countries', (NICs), and the 'economies in transition'. A 'soft membership' track through sponsorship of newly independent states has been eliminated to avoid certain abuses.

(10) *Preshipment and rules of origin* Several interesting additions to the international trade rules are contained in a new treaty text of the Uruguay Round relating to pre-shipment inspections and to rules of origin. The text on pre-shipment inspections is designed to allow governments to establish procedures whereby a foreign buyer can obtain an inspection of goods ordered before those goods are shipped, with the possibility of a certification that the goods meet contractual criteria and standards, and to prevent fraud. But the text is also designed to prevent such procedures from being abused for discriminatory or other purposes. The text on rules of origin, although fairly limited (but calling for further negotiation of such rules with a 'work program for the harmonization' of such rules), sets out certain disciplines during a transition period. Particularly relevant to regional preference arrangements, rules of origin are recognized to have the potential to damage the principles of liberal trade.[10]

(11) *Regional trade agreements* One of the more troublesome chapters of the GATT is its provisions (in Article XXIV) regarding free trade agreements, customs unions and interim agreements leading to a free trade area (FTA) or customs union (CU). This article grants a rather broad exception to some of the GATT rules, especially the most-favoured nation (MFN) principle of non-discrimination, for agreements that meet certain criteria spelled out in the article. Because the criteria are not very precise, the GATT discipline on regional trade agreements has been quite loose and has been subject to dispute and possible abuse. The UR texts take a small first step towards the creation of greater discipline

in this regard, providing some definitions and interpretations of clauses in GATT Article XXIV.

(12) *GATT grandfather rights* Because the GATT had been applied only 'provisionally' (a concept I explore in Chapter 2), there existed a certain number of 'grandfather rights', derived from a treaty clause in the Protocol of Provisional Application that allowed certain 'existing legislation' to prevail legally over certain GATT rules. These exceptions created some difficulties and perceptions of unfairness. With the new WTO and its 'definitive' application of treaty rules, these grandfather rights have now been abolished although some of them reappear in other legal forms.[11]

(13) *Dispute settlement procedures* Despite its 'birth defects', one of the many achievements of the GATT has been the four-decade development of a reasonably sophisticated dispute settlement process. However, a certain number of flaws have been recognized in these procedures. The Uruguay Round, for the first time, establishes an overall unified dispute settlement system for all portions of the UR Agreements, and a legal text (rather than just customary practice) to carry out those procedures. These new procedures include measures to avoid 'blocking', which occurred under previous consensus decision-making rules, and for the first time a new 'appellate procedure', which will replace some of the procedures that were vulnerable to blocking.

(14) *WTO Charter* Finally, one of the interesting achievements of the Uruguay Round is the development of a new institutional Charter for an organization that will help facilitate international cooperation concerning trade and economic relations, and will fundamentally change the GATT system to accommodate the vast new terrain of trade competence thrust on the trading system by the Uruguay Round. Some people have even said that this may be the most important element of the Uruguay Round result.

Interestingly enough, the original 1986 Punta del Este agenda did not refer to the possibility of a new international trade organization. Official proposals for such an organization were first made early in 1990. It was only in the December 1991 composite draft text of potential treaty clauses of the various UR negotiating groups[12] that there was included in the official negotiating draft texts a tentative draft agreement for a new organization, at that time titled 'Multilateral Trade Organization' (MTO). This draft had a number of flaws which were recognized by some governments, but through hard work the negotiators were able to revise the draft and iron out most of them. Thus, in the December 1993 (nearly) final draft of the Uruguay Round, a 'Charter' for the new organization – retitled the World Trade Organization – was agreed, and later came into force.

The objective of this short book[13] will be to focus on the 'constitution' of the WTO, in the broad meaning of the word 'constitution'. That is, it will consider the institutional structure of the WTO, including the structure of the organization, its treaty base, its very important procedures for dispute settlement, and the relationship of these to GATT, its predecessor. It will not be feasible here to go into the many substantive issues of international trade policy and regulation that are contained in the Uruguay Round results.[14] Instead, the intent is to present an overview of the institutional and 'constitutional' aspects of the WTO, which provide an 'umbrella' for the whole treaty with its many intricacies. In that sense, this book is sort of a sequel to my 1990 Chatham House Paper entitled *Restructuring the GATT System.*[15]

## 1.2 The policy reasons supporting the establishment of a new organization

Many factors[16] supported the ultimate decision of the UR negotiators to establish a new organization. It was thought that a new WTO Charter would assist a better implementation of the Uruguay Round results, and offer a better institutional structure to fill the 'Bretton Woods Gap'.

There are a number of particular characteristics and advantages of the new WTO Charter. First, the Charter for the WTO can be described as a 'mini-charter'. It is devoted to the institutional and procedural structure that will facilitate and in some cases be necessary for effective implementation of the substantive rules that have been negotiated in the Uruguay Round. The WTO is *not* an ITO (the 1948 draft charter for an International Trade Organization which never came into force).[17] The WTO Charter text itself does not include substantive rules, but it incorporates the substantive Agreements resulting from the Uruguay Round into 'Annexes'. In many cases criticisms aimed at the WTO during the implementation debates are really criticisms aimed at some of the substantive provisions of the UR results, and should not be considered a criticism of the WTO institutional Charter as such. Incidentally, the word 'charter' is not used officially in the Uruguay Round Agreement, but is often used informally, and similarly in this book, to describe the portion of that agreement set out at the beginning of the 'Final Act' of Marrakesh, entitled 'Agreement Establishing the World Trade Organization'.[18]

Second, the WTO will essentially continue the GATT institutional ideas and many of its practices, in a form better understood by the public, media, government officials and lawyers. To some extent, a number of the GATT 'birth defects' are overcome in the WTO.[19] The WTO Charter (XVI:I) expressly states the organization's intention to be guided by GATT 'decisions, procedures and customary practices' to the extent feasible. The practice of consensus is better defined and for the first time becomes a legal procedure in some important decisions, rather than just a practice. The 'guidance' clause of the WTO Charter emphasizes the importance of the records from the GATT period, some of which are already basic to WTO diplomatic and jurisprudential thinking.[20]

Third, the WTO structure offers some important advantages for assisting the effective implementation of the Uruguay Round. For example, a 'new GATT 1994' was created to supersede the 'old GATT 1947'. This procedure avoided the constraints of the amending clause of the old GATT, which might have made it quite difficult to bring the Uruguay Round into legal force. At the same time, the WTO ties together the various texts developed in the Uruguay Round and reinforces the 'single package' idea of the negotiators (namely, that countries accepting the Uruguay Round must accept the entire package, with a few exceptions). No longer will the Tokyo Round approach of side codes, resulting in 'GATT *à la carte*', be the norm.

Fourth, the WTO Charter establishes (for the first time) the basic explicit legal authority for an organization, a Secretariat, and a Director-General and staff. It does this in a way similar to many other international organizations, and it also provides the explicit obligation for nations to avoid interfering with the officials of the organization.[21]

Fifth, another important aspect of the WTO structure is that it facilitates the extension of the institutional structure (GATT-like) to the new subjects negotiated in the Uruguay Round, particularly services and intellectual property. Without some kind of legal mechanism such as the WTO, this would have been quite difficult to do since the GATT itself applies only to goods. The new structure separates the institutional concepts from the substantive rules. The GATT 1994 remains a substantive Agreement as a WTO Annex (with many of the amendments and improvements developed throughout its history, including in the Uruguay Round). However the WTO has a broader context. Similarly, the WTO will be able to apply a unified dispute settlement mechanism, and the Trade Policy Review Mechanism, to all of the subjects of the Uruguay Round, for all nations that become members.

Sixth, the WTO Charter may offer better opportunities for the future evolution and development of the institutional structure for international trade cooperation. Even though the WTO Charter is minimalist, the fact that there is provision for explicit legal status and the traditional organizational structure helps in this regard. With the WTO focusing on the institutional side, it could also offer more flexibility for future inclusion of new negotiated rules or measures which can help nations to face the constantly emerging problems of world economics. However, the many constraints on the power and authority of the WTO could also be a source of hesitancy and even stalemate, as we discuss later.

### 1.3 Policy and jurisprudential implications of the new organization

It is probably impossible to over-estimate the importance and profound implications that the WTO is bringing to diplomacy and international economic relations. Already various shifts in diplomatic attitudes and negotiating strategies have been reported as a result of the WTO and its new dispute settlement procedures. Many perplexing new questions are being raised. Many of these will be addressed in this book, but not so many can be answered definitively. For example, I shall briefly explore the allocation of power among the various bodies and institutions of the WTO. I shall also look at the legal relationship between the WTO and its predecessor the GATT. Similarly, I shall touch upon some of the tensions between competing policies, such as those between liberal trade policies on the one hand and increased surveillance over product safety and environmental concerns on the other. I shall also explore the nature of the new dispute settlement system, which in some ways is proving very formidable and is certainly being utilized extensively. Some diplomats seem quite apprehensive about this new procedure and its 'automaticity', which will be considered later. Finally, I shall briefly look at some of the future dilemmas and problems facing the organization, and speculate about the direction the organization may take. In a number of chapters, the issue that is sometimes called 'giving up sovereignty' will be addressed.

The growing importance of the new organization and its institutional/ constitutional procedures is evidenced by its activities and growth during its first three years. For example, as of May 1998 the number of members of the WTO had grown to 132;[22] there are also about thirty nations still negotiating for membership. It seems reasonably clear that few nations of the world feel they can stay out of this organization. This is a recognition of the growing globalization of economic affairs, and the apparent need of nation-states for some kind of an overall institutional structure to assist in resolving many of the problems that are being thrust upon them by such globalization. Already, over 100 disputes have been formally brought to the WTO under its new dispute settlement procedures.

The WTO Charter calls for a ministerial meeting not less frequently than every two years, and the first of these meetings was held in Singapore in December 1996.[23] Although not an overwhelming success, the results of this meeting, including the various discussions leading to policy compromises, have had considerable implications for the future. Furthermore, shortly after the Singapore meeting, nations concluded an important agreement relating to 'Trade and Technology Goods and Services', and an astonishing fundamental agreement relating to tele-communications.[24] Many other activities and negotiations are scheduled for the new organization in the near future.

## 1.4 The jurisprudence questions

Increasingly in recent years, one has heard references to 'international economic law'.[25] Unfortunately, this phrase is not well defined. Various scholars and practitioners have differing ideas about its meaning. Some would have it cast a very wide net, and embrace almost any aspect of international law that relates to any sort of economic matter. Considered broadly, almost all international law could be called international economic law, because almost every aspect of international relations touches in one way or another on economics. Indeed, it can be argued from the latter observation that there cannot be any separate subject denominated as 'international economic law'.

A more restrained definition of 'international economic law' would, however, embrace trade, investment, services when they are involved in transactions that cross national borders, and those subjects that involve the establishment on national territory of economic activity of persons or firms originating from outside that territory.

In any event it is clear that the subject of international trade, whether in goods or in services (or both), is at the core of international economic law. This book focuses on the institutional rules for the world trade in products and services, but the implications of those rules for other subjects of international economic relations should be obvious. The rules of product trade, centrally served by the GATT, are the most complex and extensive international rules that exist regarding any subject of international economic relations. As such, it is natural that they would have some influence on the potential development of rules for other international economic subjects,[26] particularly the subjects developed in the Uruguay Round context, including services and intellectual property. In addition, there is mention of a 'GATT for investment' and the possibility of a WTO approach for certain other subjects.

A critical question, almost always asked by anyone confronted with an international law rule, is 'Why do they matter?' Put another way, there exists much cynicism about the importance or effectiveness of international law rules. Frequently the public can read of violations of such rules by major and minor nations. In some cases such violations, even when admitted to be such (often there is bitter and inconclusive argument on this question), are rationalized or declared 'just' by national leaders.[27] Thus the cynicism about international rules cannot be surprising.

A more careful examination of the role and effectiveness of international rules is necessary, however. First, it should be observed that not all domestic rules are always obeyed either. And there are many international rules that are remarkably well observed. Why this is so has been the subject of much speculation[28] which will not be gone into here. Notions of reciprocity and a desire to depend on other nations' observances of rules lead many nations to observe rules even when they do not want to.

At least in the context of economic behaviour, however, and particularly when that behaviour is set in circumstances of decentralized decision-making, as in a market economy, rules can have important operational functions. They may provide the only predictability or stability to a potential investment or trade development situation. Without such predictability or stability, trade or investment flows might be even more risky and therefore more inhibited than otherwise. If such 'liberal trade' goals (for reasons already discussed in Section 1.2) contribute to world welfare, then it follows that rules which assist such goals should also contribute to world welfare. To put it another way, the policies that tend to reduce some risks lower the 'risk premium' required by entrepreneurs to enter into international transactions. I return to some of these ideas at the end of the book.

## 1.5 Organization and content of this book

As noted above, this book focuses on the institutional and jurisprudential aspects of the World Trade Organization. Considerable attention has been given to institutions by economists,[29] political scientists and those in other disciplines. Some scholars of these other subjects note the very great importance that institutions have for perplexities of economic development, war and peace policies, and generally questions of 'good governance'. Many of the fascinating broader contexts of this subject can be examined only in other works, but they clearly justify a close look at the institutional aspects of the WTO, which already, with only three years' experience, promise to be extraordinarily important and are already having profound effects on diplomacy and government policy in many nations. This book will briefly address these institutional and jurisprudential questions in three main chapters.

Chapter 2 will take up the historical antecedents and context of the WTO, how it evolved from the GATT, and the role (and defects) of GATT as a *de facto* organization and part of the post-Second World War 'Bretton Woods System'. It will explore the origins of the GATT, the contours of the GATT, the policy divergences within the GATT concerning a rule-oriented or negotiation/power-oriented system, the history of the Uruguay Round itself, and the implementation of the results of that Round.

Chapter 3 will then turn to the WTO 'Charter' and the institutional structure of the WTO, looking at, *inter alia,* the legal basis of the organization and its relation to the substantive texts in the Annexes and the overall organizational structure of the WTO with its Ministerial Conference and four 'Councils' which make up the most powerful of its subordinate bodies. It will also explore questions of decision-making power and the allocation of such power with its various constraints and checks and balances. It will look at membership questions, including questions concerning some countries currently negotiating to become members. And it will examine the role of the WTO in international law, and its relationship to other organizations such as the UN, IMF and WIPO.

Chapter 4 will explore the vital and dramatic contours of the new dispute settlement procedures and rules, perhaps the most important part of the new organization. This will include an historical overview of the development of the dispute settlement procedures in GATT, the outlines of the new Uruguay Round Dispute Settlement Understanding (DSU), and the workings of the various bodies such as the dramatic new appeal procedure, the legal effects of actions and reports of the dispute settlement bodies, questions of implementation of the results of dispute settlement procedures, and the relationship of all this to other international organizations including regional trade structures such as the NAFTA.

Finally, Chapter 5 will draw some tentative conclusions and point to problems looming in the near and more distant future.

# Chapter 2

# Bretton Woods, the ITO, the GATT and the WTO

## 2.1 Introduction

Looking back over the 1947–96 history of the General Agreement on Tariffs and Trade allows one to reflect on how surprising it was that this relatively feeble institution with many 'birth defects' managed to play such a significant role for almost five decades.[1] It certainly was far more successful than could have been predicted in the late 1940s.

The GATT, often described as the major trade organization and the principal treaty for trade relations, was technically neither. As a treaty, it never came into force, but was always (until 1995) applied 'provisionally' by the Protocol of Provisional Application (PPA).[2] In addition, technically the GATT was not intended to be an organization. The negotiators, in the drafting conferences in 1946 (New York), 1947 (Geneva) and 1948 (Havana), expected the International Trade Organization that was to be created by their draft treaty-charter to be the institutional framework to which the GATT (an agreement among 'contracting parties' to liberalize trade restrictions) would be attached. When the US Congress refused to approve the ITO Charter and that charter was declared dead by 1951, the GATT, which came into (provisional) force in 1948 by the terms of the PPA, became the focus of attention as a possible institution through which nations could solve some of their trade problems. An attempt in 1955 to create a small mini-organization to solve institutional problems also failed. Yet the GATT, through a series of major trade rounds designed gradually to reduce tariffs and other trade barriers (culminating in the Uruguay Round, which was the eighth round), along with an increasingly important set of relatively precise (and complex) rules, was able to achieve an astonishing amount of world trade liberalization. It would be hard to avoid the realistic conclusion that the GATT, as it actually operated, falls well within any reasonable definition of 'international organization', despite the original intent of the draftspersons.

World economic developments have pushed the GATT to an even more central role during the 1980s and 1990s. Ten or twenty years ago very few people, even in the advanced industrial societies, would have known about the 'GATT', or recognized its name. Currently, however, the GATT and its various activities often figure prominently on the front pages of the major newspapers of the world. However, the relative lack of institutional treaty clauses, and the ambiguity of those that were contained in the GATT, became increasingly troublesome as the GATT grew in scope and detail to cope with a fascinating set of concrete problems of international economic relations.

The growing economic interdependence of the world has been increasingly commented upon. Events that occur halfway round the world have a powerful influence on the other side of the globe. Armed conflict and social unrest in the Middle East affect farmers in Iowa and France and automobile workers in Michigan and Germany. Interest rate decisions in Washington have a profound influence on the external debt of many countries of the world, which, in turn, affects their ability to purchase goods made in industrial countries and their ability to provide economic advancement to their citizenry. Environmental problems have obvious cross-border effects. More and more frequently, government leaders find their freedom of action circumscribed because of the impact of external economic factors on their national economies.

Although the world has been blessed with fifty years of relative freedom from armed conflict (the two world wars were separated by only twenty years), there is a fundamental basic concern about the actions necessary to 'preserve the peace'. The relationship between economic trends and armed conflict has always been recognized and, thus, the implementation of international economic policy has a potentially powerful influence on the fundamental goals of current international relations – avoidance of armed conflict. Yet, often economic affairs are left to technical persons or ministries charged with less 'global objectives', so that there is a continuing risk of forgetting these linkages.

Because of the strange and quirky beginnings of the GATT, the institution suffered from a number of relatively serious 'constitutional defects'. Indeed, given the increasingly accelerated pace of change in economic relations in the world, the faster flow of economic influences across national borders and the increasing intricacy, and thus difficulty, of understanding a variety of economic influences, many persons began to question whether the existing international institutions, particularly the GATT, would be able to cope with the new problems arising in the world.

The GATT was (and is) part of a broader system – the 'Bretton Woods System', which includes the major monetary institutions (the IMF and the World Bank) as well as a number of other treaty instruments. This entire system needs to be examined, since the GATT is only one part of the whole. However, that task is beyond the scope of this short study.

The purpose of this study is to examine the institutional and 'constitutional' structure of the WTO, in the context of a number of fundamental issues and problems facing the world's principal international trade regime, and to suggest possible revisions in that structure. By 'constitutional', I mean the institutions and the basic treaty structure of the WTO, and its relationship to the GATT, and its decades of decisions, reports and treaty instruments.[3] It is this larger landscape that forms the 'constitution' of the world's trading system as we can observe it today. It is also this rather vast network that adds considerably to the complexity and difficulty of understanding of the institution. I have published other works relevant to this topic,[4] and the present study will draw extensively upon the works already done, although shaping the text for some of the particular questions which it is designed to address.

This chapter will present the background into which the new WTO was placed. Obviously, this requires looking at the GATT and the general context of the Bretton Woods system. This history, as noted in Chapter 1, has a particularly strong significance in the case of the WTO. The negotiators who created the WTO were eager to preserve the 'jurisprudence', or what in the context of the European Community is often called the *'acquis'* or acquired practice and experience, of the previous institution. Thus, as noted in Chapter 1, 'the WTO shall be guided by the decisions, procedures and customary practices' followed by the GATT.

This 'guidance' language may look fairly straightforward, but in actual practice it cannot be understood without understanding some of the context of GATT history, including the problems and 'birth defects' of the GATT. In addition, it is useful to set forth at least a brief overview of some of the principles and rules of the GATT (still in effect through the WTO treaty), and then to look at the history of the Uruguay Round as it reflects on the significant new institutional structures of the trading system. In a similar fashion, this chapter will identify a few important jurisprudential issues that will influence the further development of the WTO and will be discussed in the context both of the institutional structure of the WTO as an organization (Chapter 3), and of the more rigorous dispute settlement procedure (Chapter 4).

## 2.2 History of the GATT and its birth defects

The major initiatives leading towards the GATT were taken by the United States during the Second World War, in cooperation with its allies, particularly Great Britain.[5] There were two distinct strands of thought that influenced those countries during the war period.[6] One of these stemmed from the programme of trade agreements begun by the United States after the enactment of the 1934 Reciprocal Trade Agreements Act. With this Act the US Congress (responding to the unfortunate 1930 Smoot Hawley Tariff Act) delegated to the US President power to enter into reciprocal agreements to lower tariffs. Under this authority, renewed from time to time, by 1945 the United States had entered into 32 bilateral agreements reducing tariffs. Later versions of these agreements contained most of the substantive clauses later found in the GATT.

The second strand of thinking during the Second World War period stemmed from the view that the mistakes concerning economic policy during the interwar period (1920–1940) were a major cause of the disasters that led to the Second World War. The Great Depression was blamed in part for the war, as was the harsh reparations policy towards Germany.[7] In this interwar period, particularly after the damaging 1930 US Tariff Act, nations took many protectionistic measures, including quota restrictions, which choked off international trade. Political leaders of the United States and elsewhere made statements about the importance of establishing postwar economic institutions that would prevent these mistakes from happening again.

The Bretton Woods conference, held in 1944, was devoted to monetary and banking issues, and it established the Charters of the International Monetary Fund (IMF) and the World Bank (International Bank for Reconstruction and Development), but it did not take up the problems of trade as such. The conference was held under the jurisdiction of ministries of finance, while trade was under the competence of different ministries. (It is interesting to speculate, in the light of these trade conferences, how history might have been different if the Bretton Woods conference had indeed taken up the entire subject matter of economic relations including trade.) Nevertheless, the 1944 conference is on record as recognizing the

15

need for a comparable institution for trade, to complement the monetary institutions.[8]

The two strands of thinking about an organization for international trade began to merge in 1945. In the United States, the Congress enacted the 1945 renewal of the reciprocal trade agreements legislation for a three-year period.[9] In December of that year the US government invited a number of other nations to enter into negotiations to conclude a multi-lateral agreement for the mutual reduction of tariffs. In the same year the United Nations was formed, and in February 1946 its subordinate body, ECOSOC, at its first meeting adopted a resolution calling for a conference to draft a charter for an 'International Trade Organization'.[10] The United States at this time published a draft ITO Charter, and a preparatory committee was formed and met in October 1946 in London.

The principal meeting was held in Geneva from April to November 1947, and was followed by a meeting to complete the ITO Charter in Havana, Cuba in 1948.

The history of the preparation of GATT is intertwined with the preparation of the ITO Charter. The 1947 Geneva meeting was actually an elaborate conference in three major parts. One part was devoted to continuing the preparation of a charter for a major international trade institution, the ITO. A second part was devoted to the negotiation of a multilateral agreement to reduce tariffs reciprocally. A third part concentrated on drafting the 'general clauses' of obligations relating to the tariff obligations. These two latter parts together would constitute the General Agreement on Tariffs and Trade.

The 'general clauses' of the draft GATT imposed obligations on nations to refrain from a variety of trade-impeding measures. Many of these clauses had evolved in the US bilateral trade agreements, and were seen as necessary to protect the value of any tariff-reducing obligations.[11] The GATT, however, was not intended to be an organization. Indeed, US negotiators were criticized by committees of the US Congress during 1947 for tentatively agreeing to clauses which seemed to imply an organization. The US President and his negotiators recognized that an ITO Charter would have to be submitted to Congress for approval. But from the US point of view, the GATT was being negotiated under authority of the 1945 extension of the trade agreements authority. The congressional committees pointed out that this 1945 Act did not authorize the President to enter into an agreement for an organization – it only authorized agreements to reduce tariffs and other restrictions on trade. So the US negotiators returned to Geneva and redrafted the general

GATT clauses to avoid the suggestion of an organization. Thus, multilateral decisions under GATT were taken by the 'CONTRACTING PARTIES acting jointly', and not by any 'organization' body.[12]

The Geneva negotiators in 1947 pursued the goal of preparing a draft ITO Charter (to be completed at Havana in 1948), and also of negotiating elaborate schedules of tariff reductions appended to the 'general clauses' of GATT. These schedules consisted of thousands of individual tariff commitments applied to all GATT members through the most favoured nation (MFN) obligation.[13]

Since the GATT was designed to be merely a multilateral treaty, it would be similar to the bilateral treaties that preceded it, but designed to operate under the umbrella of the ITO, when the ITO came into being. The general clauses of GATT were the same as those in the chapter of the draft ITO charter which was devoted to trading rules, which in turn had been heavily influenced by clauses in bilateral trade treaties. In concept, the parallel GATT clauses would be revised to bring them into conformity with those of the ITO Charter,[14] when the latter came into being.

The Havana Conference in 1948 completed the draft ITO Charter, but the ITO never came into effect, because the US Congress failed to approve it. The US President submitted the Havana Charter (ITO draft) to the Congress in mid-1948, but after several years it became clear that the Congress would not approve the Charter, and in 1951 the President announced that he would no longer seek approval.[15] The irony was that it was the United States that had taken the principal initiative to develop the ITO Charter in the first place.

How is it that the GATT as such never came into force, and yet came to be known as the principal institution of international trade? The answer technically lies in the Protocol of Provisional Application (PPA), through which the GATT was applied as a treaty obligation under international law. This situation was a direct result of the history outlined above, but it takes some further explaining.

The GATT was completed by October 1947. Although it was to be subordinated to the ITO, the ITO Charter was to be finished only later, in 1948. Yet many negotiators felt that the GATT should be brought into force much sooner, for two main reasons. First, although the tariff concessions were still secret, the negotiators knew that the content of the concessions would begin to be known. World trade patterns could thus be seriously disrupted if a prolonged delay occurred before the tariff concessions came into force.[16]

Second, US negotiators were acting under the authority of the US trade legislation which had been renewed in 1945, under which they would not need to submit the GATT to Congress. But the 1945 Act expired in mid-1948.[17] Thus, there was a strong motivation on the part of the United States to bring the GATT into force before this Act expired. It was unlikely that this could be done if the participants in these events waited until after the 1948 Havana Conference and the completion of the ITO Charter.

On the other hand, there were several difficult problems involved in bringing the GATT into force. Some could be handled by amending the GATT at a later date to bring it into conformity with the results of the later Havana Conference. However, some nations had constitutional procedures under which they could not agree to parts of the GATT without submitting this Agreement to their parliaments. Since they anticipated the need to submit the final draft of the ITO Charter to their parliaments in late 1948 or the following year, they feared that to spend the political effort required to get the GATT through the legislature might jeopardize the later effort to get the ITO passed; they preferred to take both Agreements to their legislatures as a package.[18]

The solution agreed upon was the adoption of the Protocol of Provisional Application.[19] By this protocol eight nations agreed to apply the GATT 'provisionally on and after 1 January 1948', while the remaining members of the twenty-three original GATT countries would do so soon after. The Protocol contained several other important clauses which resulted in changing the impact of the GATT itself.

The much more important impact of the PPA, however, was its manner of implementing the GATT. Parts I and III of GATT were fully implemented without a PPA exception, but the PPA called for implementation of Part II 'to the fullest extent not inconsistent with existing legislation'. Part I contained the MFN and the tariff concession obligations, while Part III was mainly procedural. Part II (Articles III–XXIII) contained most of the major substantive obligations, including those relating to customs procedures, quotas, subsidies, anti-dumping duties and national treatment. As to these important obligations, each GATT Contracting Party was entitled to 'grandfather rights' for any provision of its legislation existing when it became a party which was inconsistent with a GATT Part II obligation.

Since the ITO did not come into being, a major leg was missing from the furniture intended for post-Second World War international economic institutions – the 'Bretton Woods' system. It was only natural that that institution that did exist – the GATT – would find its role changing dramatically as nations turned to it as a forum to handle an increasing number of problems concerning their trading relationships. More countries became Contracting Parties (CPs). Because of the fiction that the GATT was not an 'organization', there was considerable reluctance at first to delegate any activity even to a 'committee'. Gradually that reluctance faded, and soon there was even an 'Intersessional Committee'[20] which met between sessions of the CONTRACTING PARTIES.

No secretariat existed for the GATT. After the 1948 Havana Conference, however, an 'Interim Commission for the ITO' (ICITO) was set up in the typical pattern of preparing the way for a new international organization. A small staff was assembled to prepare the ground for the ITO, and this staff[21] serviced the needs of the GATT. As years passed and it became clear that the ITO was never to come into being, this staff found that all of its time was devoted to the GATT, and it became de facto the GATT secretariat. (Technically, it was sort of a 'leased' group, whereby the GATT 'reimbursed' the ICITO for the costs of the secretariat.)

In the early 1950s the GATT CPs decided that it would be necessary to review the GATT, and amend it so as to prepare it better for its developing role as the central international institution for trade. The CPs' ninth regular session scheduled for 1954–55 was designated as a 'review session', and at this exceptionally long session extensive protocols were prepared to amend the GATT, one for those parts of the GATT requiring unanimity to amend; another for the other parts requiring only two-thirds acceptance. Ultimately the latter protocol came into effect amending portions of Part II of GATT, but the protocol requiring unanimity never came into force and was withdrawn in 1967.[22]

The 1955 Review Session also drafted a new organizational protocol. Under this protocol an Organization for Trade Cooperation (OTC) was to be established to provide the institutional framework for the developing organizational role of the GATT. This short treaty agreement was much less elaborate than the ITO, but even it failed to get the approval of the US Congress, so the OTC was also stillborn.[23]

The last formal amendment to the GATT was a 1965 protocol to add Part IV dealing with problems of developing countries.[24]

Thus, the GATT limped along for nearly fifty years with almost no basic 'constitution' designed to regulate its organizational activities and procedures. Even so, through experimentation, trial and error the GATT evolved some fairly elaborate procedures for conducting its business. That it could do so with the flawed basic documents on which it had to build is a tribute to the pragmatism and ingenuity of many of its leaders over the years.

The GATT had an admirable record of tariff rate reductions, at least for industrial products imported by industrial countries. Of course, as tariffs were lowered, the attention of domestic producer interests turned to other devices to inhibit competition from imports. These 'non-tariff measures' (NTMs) are the crucial terrain of trade policy today, and inventories can easily list thousands of NTMs. Regarding these, the GATT record was far less admirable. The proliferation of so-called 'grey area measures' – neither clearly illegal or legal – was troublesome. The 'loopholes' and ambiguities of the GATT, coupled with its inability to adjust to the new 'protectionist technologies' such as voluntary restraint measures, concerned thoughtful persons who tried to appraise the GATT's ability to provide the necessary discipline on nations for a successful trade policy. The wide-spreading 'grey area' measures on textiles, autos, steel and now computer parts were all troublesome in this regard.

In addition, the GATT was unable effectively to discipline national government trade measures on agriculture products. (The 1955 waiver on agriculture given to the United States did not help.) Furthermore, a number of developing countries were able to take advantage of various GATT exceptions to maintain very protectionist regulations. Similarly, the GATT was not able to develop a satisfactory mechanism for disciplining state trading activities. Many of these problems were related to the constitutional defects of the GATT, although they were by no means caused solely by them.

Clearly, the most significant success of the GATT history during its more than forty years was the reduction of tariff levels among the Contracting Parties. For the most part this has occurred as a result of eight intensive negotiating rounds, beginning with the first, which occurred in Geneva in 1947 at the time the GATT was originally drafted. As a result of these rounds, tariffs on industrial products imported into the industrial nations were reduced to a point where, in the view of some economists, they are no longer significant, with a few exceptions. The exceptions include some 'peak levels' of particular products for which tariffs still remain high, and also certain relationships between close neighbour trading partners (such as the United States and Canada), where even a few percentage points of a tariff can influence investment and other economic decisions.

The first five of these negotiating rounds concentrated primarily on tariffs. The sixth, the Kennedy Round, undertook to look seriously at non-tariff barriers, but that goal was only minimally achieved.

The Tokyo Round in the 1970s was the first major negotiating round to make non-tariff barriers the priority objective of the negotiation. Negotiating in a multilateral context on the reduction of non-tariff barriers is much more complex than is the case for tariffs. As the early decades of the GATT progressed, and tariffs were substantially reduced, non-tariff barriers became significantly more important. Many domestic producer interests would begin turning to a variety of non-tariff barriers (more than a thousand) as a way to minimize the competition from imports, since tariffs would no longer provide that type of protection.

The focus on non-tariff barriers, therefore, became a substantial challenge to the GATT 'constitution'. Not only was negotiation for reducing these barriers much more complex, therefore requiring a different sort of institutional framework, but the implementation of any non-tariff measure agreements resulting from the negotiation were much more difficult to achieve.

Table 2.1 summarizes the eight trade negotiating rounds held under GATT.

**Table 2.1: GATT negotiating rounds**

| Round | Dates | Number of countries | Value of trade covered ($bn) |
| --- | --- | --- | --- |
| Geneva | 1947 | 23 | 10 |
| Annecy | 1949 | 33 | Unavailable |
| Torquay | 1950 | 34 | Unavailable |
| Geneva | 1956 | 22 | 2.5 |
| Dillon | 1960–61 | 45 | 4.9 |
| Kennedy | 1962–67 | 48 | 40 |
| Tokyo | 1973–69 | 99 | 155 |
| Uruguay | 1986–94 | 120 | 3,700 |

In the Tokyo Round, as described earlier in this monograph, nine different special agreements on non-tariff measures were completed, six or seven of which were sometimes called 'codes', since they involved reasonably concrete obligations. Nevertheless, the implementation of some of these codes was troubled, for several reasons. First, some of the codes (particularly the agreement concerning subsidies) contained very ambiguous language which reflected the lack of real agreement among the negotiating partners in the Tokyo Round. Second, the dispute settlement procedures sometimes contained in these codes have not always worked satisfactorily, or have been the subject of controversy about whether a dispute should be brought under a general GATT procedure, or under a particular code procedure. Finally, the 'codes' substantially added to the administrative and institutional burden of GATT, possibly tripling the amount of activity involved. This posed a strain on some of the smaller less developed countries. In addition, the whole question of the legal relationship of the codes to the GATT itself was troublesome. A major advance of the Uruguay Round result and the WTO is to bring these updated 'side agreements' into the core of the WTO/GATT legal structures, although a number of difficult legal questions about the relationships of these various texts to each other and to the GATT still exist.

### 2.3 Overview of the fundamental principles of the GATT

This book is purposely focused on the institutional structure of the trading system, particularly the WTO and its dispute settlement procedures; it is not intended to go into the many intricate substantive rules of that system.[25] However, to explore the institutional structure without any mention of the substantive rules is a bit artificial. It is helpful to know at least a little about the more fundamental rules and basic policies that are the subject of this institution. This section is intended to provide a brief overview of those fundamental rules.

The GATT is a treaty that deals almost entirely with trade in products. The Uruguay Round for the first time produced a comparable treaty for trade in services (broadly defined), namely the General Agreement on Trade in Services. It also created a new treaty dealing with intellectual property called the Trade-Related Intellectual Property Agreement. These three treaties form the core and bulk of the substantive international rules that will be administered by the WTO. What do these treaties provide?[26]

*GATT 1947 and 1994*
The General Agreement on Tariffs and Trade, completed in late 1947 and amended and embellished with a variety of treaty instruments (about 200) in 1994, provides an important 'code' of rules applying to government actions which regulate international trade. GATT 1947 refers to the original GATT, while GATT 1994 is the version incorporated into the WTO Annex 1 and is the updated GATT along with its various associated treaty texts, 'side agreements' (as amended or revised), etc.

The basic purpose of the GATT is to constrain governments from imposing or continuing a variety of measures that restrain or distort international trade. Such measures include tariffs, quotas, international taxes and regulations which discriminate against imports, subsidy and dumping practices, state trading, as well as customs procedures and a plethora of other 'non-tariff measures' which discourage trade. The basic objective of the rules is to 'liberalize trade' so that the market can work to achieve the policy goals established for the system. An additional and very important rule is the most favoured nation clause of Article I (MFN), which provides that government import or export regulations should not discriminate between other countries' products. Similarly, Article III establishes the 'national treatment' obligation of non-discrimination against imports. Article II establishes that the tariff limits expressed in each contracting party's 'schedule of concessions' shall not be exceeded. The thrust of the General Agreement is to channel all 'border protection' against imports into the tariff, and to provide for agreements for tariff reductions, which are 'bound' in the schedules and reinforced by Article II rules and the rest of the agreement. Additional GATT clauses set constraints on the way governments administer customs (tariffs, quotas, etc.) at the border, in order to prevent arbitrary and unfair decisions or policies from undermining the other rules of GATT.

The General Agreement also has a number of exceptions, such as those for national security, health and morals, safeguards or escape clauses (for temporary restraint of imports), free trade agreements and customs unions, plus a 'waiver' power.

## GATS and TRIPS

The GATS and the TRIPS now add several more fundamental principles to the list for the WTO. One of the interesting questions is the degree to which the basic GATT rules mentioned above can be applied satisfactorily to the new subjects of services and intellectual property. These Agreements attempt to apply the MFN and national treatment rules and the 'scheduled commitments' approach, but the subject matters addressed are so different from goods that the negotiators had to develop modifications of the rules that applied to goods. In addition, one can detect in the GATS and TRIPS agreements some new 'fundamental' approaches for those subjects. For example, in GATS there is an ingenious schema of 'modes of delivery' for services, which forms a core outline for scheduled commitments. The TRIPS agreement makes significant reference to some of the long established and key intellectual property treaties, such as the Bern and Paris treaties,[27] and establishes an elaborate series of minimum standards which governments must apply to protect intellectual property.

The TRIPS agreement also sets forth very extensive rules and principles which governments must satisfy to provide private intellectual property (IP) rights holders adequate national legal powers to enforce their IP rights. In many ways, the new fundamental rules and principles for these two new subjects will be a whole new ball game for diplomats and jurists.

## 2.4 The Uruguay Round negotiation and the birth of the WTO

Soon after the completion of the Tokyo Round in 1979, it was obvious to most trade policy members that a new round would be necessary.[28] In part, this reflected the 'bicycle theory' of trade policy, namely that, unless there is forward movement, the bicycle will fall over. If there were no initiatives on trade policy, the temptations of national governments to backslide would be very great. But in addition, the world was becoming increasingly complex and interdependent, and it was becoming more and more obvious that the GATT rules were not satisfactorily providing the measure of discipline that was needed to prevent tensions and damaging national activity. Very significant and substantial new subjects were proposed for GATT competence (including services and intellectual property), and these would require a prolonged period of consultation, diplomacy and negotiation.

In 1982 the GATT held a Ministerial Meeting (the first since the 1979 completion of the Tokyo Round), one of the objectives of which was to consider the launching of a new trade round. That objective essentially failed, and the results of the 1982 Ministerial Meeting have been considered relatively unsuccessful.[29] There was an attempt at that meeting to reform the GATT dispute settlement procedures, but this attempt did not have very much success.

In the following years, further attention was given to the possibility of a new round, often under the leadership of the United States. There was particular controversy about the content of negotiations in a new trade round, with the United States and a few other countries pushing strongly for a very broad content that would include such new subjects as services and intellectual property, as well as some investment measures and the all-important subject of agriculture; other countries opposed to these broad initiatives opposed the launching of a new trade round altogether. However, the supporters of a new round won out, and in September 1986 at Punta del Este, Uruguay, a large Ministerial Meeting was held for the purpose of developing the framework for a new trade round, to be known as the 'Uruguay Round'. (Even though the launching meeting was in

Uruguay, most of the meetings occurred in Geneva or at major national capitals.)

The Declaration of Punta del Este contained the mandate for this round,[30] and it was very broad indeed. The Declaration was deemed a considerable success for the United States and a number of other countries that had been supporting a broad mandate. One of the key questions – whether services would be negotiated – was answered largely in the affirmative, although not without some compromise. Indeed, the inclusion of services in the negotiating round amply demonstrates the importance of institutional measures. The structure of the Punta del Este Declaration made it clear that the question of whether services would ultimately be part of the GATT structure (or that of some other organization) was left open by that Declaration. Thus, the structure of the negotiation on the one hand dealt with trade in goods, while on the other it set up a separate committee and negotiating structure for trade in services. Nevertheless, as time went on, the opinions of many officials and diplomats gradually accepted the idea that the GATT system would have competence over trade in services.

After Punta del Este, the Contracting Parties met to establish a series of negotiating groups and a schedule for their meetings. In general, the list of negotiating groups follows quite closely the list of subjects included in the Punta del Este Declaration. Fourteen negotiating groups were set up to work on the problems of trade in goods,[31] and a separate negotiating structure was set up for negotiations on trade in services. An elaborate meeting schedule was formulated, and governments geared up to handle these meetings.

In the ensuing years, it was decided there would be a mid-term review towards the end of 1988, which would be a meeting of GATT Contracting Party Ministers of Trade, for the purpose of surveying the progress of the negotiation and establishing directions for the remainder of the negotiation. This was held in Montreal, Canada. Originally it was thought that there might be some concrete agreements that could be accepted and possibly even implemented as a result of the mid-term review, but as the time for that review approached, it appeared less and less likely that this would occur. In the end, there were no real agreements to be implemented, with the possible exception of some improvements in the dispute settlement process. Rather, the agreements set forth the framework of the further negotiations.

It is probably not surprising that there was a lack of agreement at Montreal. The two largest trading blocs were represented at that meeting by officials who were leaving their positions. In the United States, the November 1988 presidential election had established that the Bush administration would succeed the Reagan administration, but Reagan administration officials were still in charge at Montreal, and it was not always clear who the Bush officials to succeed them would be. Similarly, and coincidentally, in the European Economic Community the position of Commissioner for External Relations (the US trade negotiator's counterpart) was shifting from Commissioner Willy De Clercq to Commissioner Frans Andriessen. As it turned out, there was a bit of reciprocal and symmetrical irony with respect to these two trading powers: in the US the trade representative Clayton Yeutter was moved to the position of Secretary of Agriculture; in the European Community, the Commissioner for Agriculture, Frans Andriessen, was moved to the position of trade negotiator!

If the mid-term review was timed to occur shortly after the US presidential elections as a way for the GATT Contracting Parties to 'reconnoitre the situation' in the light of the US election result, it may have afforded that opportunity to the Contracting Parties. The other side-effect, however, was to insert an element of paralysis, or inability to make the necessary compromises, in order to achieve an agreement at Montreal. On the other hand, over the ensuing months the new administrations were in place and, since their positions were relatively uncompromised by their predecessors, they were able to move forward and achieve some sort of a consensus, with the assistance of the good offices of the GATT Director-General. By April 1989 the result of this process was the set of agreements of the mid-term review.[32]

The Uruguay Round obviously presented fundamental institutional questions for the GATT. The Punta del Este Declaration itself contained some reference to these matters, for example the dispute settlement procedures and 'functioning of the GATT system (FOGS)'. The new subjects, however, posed some potentially more difficult questions, such as: could the GATT system, as it was then working, embrace these new subjects, such as trade in services and intellectual property? How would the intellectual property issues relate to the the World Intellectual Property Organization (WIPO)? How would the Services Agreement be administered by a GATT text that basically was designed only for goods? The Punta Declaration and the 1986 launching Ministerial Meeting tended to defer some of these fundamental institutional questions. During the early years of work of 'FOGS' the negotiating group did not address these issues either, focusing instead on the development of a trade policy review mechanism, and worrying about the relationship of monetary institutions to the trade institution.

The Punta del Este Declaration said nothing about the establishment of a new organization to replace the troubled GATT institution. It was only in early 1990 that the first official government proposal (by Canada) was publicly made for the establishment of a new organization, to be called the 'World Trade Organization', to help effectively administer and bring into force the vast new subject terrain that was anticipated from the Uruguay Round. Before that, in the summer of 1989, an informal and partly academic meeting including a number of key negotiators had been held in Geneva during which the idea of a new organization was discussed.[33]

The Canadian government made its proposal in public announcements and press releases in early April 1990, followed by discussions at a special meeting of thirty trade ministers participating in the Uruguay Round negotiations.[34] Canada was particularly well placed to put forward such a proposal. It belonged to the very powerful 'quad' group[35] (consisting of the United States, European Community, Japan and Canada), but it was the smallest of that group, and the one least likely to meet 'automatic' objections to any rather novel proposal, unlike the large powers which often received an antagonistic response from many of the small countries of the world when they put forward initiatives.

Discussions about a new organization began to develop in some delegations, particularly within the European Community. The Community, however, felt that the name that should be used for such an organization should be the Multilateral Trade Organization (MTO).

A Ministerial Meeting for the negotiation was held in December 1990 in Brussels. This was the meeting that was supposed to conclude the Uruguay Round, but it resulted in an impasse, for a number of reasons. Perhaps most prominent was the inability of the United States and the European Community to agree on the agricultural measures to be included in the Uruguay Round Agreement. The documents for this meeting (not adopted), including the proposed Ministerial Declaration,[36] did not include any detailed proposals for a new organization, although there was mention of the need to have some institutional innovations in order to carry out the results of the Uruguay Round.

Thus, at the beginning of 1991 the negotiation was at a virtual halt, and the diplomats and officials were trying to reach agreement on how to proceed. The United States fast-track[37] procedure (deemed essential by most of the diplomats in the negotiation) for congressional approval of the Uruguay Round was to expire on 1 June 1991, unless it was extended by a procedure in the US Congress (which was done).[38] (At the same time, the Congress authorized the fast track for the trilateral negotiation for a 'North American Free Trade Agreement' – NAFTA – among Canada, the United States and Mexico). Various discussions and drafting ideas were developed during 1991. At the end of the year the Secretariat, under the direction of the Director-General Arthur Dunkel, was able to get the various negotiating groups in the Uruguay Round to present drafts representing the current state of the tentative agreements on the many different parts of the negotiation. These various drafts were pasted together into a large document embodying all of the work that had yet gone on in the Uruguay Round. The master-draft, appropriately called the 'Dunkel Text', was immediately made public worldwide.[39] Contained in this document was the first full draft of a new organization 'Charter' that was put forward as part of the multilateral document for consideration by the negotiators. At this point the organization was still being referred to as the 'Multilateral Trade Organization'.

The Dunkel Text was extraordinarily important. For the first time it allowed more than a hundred governments throughout the world to see what the potential of the Uruguay Round might be, with its many different strands of significant potential treaty texts. Governments could then make policy decisions about the trade-offs between advantages that they would receive from the overall Uruguay Round text, and the disadvantages to them. Gradually a general consensus could be detected in support of the completion of the Uruguay Round very much along the lines of the Dunkel Text. With respect to the establishment of a new organization, negotiations occurred on and off within certain negotiating groups. The US, perhaps alone of the quad and other major participants in the negotiation, refused to commit itself to the establishment of a new organization at that time. Indeed, US attention was being diverted by the negotiation for a NAFTA.[40] Under the extended version of the fast-track legislation of the US Congress, the (nearly) final negotiating draft was due on 1 March 1993, to be followed by three months of discussion among parliaments and the US Congress, and then the final signing by 1 June 1993.[41] In the autumn of 1992, however, the presidential election in the United States resulted in a new administration taking office in January 1993, and this administration was not quite ready to decide what it wanted to do regarding the Uruguay Round. Consequently, the fast track had to be amended again after the administration decided to go ahead, so that the critical dates were now 15 December 1993 for the (nearly) completed draft to be notified to the Congress, followed by four months of discussion, and then the final Ministerial Meeting in mid-April at Marrakesh, Morocco, on 15 April 1994. (Once the signing had occurred, then under the US fast track the President could decide at what point he would present the treaty to the Congress for its approval.)

Consequently, the very intensive effort to finish the Uruguay Round occurred during the three or four months just before 15 December 1993. Extensive activity with many long (and sometimes overnight) sessions of negotiation occurred. Considerable revisions were made in a 'Charter' for a new MTO. Although the United States participated in these revisions, it still had not committed itself to accept the idea of a new organization. At the same time, many inconsistencies and drafting problems and disparities in the Dunkel Text had to be addressed, although not all of these were corrected.

It was only in the last few hours of the day preceding the 15 December deadline that the United States indicated that it would accept the new organization.[42] But the US acceptance was conditional upon a different name from 'Multilateral Trade Organization', namely the 'World Trade Organization'. There are many ironies in this last-minute decision. The United States, being the most hesitant about a new organization, seemed to be opting for a title that had a broader and more expansive connotation than what could be inferrred from 'Multilateral Trade Organisation'. The decision was made so late that all of the documents that were already prepared to be transmitted to the Congress by the December 15 deadline used the earlier title. The negotiators therefore attached to the front of this document a statement instructing readers to change 'MTO' wherever it was found in those texts to the new title 'WTO'.[43] Thus, either knowingly or not, the United States was instrumental in causing the new organization to assume the title that had originally been indicated for it by the Canadian government proposal in the spring of 1990![44]

In 1994 the Agreement was signed as planned on 15 April, and then governments went about the task of following their various constitutional procedures for approving the text. The goal was for the Agreement to come into effect on 1 January 1995, but that left very little time for all the necessary constitutional procedures in many of the major trading entities.[45]

## 2.5 National government implementation

After the Final Act of the Uruguay Round results was signed at Marrakesh on 15 April 1994, most nations needed to follow up with domestic constitutional or other procedures in order to accept the agreement definitively. With over 120 nations in the negotiation, over 113 of which were present at Marrakesh,[46] the variety of procedures was enormous.[47] Each nation had its procedure. In some cases a nation's diplomat could sign with definitive acceptance at the Ministerial Meeting at Marrakesh.[48] In most cases the signing was understood to be 'ad referendum', i.e. that the governments concerned must go back to their capitals and arrange for parliamentary or other actions of legal approval. Since the Agreement was scheduled to come into force on 1 January 1995, this left only a meagre eight months or so to accomplish these procedures. Yet, remarkably, by 1 January 1995 at least 76 governments had taken the necessary domestic legal action to approve the agreement and become members of the new WTO which came into existence that day. Subsequently many more nations have become members,[49] with still more negotiating for membership.[50] Also remarkable was the fact that by 1 January 1995, all the major trading entities in the Uruguay Round had approved the agreement. A brief discussion of the procedures of several of these follows.

*United States*[51]

Approval of international agreements is much more complex than is commonly understood. The US Constitution explicitly provides only one procedure for approving 'treaties', but there are in fact five different procedures, although in US domestic law terms the other procedures deal with 'agreements' (which under international law terminology are clearly 'treaties'). The procedure used for many trade treaty approvals in the United States has for decades (even centuries) been a 'statutory' approach, by which an agreement, called a 'Congressional–Executive Agreement', is approved by normal legislation which delegates to the President the authority to enter into ('ratify') such agreement. All GATT trade agreements were pursuant to this procedure, either by advance delegation or by a statute enacted after the agreement was negotiated and signed. At the end of the Uruguay Round this was the procedure followed by the United States, although some constitutional objections were made (and failed to prevail).[52] The US Uruguay Round Implementing Act was enacted in December 1994, in time for the WTO launch.[53]

Since the Trade Agreements Act of 1974, the US Congress has considered approval of all major trade agreements (GATT rounds and Free Trade Agreements such as NAFTA) under a procedure known as the 'fast track'. While somewhat intricate and based on an interesting history, the fast track is essentially a 'statutory' treaty approval, mentioned above, but with certain specific procedural characteristics designed to accommodate special problems of international trade negotiations. Basically, foreign nations are not very happy to negotiate seriously in the context of a rule that requires the result of a negotiation to be submitted to Congress, which then can effectively 'reopen' the negotiation and demand (by amending the proposed law) additional terms. Foreign nations want assurance that the results of the many compromises involved in an intricate trade negotiation will at least be voted on as a whole. Therefore the fast-track procedure calls for an initial period of intense consultation between the US executive and Congress about a preliminary draft treaty. These consultations are considered by the executive and its diplomats negotiating the treaty, and after the treaty is completed and signed the President will submit proposed legislation that will authorize the President to accept the treaty, and will ensure legislation of the measures necessary to carry out the obligations in the treaty.

When the proposal is made to Congress, the fast-track rules have several features:

(1) the bill cannot be amended;
(2) congressional committees must consider and report the bill to the floor of the two houses within rather strict time limits; and
(3) debate in both houses (House of Representatives and Senate) is strictly limited. These rules have some other features that will not be detailed here, and the rules themselves are not statutory, but are in the rules of procedure of the House and the Senate, respectively. Thus, the fast track is somewhat vulnerable to attack by certain parliamentary procedures. But so far it has managed to operate largely as planned.

Whether a treaty itself becomes part of US domestic law is a separate question which depends on the US doctrine of 'self-executing treaties'. However, as to the trade treaties of 1979 and subsequently, statutory phrases and legislative history provide that the treaties are not self-executing, with some possible minor exceptions. Thus, the US domestic law does not include the text of the statutes, but of course the implementing legislation is part of domestic law, and often that legislation includes language drawn directly from the treaty.[54]

## *European Community*[55]
The European Community followed an even more complex procedure. There were uncertainty and conflicting views about whether the approval

of the UR agreement required only EC action, or required in addition the approval of each of the member states. The EC action on an international agreement devoted solely to 'commercial policy' requires a proposal by the EC Commission to the Council, and an affirmative vote (pursuant to Article 113 of the EC treaty) of a 'qualified majority'. Some other related matters require a unanimous vote of the Council. In most cases of such international agreement, the European Parliament since 1992 must 'consent' to the agreements.[56] However, objections to sole or exclusive EC jurisdiction were taken to the EC Court of Justice (which sits in Luxembourg), and that Court rendered a judgment on 15 November 1994 (six weeks before the WTO due date!) which concluded that certain subjects of the UR Agreement still fell within the competence of the member states (or at least required 'mixed agreement' of both member states and EC institutions). These subjects included particularly those of the UR text on trade in services (General Agreement on Trade in Services) relating to cross-border delivery of services requiring movement of natural persons, some issues of financial services, and possibly some other subjects for which member-state governments retained competence. Similarly, issues of intellectual property, the subject of the Trade Related Intellectual Property agreement, were still under the competence of member states. For a variety of reasons, including some 'EC constitu-tional anxieties' of certain member states about the EC voting requirements, the EC Commiss-ion proposed that the entire UR Agreement (single package) would be approved only if the Council voted unanimously to do so upon consent of the European Parliament, and, partly because of the Court ruling, it was also decided that each member state must ratify the UR agreement. All these entities completed their necessary procedures before the deadline.[57]

One interesting facet of the EC approval was a question of whether the UR agreements would be 'directly applicable', so as to become directly part of the internal law of the EC (and its member states). This has been a subject of considerable controversy within the EC and its Court for decades.[58] In the final decision of the Council to approve the UR results, the preamble states explicitly that the UR texts themselves would not be deemed directly applicable.[59] This somewhat parallels the US approach for this agreement.

### *Japan*[60]

In Japan, treaties must be approved by parliament, but as a parliamentary democracy, it has no sharp division between executive and parliament as in the United States, nor is Japan a 'federal state' that gives rise to power distinctions between states or provinces (or member states of a regional union), such as are found in the European Community. Nevertheless there were some policy conflicts that had to be overcome, and recent changes of political control of the parliament in Japan made treaty approval more complicated and difficult. Yet in the end, and in time, the Japanese parliament approved the Uruguay Round agreement. Although the Japanese constitution appears to provide that treaties have the force of law and prevail over even later statutes, in practice there are some nuanced differences in how courts react, and a distinguished scholar says that 'when individuals challenge the conformity of Japanese law to the WTO Agreement, it is unlikely that Japanese courts will declare the law to be null and void, especially because the direct applicability of the WTO Agreement is denied in the United States and possibly also in the European Union'.[61]

## 2.6 The 'sovereignty' question

As noted at the beginning of this book, the implications of the UR Agreement are undoubtedly not fully understood yet by any government that has accepted them. In the United States during 1994 there was considerable discussion about the impact of the UR treaty and the WTO on 'US sovereignty'. (Indeed, in another work I termed this the 'Great Sovereignty Debate of 1994'[62].) While the term 'sovereignty' has been much criticized as out of date and archaic, nevertheless, some of the issues in this 'great debate' are vital and contemporary. To a large extent these issues concern 'allocation of power' as between a nation-state and an international regulatory system. To give a few examples, there are questions as to whether a product safety standard should be controlled by an international body or a nation-state government, or even by sub-federal government units. There are also questions about how to apply certain well-established international policies such as 'most favoured nation' treatment (non-discrimination as between different nations) or 'national treatment' (non-discrimination as between domestic products or services and imported products or services). In addition, there are questions about whether or not disputes about these and other issues should be resolved by an international body. We will come back to some of these sovereignty issues in later chapters, since they engage subjects discussed there. In fact, a close analysis of sovereignty turns out to be very complex, and the subject can be 'decomposed' into dozens of more specific issues.[63]

Clearly, acceptance of any treaty in some sense reduces the freedom of scope of national government actions. At the very least, certain types of action inconsistent with the treaty norms would give rise to an international law obligation, and the degree of constraint might then vary with the institutional mechanisms for enforcement, but also with the national domestic government structure or political attitude towards international norms. Some sceptics might dismiss an international norm as ineffective and thus not constraining. But if a treaty norm were 'self-executing' or 'directly applicable' in a domestic legal system, it could have a greater constraining effect.

Even without those effects, a treaty can have important domestic legal effects, such as influencing how domestic courts interpret domestic legislation. Beyond that, a treaty norm even without domestic legal effect can have weight in some domestic policy debates where some advocates will stress that positions contrary to their views would raise 'serious international or treaty concerns'. Thus the 'sovereignty objection' can be seen to be directed more to the question of where a decision should be made, and what influences on that decision should be permitted.

It can also be observed that the lack of direct effect of a treaty in domestic law is considered a possible protection against 'sovereignty diminution'. This is because, without direct effect, a nation normally can decide how to respond to a complaint that its actions have breached international law, and one possible response is to ignore the complaint and live with the breach. This may not be particularly admirable, but it can act as sort of a buffering process or 'safety valve' against international action which might be deemed overreaching or otherwise inappropriate.

Finally, it should be noted that the legal ability to withdraw within a reasonable period of notice arguably reduces the worry about 'infringement on sovereignty'. This option seemed to be interesting to some of those worried about the sovereignty arguments. The Uruguay Round treaty provisions allow withdrawal upon six months' notice. Whether this is a realistic option for nations today, in the light of their considerable dependence on international trade and the trade system of the GATT/WTO, is a somewhat different question which can also be considered.

Related to the considerations mentioned above, some general objections to a treaty are driven by the substance of particular issues. Many US environmentalist advocates and groups in the 1994 debate were concerned that specific treaty clauses would 'trump' US environmental law or even state law such as that of California, in a way to 'harmonize downward' the more stringent US law about which the environmentalists were justifiably proud.[64] Thus, important questions were raised about the legal and practical effect of the WTO and UR treaty norms on particular subjects, and 'sovereignty objections' became objections to the substance of the international norms, at least to the extent that those norms appeared not to give enough leeway to domestic US political institutions to decide 'more appropriate' higher standards.

# Chapter 3

# The WTO – Charter and organization

## 3.1 Introduction to the WTO as an institution

Perhaps the most dramatic result of the Uruguay Round negotiation was the establishment of a new organization to replace the GATT institutional function (such as it was), as described in the previous chapter. This result was achieved by the 'Agreement Establishing the World Trade Organization', which informally is called the 'Charter' of the WTO, but is actually the leading portion of the 26,000-page treaty (including extensive annexes) that was the 'single package' result of the Uruguay Round. The WTO 'Charter' itself is a short document (about fifteen pages), and in this sense is more closely inspired by the 1955 proposed 'mini-charter' for an Organization for Trade Cooperation (ten pages)[1] than by the 1948 proposed International Trade Organization (106 articles and over 100 pages).[2] Neither of these latter, of course, ever came into effect.

In the light of the negotiating history for the WTO and its many annexed parts, it is not surprising that these 1,000 pages of text plus extensive schedules are not particularly polished or coherent, to say nothing of the problem of numerous ambiguities which are probably inevitable for a negotiation with so many participating countries.[3] Nevertheless, the essential basic characteristics of a 'legitimate' international organization are now established as binding treaty law in the Charter, as we will explore in the next section.

To a large extent the Uruguay Round treaty corrects many of the 'birth defects' of the GATT.[4] No longer can government officials and diplomats easily and mistakenly describe the institution and its rules and decisions as 'non-binding'; nor can political interests in some countries such as the

United States claim that the treaty is not binding or authoritative because it has never been approved by the US Congress. Grandfather rights are generally a thing of the past, and many (but not all) of the potential problems of the GATT open-ended treaty clauses concerning decision-making authority have been largely corrected, as we shall see.[5] The new dispute settlement procedures (the subject of Chapter 4) mostly unified the multiplicity of dispute procedures under the prior GATT and its many 'side agreements' (mostly from the Tokyo Round). The legal process of adopting a whole new treaty technically replacing the GATT and the various 'side codes' avoided the legal and practical problems of the GATT amending provisions. The 'single package' concept essentially required all WTO members to accept as binding international law obligation almost all of the prior rules and texts as amended.[6] Other traditional international law attributes of a legitimate international organization are also established.[7]

### 3.2 Legal structure of the WTO Treaty

The GATT legal structure was always clouded by its 'provisional' status, 'birth defects' and significant ambiguities concerning the legal status of particular texts. It was a complex mixture of almost 200 treaty texts (protocols, amendments, rectifications, etc.), and was affected by numerous decisions and waivers of the CONTRACTING PARTIES of the GATT acting jointly. Even in the GATT treaty text, an Annex I provided 'interpretive notes' for various Articles, so a careful lawyer would need to be watchful for these or other texts that affected certain treaty clauses.[8] The domestic law status of the GATT in some national legal systems was also murky.[9] After the Tokyo Round 'side agreements' entered into force in 1979 or later, there were a number of uneasy relationships between text in some of those agreements and the GATT text itself.

In some ways the Uruguay Round (UR) texts and the WTO Treaty have improved these matters, but in other ways this new treaty has created a number of new legal problems. In part this was a result of the particular preparatory history. As noted earlier,[10] the substantive treaty obligation texts are appended to the WTO Charter; in particular Annex 1A, which embodies the GATT (now GATT 1994) and the goods rules, contains, in addition to the GATT 1994 text (basically the GATT of 1947 as amended to the date of the UR completion), a long list of 'agreements', understandings, declarations, decisions and other texts.[11] The 'agreements' are mostly the Tokyo Round side agreements as modified by the UR negotiation, but now no longer 'optional' under the 'single package' concept.

The ways in which these various texts interrelate is not always clear. Indeed, lawyers for some of the negotiating parties tried to clarify some of these problems, but time did not permit such efforts, and negotiators were often afraid to change any of the texts (at least after the 1991 Dunkel Text was promulgated) because they feared that such a change would 'reopen' substantive issues previously laid to rest, or would otherwise be too contentious or would arouse suspicions. As a result, many of the legal relationships among the various complex texts will be likely to need resolution through a dispute settlement process, usually requiring attention of the new Appellate Body.[12]

Thus, the structure of the treaty is technically as follows. The overall treaty is the 'Final Act Embodying the Results of the Uruguay Round of Multilateral Trade Negotiations',[13] and the first element is the WTO 'Charter'. This Charter contains four important *annexes*, which comprise most of the treaty's pages and all of the 'substance', as contrasted with the Charter *clauses*, which deal with institutional and procedural matters. One possible reason for this structure may be to suggest that the processes for changing the annexes might be more flexible and efficient than for changing the Charter, so that the institution could keep abreast of fast developing changes of economic circumstances. Whether this will in fact be the case will be discussed later.[14] The following is a brief description of the annexes, but an appendix gives a full list in outline form of the texts of these annexes.[15]

### Annex 1

This annex contains the large texts, termed 'Multilateral Trade Agreements', that comprise the bulk of the UR results. All these are 'mandatory', in the sense that they impose binding obligations on all members of the WTO. This reinforces the 'single package' idea of the negotiators, departing from the Tokyo Round approach of 'pick and choose' side texts, or 'GATT *à la carte*'. The Annex 1 texts include:

- Annex 1A GATT 1994, the revised and all-inclusive GATT agreement with related agreements or 'codes', and the vast 'schedules of concessions' that make up the large bulk of pages in the official treaty text. The schedules for each of the major trading countries, i.e. the United States, Japan and the European Union, each constitute a volume of printed tariff listings. The Annex 1 'interpretive notes' continue in effect.

- Annex 1B GATS, the General Agreement on Trade in Services, with its schedules of specific commitments and annexes.
- Annex 1C TRIPS, the Agreement on Trade-Related Intellectual Property measures.

Annex 1A is by far the largest of these annexes and contains the GATT 1994, which is essentially the old GATT as modified by amendments, the Tokyo Round 'codes', renegotiated in the Uruguay Round and some new Uruguay Round agreements. In addition to the GATT 1994, Annex 1A includes:

- Agreement on Agriculture
- Agreement on Sanitary and Phytosanitary Measures
- Agreement on Textiles and Clothing
- Agreement on Technical Barriers to Trade
- Agreement on Trade-Related Investment Measures
- Agreement on Article VI (Antidumping)
- Agreement on Customs Valuation
- Agreement on Preshipment Inspection
- Agreement on Rules of Origin
- Agreement on Import Licensing
- Agreement on Subsidies and Countervailing Measures
- Agreement on Safeguards

It also includes a series of 'understandings' and some ministerial 'decisions and declarations' which further modify the GATT. The tariff schedules (most of the 26,000 pages) are technically part of this annex. The relationship of many of the above listed agreements to GATT 1994 is not always entirely clear.

Two of these agreements concern what are probably the most contentious of the 'rules of conduct' clauses of the GATT, namely Antidumping and Subsidies and Countervailing Measures. One other concerns product standards (Technical Barriers to Trade), which is also addressed in the Sanitary and Phytosanitary Measures Agreement.

*Annex 2*
This annex contains the dispute settlement rules, called the Dispute Settlement Understanding (DSU), which are obligatory for all members, and which form (for the first time) an integrated and unified dispute settlement mechanism with some exceptions covering the WTO Charter,

and the agreements listed in Annexes 1 and 2 and made available for agreements in Annex 4.

### Annex 3

This annex contains the Trade Policy Review Mechanism (TPRM), in existence since 1988, by which the WTO will review the overall trade policies of each member on a periodic and regular basis, and report on those policies. The approach is not supposed to be 'legalistic', and questions of consistency with WTO and annex obligations are not the focus; rather, the focus is on transparency and the general impact of the trade policies, both on the country being examined and on its trading partners.[16]

### Annex 4

This annex contains four agreements that are 'optional', called 'plurilateral agreements'. This is a slight departure from the 'single package' idea, but the agreements tend to deal with subject matter that concerns a small number of countries, or is more 'hortatory' in nature. Clearly, this annex, to which additions may be made, provides some important flexibility for the Organization to evolve and redirect its attention and institutional support for new subjects that may emerge as important during the next few decades. The plurilateral agreements originally included (meat and dairy are being terminated) are:

- Agreement on Trade in Civil Aircraft
- Agreement on Government Procurement
- International Dairy Agreement
- International Bovine Meat Agreement

As impressive as the Uruguay Round results are, there clearly are a number of 'left-over' issues which the WTO system will need to address during forthcoming years, in addition to overseeing a satisfactory implementation of the UR results. The descriptions above hint at some of these, and other issues can be named:

- Enhancing and extending the liberalization of trade in agricultural products
- Future extensive negotiations on services
- Further elaboration of the rules on subsidies
- Further market access efforts

- Further negotiations in the context of trade-related investment measures
- Further negotiations concerning rules of origin
- Greater integration of developing countries as well as monitoring of the WTO/GATT rules to ensure fair treatment of those countries
- Attention to the problems of anti-dumping rules and the risks they raise for undermining some of the Uruguay Round results
- The problem of integrating the 'economies in transition' (e.g. China, Russia) into the WTO system, and of facing up to the problem of 'state trading' entities

### 3.3 Organization, structure and powers

The governing structure of the WTO follows the GATT 1947 model in part, but departs from it substantially.[17] At the top there is a 'Ministerial Conference' (MC) which meets at least every two years. Next, there are not one but four 'Councils'. These include one 'General Council', which seems to have overall supervising authority, can carry out many of the functions of the Ministerial Conference between MC sessions, and meets approximately every two months.[18] In addition, there is a Council for each of the Annex 1 Agreements:

- Council for Trade in Goods (GATT 1994)
- Council for Trade in Services (GATS)
- Council for Trade-Related Aspects of Intellectual Property Rights (TRIPS)

There is also established a 'Dispute Settlement Body' (DSB) to supervise and implement the dispute settlement rules in Annex 2. The WTO Charter provides that the 'General Council shall convene as appropriate to discharge the responsibilities of the [DSB]'. In the same manner, there is a TPRM body for the TPRM.

### 3.4 Decision-making and power distribution in the WTO: amending, interpreting, voting, transparency

Since the GATT was not viewed as an organization, it is not surprising that the GATT treaty had little in it about decision-making. Article XXV called for one-nation, one-vote and decision by a majority of votes cast unless otherwise provided. For example:

> 1. Representatives of the Contracting Parties shall meet from time to time for the purpose of giving effect to those provisions of this Agreement which involve joint action and, generally, with a view to facilitating the operation and furthering the objectives of this Agreement.

This language is remarkably broad, and although cautiously utilized (at least in the early years) was the basis for much GATT activity. For the United States, for instance, such language could have posed a danger. First, the United States could have been easily outvoted in a GATT with over 120 members,[19] over two-thirds of which are developing countries and over half of which are formally associated in one status or another with the European Community. Second, a nation's vote is cast by the executive branch of its government, and for the United States (possibly other countries as well) an executive decision to vote for a measure could result in its accepting a binding international obligation, without the participation of its legislative branch. In practice, however, this was probably not a realistic danger, since the preparatory work, the failure of the ITO and OTC, the criticism of Congress and the worry over voting strength led the CONTRACTING PARTIES to be cautious in voting additional obligations. A short withdrawal notice period and the relative ease of breaching obligations have also been sources of caution. Most efforts in the GATT were accomplished through a process of negotiation and compromise, with varying degrees of formality and a tacit understanding that agreement is necessary among countries with important economic influence.

One important question concerning the scope of authority under Article XXV was whether the CONTRACTING PARTIES had the power to make definitive interpretations of the General Agreement, which were binding on all members. For example, the CONTRACTING PARTIES, in a decision of 9 August 1949, ruled:

> The reduction of the rate of duty on a product, provided for in a schedule to the General Agreement, below the rate set forth therein, does not require unanimous consent of the CONTRACTING PARTIES.[20]

From time to time, various working groups or panels of the GATT reported their interpretations of the General Agreement, and these reports were 'adopted' by the CONTRACTING PARTIES. In addition, occasionally the chairman of the CONTRACTING PARTIES made an 'interpretative ruling', and no objection was raised in the CONTRACTING PARTIES' meeting.[21]

The GATT also had measures specifying the procedure and votes for amending the Agreement, and for waivers.

The WTO substantially changes all of this, and contains an elaborate matrix of decision-making procedures with important constraints around them. Basically, there are five different techniques for making decisions or formulating new or amended rules of trade policy in the WTO: decisions on various matters, 'interpretations', waivers, amendments, and finally the negotiation of new agreements. In addition, certain decisions are governed by the texts of Annex 4 plurilateral agreements.

A key WTO charter provision states: 'In the event of a conflict between a provision of this Agreement and a provision of any of the Multilateral Trade Agreements, the provision of this Agreement shall prevail to the extent of conflict.'[22] Thus, the WTO Agreement provisions on decisions would seem to trump GATT 1994 provisions such as GATT Article XXV, or the practice regarding formal 'interpretations'.

However, another 'conflict' rule adds some complexity. WTO Annex 1A includes a 'General interpretative note to Annex 1A', which reads: 'In the event of conflict between a provision of the General Agreement on Tariffs and Trade 1994 and a provision of another agreement in Annex 1A ... the provision of the other agreement shall prevail to the extent of the conflict'. So, if a GATT Article XVI subsidy rule is conflicting with a measure in the separate text (a former and now revised side agreement) on subsidies, the latter rule will prevail. Yet the WTO Charter rule would trump that, although the Charter rule would most likely be a procedural or institutional rule rather than a substantive trade policy rule, and so no 'conflict' would occur. Yet one cannot be completely sure about this approach.

There are other 'conflicts' in the Uruguay Round texts. For example, many of the texts including the GATT in Annex 1A have provisions for dispute settlement. However, the Annex 2 Dispute Settlement Understanding (discussed in more detail in the next chapter) provides in its Article 1 that the DSU rules and procedures shall apply to all disputes concerning 'covered agreements' listed in a DSU Appendix, although it then provides for some specific exceptions for certain texts listed in another appendix. So, despite some conflicting language regarding disputes, the DSU seems to trump most of that conflicting language.

The WTO Charter specifies that the GATT practice of decision-making by 'consensus' is to be continued for the WTO Ministerial Conference (MC) and General Council (GC), but when consensus cannot be achieved decisions will be made on the basis of the majority of votes cast, with each member having one vote, unless otherwise provided.

Regarding 'interpretations', the MC and GC have exclusive authority to adopt interpretations of the WTO Charter and the Annex 1 Multilateral Trade Agreements. Interpretations of the Annex 1 Agreements are to be based on a recommendation of the Council for that Agreement and require an affirmative vote from three-quarters of the overall WTO membership. Interpretations are not to be used to undermine Article X's amendment procedures.[23]

The MC may waive an obligation under the WTO Charter and the Annex 1 Multilateral Trade Agreements. If consensus cannot be reached, the grant of a waiver requires an affirmative vote of three-quarters of the overall WTO membership. In the case of Annex 1 agreements, the waiver request is to be submitted to the relevant council (e.g. Goods, Services or TRIPS), which will submit a report to the MC. Article IX:4 provides that any waiver granted shall specify the exceptional circumstances justifying it and a termination date. Waivers are subject to annual MC review.[24]

In the GATT there was some concern about waivers being used as a sort of 'easy track' substitute for amendments. Some GATT documents discussed this problem,[25] but the practice of GATT was rather relaxed on this point. The WTO Charter considerably stiffens the rules regarding waivers and makes explicit the power of the organization to terminate waivers (an issue of some contention in the GATT).[26]

In the GATT there was also concern about the amending rules (contained in Article XXX). The unanimity required for certain amendments had never been achieved, and the requirement otherwise of two-thirds (but not binding on hold-outs) was increasingly difficult to fulfil as the number of GATT Contracting Parties increased. This difficulty was a major factor in the Tokyo Round negotiations, leading the participants to utilize 'side codes' or special agreements on a number of GATT subjects as a way of avoiding the need for amendments. But these codes bound only those governments which accepted them, and in the Uruguay Round it was decided that a 'single package' approach should be followed, so that all governments that became members of the WTO would be obligated to observe almost all of the agreements and rules. The amending rules of this new package are somewhat similar to those of the GATT, so it is possible that the inconveniences of the GATT rules will continue to be a problem.

The amending authority (Article X) is itself quite intricate and ingenious. It obviously has been carefully tailored to the needs of the participating nations related to each of the different major multilateral agreements (GATT, GATS (Services) and Intellectual Property). Amendments for some parts of these require unanimity; for other parts a two-thirds majority is required (after procedures in the Ministerial Conference and Councils seeking consensus for amendment proposals). In almost all cases, as mentioned above, a member that refuses to accept an amendment that would 'alter the rights and obligations' is not bound by such an amendment. In such cases, however, there is an ingenious procedure (partly following the GATT model) whereby the Ministerial Conference can, by a three-quarters vote of the members, require a holding-out member to accept the amendment or withdraw from the Agreement, or to remain a member only with the explicit consent of the Ministerial Conference (i.e. the MC can grant that member a waiver). For these reasons, therefore, it is very hard to conceive of the amending provisions being used in any way to force a major trading country such as the United States, the European Union or Japan to accept altered rights or obligations. As stated above, the spirit and practice of the GATT has always been to try to accommodate through consensus negotiation procedures the views of as many countries as possible, but certainly to give weight to the views of countries that have power in the trading system. This is not likely to change.

Amendments to the following take effect only upon acceptance by all members: WTO decision-making and amendment rules (Articles IX, X); GATT Articles I (MFN) and II (Tariff Schedules); GATS Article II:1 (MFN); TRIPS Article 4 (MFN).

Amendments to Annexes 2 (Dispute Settlement) and 3 (TPRM) can be made by MC action alone (without member treaty acceptance documents), but for Annex 2 MC approval must be by consensus (Article X:8).

The WTO also provides a forum for negotiations on agreements contained in its annexes. It may also provide a forum for other negotiations on trade relations and a framework for the implementation of the results of such negotiations, by decision of the MC.[27]

Decision-making and amendments under the plurilateral agreements of Annex 4 are governed by the rules contained in each agreement. The MC may add trade agreements to Annex 4 by consensus; it may delete agreements from Annex 4 on the request of the members party to the agreement.[28]

In addition, it is important to understand the potential of the dispute settlement procedures, and the panel reports that result (the subject of the next chapter), on the change or evolution of the trade rules.

There have been some allegations that the WTO Charter is an important intrusion on national sovereignty. Apart from the general problems of how to define 'sovereignty' in a world that is increasingly interdependent, we can see that the WTO contains an elaborate matrix of decision-making procedures controlled by important constraints.

A careful examination of the WTO Charter suggests that apart from the addition of many new subjects to the substantive annexes, the WTO has no more real legal power than that which existed for the GATT under the previous agreements. This may seem surprising, but in fact, as discussed earlier, the GATT Treaty text contained language that was quite ambiguous, and could have been misused (but fortunately was not) to provide rather extensive powers.

Regarding the practice of 'consensus', as established in the GATT, several characteristics are worth noting. In the GATT, there was no explicit indication of a 'consensus practice', and the word 'consensus' was not used. The practice of consensus voting developed partly because of the uneasiness of governments about the loose wording of GATT decision-making powers, particularly that in GATT Article XXV. Because of this uneasiness, the practice developed of avoiding strict voting. Instead, the Contracting Parties for several decades took virtually all of their decisions by 'consensus'. Often even when a formal vote was required (such as for a waiver), there would generally be a negotiation for a consensus draft text before such text was submitted to member states'capitals for the formal vote.

In practice, however, the word 'consensus' was not defined in the GATT. In the legal sense, if some sort of 'consensus' could not be achieved, the fall-back was the loose majority voting authority of the GATT. In the WTO Charter, however, consensus is defined (at least for some purposes) as the situation when a decision occurs and 'no member, present at the meeting when the decision is taken, formally objects to the proposed decision'.[29] It should be noted that this is not the same as unanimity, since consensus is defeated only by a formal objection by a member present at the meeting. Thus, those absent do not prevent a consensus, nor does an abstention prevent a consensus. Furthermore, the practice in the GATT, and surely also in the WTO, is that some countries that have difficulty with a particular decision will nevertheless remain silent out of deference to countries with a substantially higher stake in the pragmatic economic consequences of a decision. Thus, the consensus practice itself involves some deference to economic power. This has certainly been the practice in the GATT, and the WTO Charter provides that the WTO shall be guided by such 'customary practices'.

The WTO is considerably more explicit about the situation where consensus fails. In a few instances, a decision must be by consensus and there is no fall-back to a majority vote (for example, adding plurilateral agreements to Annex 4, Article X:9, and amendments to the dispute settlement procedures in Annex 2). In many other situations, when consensus fails there is an explicit fall-back vote, such as three-quarters of the membership. It is considered quite difficult to achieve such a heavy fall-back vote as three-quarters of the membership (not three-quarters of those voting), since often a quarter of the membership is not involved in a particular decision and may not show up at the meeting.

Therefore, the protections of national sovereignty built into the WTO Charter rules on decision-making are substantially enhanced compared with those of the GATT.

There still exists some risk in the voting system and practice under the WTO which could be crucial in defining and constraining these risks. For example, bloc voting could develop, and there have been hints that the European Union, with its number of votes (equal to the number of its members who are also members of the WTO) and the votes of members of a series of association and affiliation agreements (all totalling more than a majority of GATT and now WTO members), could be tempted to use this voting strength in a way to achieve some of its trade policy goals (such as a waiver or selection of officers).

### 3.5 Members and membership

Since in theory the GATT was not an 'organization', it did not have 'members'. The terminology used to emphasize this theory in the Agreement was 'contracting party'. Yet we can fairly speak of 'membership', in the light of the evolution of the GATT into a de facto organization.

Apart from the twenty-three nations that were original GATT Contracting Parties (CPs), nations became GATT Contracting Parties by one of two methods. The normal method is governed by Article XXXIII of the GATT and required a two-thirds vote of approval by the existing CONTRACTING PARTIES for a nation to be accepted into GATT. The key part of obtaining sufficient votes for accession is the candidate nation's willingness to negotiate tariff concessions which existing GATT CPs deem to be adequate to fulfil their views of 'reciprocity' to the various existing GATT concessions now binding the existing GATT members. It seemed unfair to let a nation enter the GATT and receive the advantage of over forty years of various trade concessions and obligations, which the existing membership had accepted, without requiring the new nation also to commit itself to equivalent obligations. This is sometimes referred to as 'negotiating the ticket of admission'.

In this respect, WTO Article XII on accession follows the GATT (and presumably will largely follow the GATT practice for the accession procedures). Of course, accession to the WTO requires acceptance of all of the multilateral agreements, so in that respect there is added complexity.

An interesting aspect of GATT membership, which continues under the WTO Charter, is that full nation-state 'sovereignty' is not a condition of membership. Instead, the language of the GATT and of the WTO (Article XII) allows a 'separate customs territory possessing full autonomy in the conduct of its external commercial relations and of the other matters provided for in this Agreement and the Multilateral Trade Agreements' to accede to the WTO 'on terms to be agreed'. Such accession, of course, under the 'single package' idea, involves full acceptance of the WTO and Annexes 1, 2 and 3, thus including the GATT, the GATS and the Intellectual Property Agreement, as well as the DSU and the TPRM.

A second path to new membership in the GATT also existed, however. GATT Article XXVI:5(c) provided that, if a parent country has accepted the GATT in respect of a dependent customs territory (such as a colony) and that customs territory later becomes independent, such territory can become a GATT Contracting Party merely through sponsorship by the parent country. Over fifty newly independent nations aquired GATT membership by this route. The advantage to those nations was that they did not need to negotiate a ticket of admission.

One result of this provision was that in the GATT many developing countries – those that were newly independent and sponsored for Contracting Party status – had either no tariff schedule or very brief tariff schedules. Under the WTO, this is no longer the case.[30] A condition of membership of the WTO is the acceptance of a schedule of concessions and commitments for both the GATT and the GATS (Services). Later accession requires the negotiation of an agreement between the WTO and the applicant as noted above, and presumably this will apply the same conditions as apply for original membership.

Article XXXV of the GATT contained an important measure which affected to whom a Contracting Party's GATT obligations would apply. This Article, introduced in the original 1947 GATT draft when the voting requirement for new members was reduced from unanimity to two-thirds, allowed either a prior member or a new member to 'opt out' of a GATT relationship with the other at one time only – the time when the new member entered GATT.[31] This opt-out provision was used extensively against Japan in 1955 when it became a member,[32] and it has been used by other countries for a variety of reasons. Often the reason to object to a GATT relationship was political in nature, as in the case of India's original 1948 invocation of Article XXXV against South Africa.[33] This opt-out clause was carried into several of the 1979 Tokyo Round 'Codes', and has been used in some cases in connection with those codes also.[34]

Article XIII of the WTO Charter carries forward this concept of a one-time opt-out between WTO members at the time one or the other first enters the agreement. There is provision for carry-over of the opt-outs for the GATT which are still in effect, and it is applied now to all of the multilateral trade agreements in Annex 1 and also Annex 2 (dispute settlement).[35] This can have a substantial significance. It means that an applicant country may be approved for membership in the WTO, and assume that membership, but find then that it will not have a treaty obligation relationship on the most important rules, *vis-à-vis* another WTO member, because that other member has opted out. Indeed, the treaty language of the WTO Charter on this point suggests that an existing member might be willing to vote in favour of a new applicant's membership, but at the same time give notice and apply the opt-out. Under the laws existing in the United States in mid-1996, the United States Executive Branch may be required to use the opt-out clause in the event of accession by certain 'communist' countries. (This would leave the United States and the other country to continue a WTO–GATT relationship by bilateral agreement, but that agreement would be subject to annual or other reviews.) The WTO language is similar to that of the GATT, but it expands the concept beyond the GATT Agreement to other matters provided for in the WTO Agreement and the Multilateral Trade Agreements annexed thereto. 'Non-application' of a plurilateral agreement (Annex 4), however, is governed by the plurilateral agreements.[36]

Several interesting 'membership' questions existed in connection with GATT practice, one of which was the status of the European Community (EC) in GATT. It is possible to argue that the EC is a 'separate customs territory possessing full autonomy' over GATT matters so that it could itself become a Contracting Party. Yet it did not take steps to do so. The EC represented its member states (all of whom were GATT CPs) in the GATT. However, the Treaty of Rome allocates competence over member states' external trade relations with the EC institutions. The EC Commission provides a mission at the GATT (now the WTO) and asserts the sole right to speak on trade matters for the member states at the GATT (and presumably the WTO). There have been occasional instances, however, when because of this some tension has developed between the EC Commission representatives and the member states. In addition, in several instances it was decided that the Commission did not have competence to discuss a matter at the GATT, and in such cases the member states spoke and acted for themselves. When actual voting occurred in the GATT (somewhat rarely), each member state cast its vote as a Contracting Party (supposedly coordinated by the EC), and thus the EC effectively had fifteen votes.[37] The language in some Tokyo Round Agreements permitting the EC also to be a Contracting Party raised the possibility that the EC would control one more vote (its own), in addition to the votes of its member states. In the WTO, the EC total votes are limited to the number of member states.[38]

China was one of the original Contracting Parties of the GATT in 1948, but arguably withdrew from GATT in 1950. (The matter is disputed.[39]) China joined the GATT Multi-Fibre Agreement in 1984, and became an observer to the GATT in that same year.[40] In the Uruguay Round, beginning in 1986, the People's Republic of China negotiated for 'resumption' of its seat. China eagerly sought to become an original member to the new WTO, which required it to become a Contracting Party to the GATT under the appropriate procedures (somewhat ambiguous). However, China did not succeed in this quest, and is still going through the process of negotiating the appropriate agreement for its membership in the WTO.[41]

The case of Hong Kong is also very interesting in connection with GATT 'membership'. For many years Hong Kong participated in the GATT as a colonial entity of the United Kingdom, which was a GATT Contracting Party.[42] In April 1986, after a declaration of the United Kingdom under Article XXVI, Hong Kong was accepted by the GATT CONTRACTING PARTIES as a full Contracting Party. To become such a 'member', however, a determination was made that Hong Kong was an independent customs territory with full autonomy over its external trade relations. The United Kingdom's possession of Hong Kong and adjacent territories ended in June 1997 and an agreement had already been reached between the United Kingdom and the People's Republic of China about the reversion of Hong Kong to China and the status that Hong Kong would then have. Before Hong Kong was accepted as a Contracting Party to GATT, assurances were received from the People's Republic of China that Hong Kong's status would remain sufficiently independent to fulfil the GATT Article XXVI requirement.[43] Hong Kong, as a Contracting Party of GATT, completed the appropriate steps to accede as an original member to the WTO, and since 1 January 1995, the

effective date of the WTO, Hong Kong has been such a member. A 1997
WTO document reaffirms this state of affairs, at least for the present.[44]

### 3.6 Links, relationships and public participation

For any international organization today, but particularly for one like the
WTO, which has such potentially profound effects on the economic well-
being and activity of billions of citizens, there are a number of complex
and sometimes troublesome issues about how the organization relates to
other international organizations (governmental), to non-governmental
organizations (NGOs), and indeed to businesses, firms and individual
citizens. The story begins with the United Nations and then continues
with other relationships.

The WTO Charter itself contains only a few clauses relating to these
relationships, as follows:

*Article III*
*Functions of the WTO*

5. With a view to achieving greater coherence in global economic policy-
making, the WTO shall cooperate, as appropriate, with the International
Monetary Fund and with the International Bank for Reconstruction and
Development and its affiliated agencies.

*Article V*
*Relations with Other Organizations*

1. The General Council shall make appropriate arrangements for effective cooperation with other intergovernmental organizations that have
responsibilities relate to those of the WTO.

2. The General Council may make appropriate arrangements for consultation and cooperation with non-governmental organizations concerned
with matters related to those of the WTO.

The Dispute Settlement Understanding has some reference to the composition of panels, confidentiality of deliberations, and a panel's right to
seek information or advice from 'any individual or body which it deems
appropriate', which affect questions of transparency and NGO or private
person relationships, as we shall explore below.[45]

## The WTO and the United Nations

The WTO is not a part of the UN, nor is it a specialized agency of the UN, for a variety of reasons. Although the GATT was never supposed to be an organization, the ITO (as indicated in Chapter 2) was intended to become the trade complement to the financial institutions of the Bretton Woods System, and thus is likely to have become a specialized agency of the UN. Both the World Bank and the IMF entered into such a relationship with the UN (by specific and tailored agreements), and continue in that status today.[46]

As indicated in Chapter 2, in 1948, in anticipation of the ITO, a preparatory organization – the Interim Commission for the ITO (ICITO) – was formed as part of the United Nations to provide the organizational and secretariat infrastructure for the ITO pending its coming into being.[47] At the same time, the ICITO serviced the GATT since it was assumed that the GATT would be part of the ITO family and would receive its secretariat services from the ITO secretariat. By the end of the 1940s however, the ICITO secretariat was devoting virtually all its efforts to servicing the GATT, and this continued throughout GATT history. So as the GATT gradually became a 'de facto organization' it continued to rely on the ICITO for its secretariat services, and reimbursed ICITO (100% of its budget eventually). This situation continued until the GATT organization ended (one year after the WTO came into force). Thus, secretariat members were technically employed by ICITO and depended on it for their salaries and fringe benefits. In this circumstance the UN rules were generally applied to the ICITO secretariat. Employment contracts and pension benefits were legally those of ICITO (and the UN pension system). This situation actually still continues in spring 1998, although the WTO Charter calls for a WTO secretariat, and measures are under way to achieve this new legal status for the secretariat.[48] Indeed, members of the ICITO/WTO secretariat chafe at the UN regulations and have sought to become independent of it, partly because the pay scale and pension rules of the UN are deemed inadequate compared with those of other economic and financial institutions such as the World Bank, IMF and even the Organization for Economic Cooperation and Development (OECD).[49]

The question of 'specialized agency' status for the WTO link to the UN was explicitly considered and explicitly rejected by the WTO members, possibly because of the scepticism of some members about the UN budgetary and personnel policies and their alleged inefficiencies.[50]

*International governmental organizations (IGOs)*

The language of the WTO Charter only calls for an 'appropriate' relationship with IGOs. Except for the IMF and World Bank, most questions about such a relationship seem to concern observer status, and a number of IGOs were given observer status in the GATT, and now have observer status in various organs or committees of the WTO. Such status usually brings access to documents, including restricted documents. Certain functions, particularly negotiating positions, have sometimes been kept more confidential, and this can give rise to questions of access by IGOs or other entities. So far it appears that observer status in the WTO is determined by various subordinate bodies of the WTO, rather than by one decision that embraces all WTO activity.[51] Also, it appears clear that WTO members want some 'justification' or 'reason' for an IGO to receive observer status: it is not enough simply to be an IGO. As yet there does not seem to be any general rule for an IGO representative to 'participate' or speak at meetings that are observed.

The GATT had (and still has) language[52] that recognized a special role for the International Monetary Fund on certain issues relating to GATT trade rules, particularly the exception in GATT Article XII regarding balance-of-payments problems. The WTO Charter provision (quoted above) recognizes a special role 'as appropriate' for both the IMF and the World Bank. This has turned out to be a bit difficult in practice owing to divergent ideas about such a role as between the three organizations concerned. However, in 1996 a delicately negotiated text of agreement between the WTO and the IMF and World Bank was completed, recognizing a need on the part of the financial organizations to have some special access and opportunity to comment. This was particularly an issue in terms of a role for the IMF and World Bank in dispute settlement procedures.[53]

*Non-governmental organizations*

So far there seems to be no general explicit rules regarding a role for NGOs in various WTO activities. This has been a source of strong criticism of the WTO, particularly by environmental groups who argue that NGOs can bring important expertise and information to bear on WTO questions. Again, the WTO language speaks of 'appropriate arrangements'. The DSU language entitling a dispute panel to seek 'advice from any individual or body' could be used to provide some role for NGOs, at least in specific cases (and it would seem feasible to develop some general presumptions subject to overruling by panels in specific cases).[54]

Certain specific measures have been taken by the WTO to reach out to NGOs, including assisting in the organization of conferences to which NGOs have been invited and making provision for NGOs (as well as some private parties and press persons) to attend specified open sessions of the December 1996 first Ministerial Conference held in Singapore. It remains to be seen how much more the WTO can and will do to extend participation to NGOs.[55]

### 3.7 Regional trade blocs and the WTO

One of the more difficult institutional problems for the WTO is the widespread development of regional trade blocs, which in the view of some threaten to detract from and compete with the goals of multi-lateralism embodied in the WTO/GATT system.[56] Under the GATT this was already a major problem, partly because the legal principles contained in the GATT, principally the provisions of Article XXIV relating to customs unions and free trade areas, appeared to be inadequate to prevent potential abuses.

The starting point in the GATT rules is the MFN clause. This standing alone would generally work against regional trade arrangements, but GATT Article XXIV provides an ambiguous and potentially broad exception to MFN for customs unions and free trade areas that meet certain criteria. An article in the Services Agreement, GATS, provides a similar exception with some similar problems.

GATT Article XXIV is based partly on the historical precedent of special regimes of frontier traffic between adjacent countries, but also on the policy that total world welfare can be enhanced by regimes of trade that totally eliminate restrictions to trade among several countries. This is a kind of 'all or nothing' idea, which is prepared to tolerate some of the disadvantages of preferential treatment of trade in exchange for substantial liberalization of trade between several nations. It recognizes the 'free rider' or 'foot dragger' disadvantages of MFN, allowing particular departures from MFN to facilitate trade liberalization if such liberalization goes far enough to provide substantial advantages to the world. This Article is also designed to allow such departures from the MFN principle for the purpose of trade creation, while discouraging regimes leading to trade diversion.

For these reasons, the GATT exceptions for customs unions and free trade areas provide several significant limitations on the exception. First, the MFN departures are in theory allowed only for CUs or FTAs that are defined to require liberalization on 'substantially all' the trade involved. Second, regarding CUs, the GATT Article requires that the common tariff arrangements of the preferential group towards third country 'external' trade be not 'on the whole' more restrictive than the 'general incidence of' duties and regulations before the CU was formed. These are, however, difficult legal concepts to apply, and have caused much controversy in the GATT. In addition, the GATT exception allows an 'interim agreement' – one that leads to a CU or FTA within a reasonable time – to depart from MFN. This has opened a loophole of considerable size, since almost any type of preferential agreement can be claimed to fall within the exception for 'interim agreement', and 'reasonable time' is exceedingly imprecise.[57]

Indeed, despite notification of over 100 Article XXIV-type arrangements, some of which provided very loose preferences as 'interim agreements' and indicated no set date for completion of the FTA, there was no formal record of GATT 'disapproval' of such arrangements.[58]

The Uruguay Round results include an 'Understanding on the Interpretation of Article XXIV of the General Agreement on Tariffs and Trade 1994', which was designed by the negotiators to address some of these problems.[59] While not changing the actual language of Article XXIV of GATT 1994 (which, of course, is part of WTO Annex 1A), the Understanding sets forth certain interpretations and guidelines for handling some of the ambiguities in Article XXIV. Significantly, the Understanding also provides that the dispute settlement provisions of GATT 1994 (which presumably now means the WTO dispute settlement procedures) may be invoked with respect to any matter arising under Article XXIV relating to customs unions, free trade areas or interim agreements. This was an issue that had come up in a case brought against the European Community for its banana regulations,[60] and the negotiators have resolved to reinforce the opinion of the dispute panel in the two panel reports on bananas, which indicated that Article XXIV could be invoked despite an argument that the Article has some separate procedures that could arguably be applied to disputes.

While there was general agreement on the trade policy goals of multilateralism and non-discrimination modified by some objectives mentioned above in connection with the regional exceptions, countries have nevertheless sometimes been frustrated with the GATT, multilateralism and MFN. The large numbers and wide diversity of economic and trading systems represented, coupled with a 'lowest common denominator' approach, partially encouraged by the MFN clause, have made it sometimes difficult to achieve progress within the GATT towards resolving some of the issues that world trade developments have posed. This has been particularly true for new areas needing international discipline, such as trade in services, or intellectual property. Other issues that have arisen include environmental rules, competition policy, dumping rules, and of course the ongoing concern about trade in agricultural goods. The GATT dispute settlement system and its institutional structure have been criticized as inadequate for many new developments in world economic relations.[61] All of these factors have led groups of countries to consider moving beyond the GATT/multilateral system to develop more tightly knit and deeper regulation of economic relations, for small groups of nations on a preferential basis.

In addition, it has become increasingly clear that the language of GATT Article XXIV is not adequate for the developing international economic practices today. For example, neither the GATT generally nor the language of Article XXIV deals with the important question of 'rule of origin', by which preferential parties determine whether goods are entitled to receive the preference of their arrangement. Rules of origin can be very damaging to the trade of third parties, if the rules are designed to strongly favour products and parts manufactured within the preferential area.[62] Similarly, certain other trade policy laws and rules are not clearly addressed in GATT language. For example, how does a safeguard or escape clause measure operate? Can a preferential arrangement give preferences to its preference parties in the application of an escape clause? Arguably the answer should be yes, since the preferential group should be treated more like a single trading entity. A similar argument, or problem, is raised by the unfair trade rules (anti-dumping and countervailing duties), but there is now a practice of tolerating preferential agreements that do not eliminate such unfair trade rules between the preference parties.[63]

Furthermore, there are a number of issues regarding the institutional structure of preferential arrangements, particularly those relating to dispute settlement. Since one of the motivations for preferential arrangements is a certain frustration with the GATT, it is not surprising to find different procedures in some arrangements. This might detract from the eligibility of such a system for the GATT Article XXIV exception.

Another area of considerable ambiguity, even with regard to the traditional subjects of the GATT, includes the application of certain other GATT exceptions, such as the general exceptions of Article XX (e.g. health regulations and competition) and the newly prominent issues of environmental regulation. The major new subjects of trade in services and intellectual property can also be a question, at least for future development of standards and policies relating to preferential areas.[64]

Indeed, there are so many variations and so many possible preferential arrangements, that nations entering them may find it necessary to develop a new type of 'MFN' clause: a clause that will ensure to the preference parties preferences at least as favourable as those granted to other potential preferential parties when a nation belonging to one enters into additional similar arrangements.

### 3.8 Some reflections

The Uruguay Round negotiators obviously felt that it was important to create a new trade organization to correct some of the institutional problems of the GATT and to facilitate the more effective implementation of the vast Uruguay Round results including new texts on important new subjects such as services trade and intellectual property.

However, the negotiators were worried about the dangers of too much power in the new institution they were creating. Too much power could be distorting, misused and corrupting. Experienced government leaders wanted to build checks and balances into the evolving system for world trade. To some extent they did this with embellishments to the dispute settlement system and an emphasis on rule orientation. But they also did it by building into the institutional 'constitution' certain constraints on the power of the new organization and its entities and decision-making processes. A national government representative could easily be concerned about the potential of an international 'faceless bureaucracy' or even majority voting by sometimes irresponsible one-nation one-vote procedures. A particular government's democratic legislature may have spent decades developing laws and administrative procedures that delicately balanced conflicting governmental goals to achieve, for example, both a large measure of environmental protection and reasonable protection of private property. Or compromises may have been struck to achieve an appropriate relation between economic incentives compared with protection of poor and needy elements in a society. It could often be intolerable for an international body to come along and upset these careful balances and compromises, perhaps motivated by vastly different societal customs and beliefs among more than 130 nations.

But checks and balances are also a compromise. On the one hand, there are necessary measures of cooperation among different nations to avoid the dangers of a 'race to the bottom'[65] or the 'prisoner's dilemma' when nations competitively act to 'beggar neighbours' in order to enhance their own constituents, often causing overall harm to everyone. On the other hand, the dangers of such cooperation have been indicated above. Thus, the WTO Charter contains considerably more treaty text about various types of decision-making, than did, for example, the GATT. A key issue to watch over the next few years is whether the WTO as an institution has been too constrained by the various checks and balances discussed in this chapter to enable it to respond effectively to the many and rapid changes in economic and market forces that are occurring. In the final chapter of this book I will return to some of these challenges.

Clearly, the WTO is not a 'perfect' institution. It still represents some of the older ideas of conducting 'diplomacy', which called for secrecy and elitism. Observers are critical of the WTO's lack of transparency, the lack of opportunities for broad participation by various private citizen groups and NGOs, and the (sometimes) seeming lack of 'democratic legitimacy' for some of its decisions. It will be interesting to observe how this institution develops within its constitutional structure so as to reconcile the need for international cooperative action with a respect for the constraints placed on its capacity for action.

# Chapter 4

## Dispute settlement and the WTO

### 4.1 The policies of dispute settlement procedures

For a variety of reasons, dispute settlement procedures have been growing in importance as an essential part of international economic relations and the diplomacy for those relations. The last decade of GATT, 1985–94, saw greatly increased attention to the dispute settlement procedures, and that attention continued to increase after the Uruguay Round treaty introduced numerous reforms in those procedures. Both WTO and important national leaders have lauded the dispute settlement procedures in the WTO, making them almost the centrepiece of the new Organization. For example, WTO Director-General Renato Ruggiero said in a Special Report of 30 September 1996 concerning preparations for the first Ministerial Conference in December 1996 in Singapore:

> One success that stands out above all the rest is the strengthening of the *dispute settlement* mechanism. This is the heart of the WTO system. Not only has it proved credible and effective in dealing with disputes, it has helped resolve a significant number at the consultation stage. Furthermore, developing countries have become major users of the system, a sign of their confidence in it which was not so apparent under the old system.[1]

The Ministerial Declaration resulting from the December 1996 WTO Ministerial Meeting at Singapore endorsed this view, stating:

The Dispute Settlement Understanding (DSU) offers a means for the settlement of disputes among Members that is unique in international agreements. We consider its impartial and transparent operation to be of fundamental importance in assuring the resolution of trade disputes, and in fostering the implementation and application of the WTO Agreements. The Understanding, with its predictable procedures, including the possibility of appeal of panel decisions to an Appellate Body and provisions on implementation of recommendations, has improved Members' means of resolving their differences. We believe that the DSU has worked effectively during its first two years. We also note the role that several WTO bodies have played in helping to avoid disputes. We renew our determination to abide by the rules and procedures of the DSU and other WTO Agreements in the conduct of our trade relations and the settlement of disputes. We are confident that longer experience with the DSU, including the implementation of panel and appellate recommendations, will further enhance the effectiveness and credibility of the dispute settlement system.[2]

Officials of the United States have several times expressed satisfaction with the procedures and noted their importance in the diplomacy of the United States.[3]

However, throughout the history of the GATT, and now in the WTO, there has been some ambivalence about the appropriate role of dispute settlement procedures. To over-generalize a bit, there were roughly two viewpoints: one favours a 'negotiation' or 'diplomacy'-oriented approach whereby dispute settlement procedures should not be juridical or 'legalistic', but should simply assist negotiators to resolve differences through negotiation and compromise. Another approach views the dispute settlement procedure as a relatively disciplined juridical process by which an impartial panel could make objective rulings about whether or not certain activities were consistent with GATT obligations.

I suggest that the rule-oriented approach, particularly concerning international economic affairs, has considerable advantage. It is this approach that focuses the disputing parties' attention on the *rule*, and on predicting what an impartial tribunal is likely to conclude about the application of a rule. This in turn will lead parties to pay closer attention to the rules of the treaty system, and hence can lead to greater certainty and predictability – essential in international affairs, particularly *economic* affairs driven by market-oriented principles of decentralized decision-making, with participation by millions of entrepreneurs. Such entrepreneurs need a certain amount of predictability and guidance so that they can make the appropriate efficient investment and market development decisions.[4]

With a rule-oriented approach, then, there often could be some reduction in risk for the various decisions and for longer-term planning. Thus, the need for a higher rate of return to accommodate the 'risk premium' of a venture would be reduced, and the risk premium lowered. This should result in a general increase in the efficiency of various economic activities, contributing to greater welfare for everyone.

The phrase 'rule orientation' is used here to contrast with phrases such as 'rule of law', and 'rule-based system'. Rule orientation implies a less rigid adherence to 'rule' and connotes some fluidity in rule approaches which seems to accord with reality (especially since it accommodates some bargaining or negotiation). Phrases that emphasize too strongly the strict application of rules sometimes scare policy-makers, although in reality the different phrases may amount to the same thing. Any legal system must accommodate the inherent ambiguities of rules and the constant changes of practical needs of human society. The key point is that the procedures of rule application, which often centre on a dispute settlement procedure, should be designed so as to promote as much as possible the stability and predictability of the rule system. For this purpose the procedure must be creditable, 'legitimate', and reasonably efficient – not easy criteria.

The advantages of the rule approach are emphasized in a Wilberforce Lecture delivered by Dr Claus-Dieter Ehlermann in London in 1991, in which he said:

> The current President of the EC Commission, Jacques Delors, has repeatedly emphasized that the power of attraction exhibited by the EC towards the new European democracies, in particular towards the States of Central and Eastern Europe which have recently escaped from Communism, rests in part on the fact that it is a Community based on the rule of law. Within the EC, relations between States are governed by legal rules.
>
> . . .
>
> Growing transnational economic interdependence and the activities – perhaps even the example – of the Community have had a remarkable 'legalizing' influence on the world's most important international economic body, the GATT. Traditionally, many participants (including some Community representatives) tended to

61

view the GATT as a platform exclusively designed for negotiations, characterizing its provisions as 'soft law' and denying its legally binding nature. That view has considerably changed during the last years.

The Uruguay Round represents the most ambitious attempt ever to reform the multilateral trading system and to expand its coverage to new areas such as trade in services and the protection of intellectual property. The international trade law resulting from the Uruguay Round will be an extremely dense and complex set of norms, which parallel most aspects of the Community's internal market legislation. Many of the results reached in the Uruguay Round are largely drawn from Community proposals which in turn are inspired by the recent evolution of the Community's internal legislation. The Community has even proposed to establish the GATT as a true international organization.

The tendency towards a more legal approach is most obvious in the evolution of dispute settlement procedures. As a consequence of the rapid integration of markets, the extension of GATT rules to new areas and the increasing sophistication of protectionist devices, the number of trade disputes has increased considerably. Most participants in the GATT have come to the conclusion that more automatic and more credible dispute settlement procedures are necessary. It is likely that a right to such a procedure will be recognized, that the possibility of blocking the adoption of GATT panel reports will be greatly reduced if not eliminated and that there will be a GATT procedure for authorizing trade sanctions in case of non-compliance with the results of such a procedure. Even the establishment of an appeal mechanism made up of independent experts has been proposed by the Community and is agreed ad referendum. This appeal mechanism may well evolve towards a fully fledged international trade court. The GATT dispute settlement procedures are, of course, intergovernmental and cannot be used by private parties. There is, however, an increasing tendency of governments to take up complaints by private parties and involve outside lawyers in the preparation of cases they bring before the GATT.

Even beyond GATT, there is little doubt that the role of law in international relations generally has increased. It is remarkable how, after the lean years of the late 1960s and 1970s, the International Court of Justice has inspired new confidence from States: presently some eleven cases are pending before the Court and its Chambers.[5]

In this chapter we will explore the rule system of the WTO as reflected mainly in the new and innovative WTO dispute settlement procedures. To do this appropriately, however, we need first to take a retrospective look at the history of the GATT on this subject, partly because to understand this history is greatly to enhance the understanding of the WTO procedures, but also because, as indicated in earlier chapters, the WTO Charter explicitly provides that the WTO shall be 'guided by' GATT history, and one purpose of this provision is to preserve the 'jurisprudence of GATT', which is represented mainly by the GATT dispute settlement reports.

In considering the WTO dispute processes, the goal for this chapter is not just to describe the procedures and the practice under them, but also to probe a number of fairly fundamental jurisprudential questions about these procedures. Some of these questions have been apparent for some time; others have begun to emerge only during the early years of actual application of the WTO Agreement. These questions include the following (but this is by no means a complete inventory), to be addressed in the next sections of this chapter.

(1) Is the process primarily rule-oriented or diplomacy-negotiation-oriented (an issue with 40 years of history)?

(2) What should be the 'standard of review' or 'margin of appreciation' to be applied by dispute panels in reviewing national government decisions called into question by a dispute complaint?

(3) How should the panel process treat questions of fact?

(4) What is the legal obligation of national governments to submit to the dispute procedures of the WTO?

(5) How should procedural and 'preliminary' questions be decided in the WTO system? Must these go to a panel which has to be constituted, or will there develop a process or practice for some of these questions to be handled by standing institutions?

(6) What is the relationship of WTO jurisprudence to the concepts of general international law?

(7) In particular, what should be the approach of the panels about treaty interpretation, including the sensitive issue of reliance on preparatory work?

(8) What is the legal obligation resulting from a dispute process final adopted report? Is there an obligation to carry out the adopted recommendations of the dispute report, or is there only an obligation to 'compensate' for non-performance?

(9) What is the fundamental role of the new Appellate Body? Is it the equivalent of a constitutional court? How cautious or 'judicially restrained' should it be?

## 4.2 The GATT dispute settlement procedure and its evolution

As indicated in the previous section, one of the interesting and certainly more controversial aspects of the GATT as an institution was its dispute settlement mechanism. It is probably fair to say that this mechanism was unique. It was also flawed, owing in part to the troubled beginnings of the GATT.[6] Yet these procedures worked better than might have been expected, and some could argue that in fact they worked better than those of the World Court and many other international dispute procedures.[7] A number of interesting policy questions are raised by the experience of the procedure, not least of which is the question mentioned in Section 4.1 concerning the fundamental objective of the system – to solve the instant dispute (by conciliation, obfuscation, power-threats or otherwise), or to promote certain longer-term systemic goals such as predictability and stability of interpretations of treaty text.

The difference of opinion about the basic purpose or goals of the dispute settlement process in the GATT system has not often been explicit, and the same individuals sometimes express a preference for opposite poles of this difference without realizing it.[8] Of course, the matter is more one of appropriate balance along a spectrum than it is of choosing one extreme or the other; but nevertheless it is important to understand the difference, and describing the dichotomy helps us to do so.

There are at least two important questions, one historical and one of future policy. The historical question is whether the GATT preparatory work and practice through its decades established a goal of dispute settlement oriented more towards 'conciliation and negotiation' or towards 'rule orientation'. The future policy question is, which of these *ought* to be the goal?

With regard to the first question, the record is somewhat mixed. Despite the many statements of some writers[9] and diplomats that the GATT is merely a 'negotiating forum' primarily designed to 'preserve a balance of concessions and obligations',[10] there is considerable historical evidence to the contrary. At least one draftsman of GATT said at the preparatory meetings that 'the Agreement ... should deal with these subjects in precise detail so that the obligations of member governments would be clear and unambiguous. Most of these subjects readily lend themselves to such treatment. Provisions on such subjects, once agreed upon, would be self-executing and could be applied by the governments concerned without further elaboration or international action'.[11]

The original intention was for GATT to be placed in the institutional setting of the ITO, and the draft ITO Charter called for a rigorous dispute settlement procedure which contemplated effective use of arbitration (not always mandatory, however), and even appeal to the World Court in some circumstances.[12] Clair Wilcox, Vice-Chairman of the US Delegation to the Havana Conference, notes that the possibility of suspending trade concessions under this procedure was

> regarded as a method of restoring a balance of benefits and obliga-tions that, for any reason, may have been disturbed. It is nowhere described as a penalty to be imposed on members who may violate their obligations or as a sanction to insure that these obligations will be observed. But even though it is not so regarded, it will operate in fact as a sanction and a penalty.[13]

He further notes the procedure for obtaining a World Court opinion on the law involved in a dispute, and says:

> A basis is thus provided for the development of a body of interna-tional law to govern trade relationships.[14]

Although the ITO Charter would have established a rather elaborate dispute settlement procedure,[15] the GATT had only a few paragraphs devoted to this subject.[16] One can argue that there are a number of 'dis-pute settlement' procedures distributed throughout the GATT (raising the issue of what we mean by that phrase),[17] but the central and formal procedures clearly are those found in Articles XXII and XXIII. The first of these simply establishes the right to consult with any other Contracting Party on matters related to the GATT – a right that does not impose a major obligation, but that is nevertheless useful.[18] Such language should be interpreted to rule out the all too frequently heard argument against allowing a request to consult on some potential legislative or executive action, namely that the matter was 'premature'.

Article XXIII was the centrepiece for dispute settlement in the GATT. It also provided for consultation as a prerequisite to invoke the multilateral GATT processes. Three features of these processes can be stressed:

(1) They were usually invocable on grounds of 'nullification or impair-
    ment' of benefits expected under the Agreement, and did *not* depend
    on actual breach of legal obligation.
(2) They establish the power for the CONTRACTING PARTIES not only to
    investigate and recommend action, but to 'give a ruling on the matter'.
(3) They gave the CONTRACTING PARTIES the power in appropriately
    serious cases to authorize 'a Contracting Party or Parties' to suspend
    GATT obligations to other Contracting Parties.

Each of these features has important interpretations and implications, and
although Article XXIII does not say much about them, the procedures
followed to implement these principles have evolved over the four
decades of practice into a rather elaborate process.[19]

Originally the key to invoking the GATT dispute settlement mechanism was almost always 'nullification or impairment',[20] an unfortunately
ambiguous phrase, and one that might connote a 'power'- or 'negotiation'-
oriented approach. It was neither sufficient nor necessary to find a 'breach
of obligation' under this language, although later practice has made
doing so important, as we shall see. An early case in GATT[21] defined the
nullification or impairment (N or I) phrase as including actions by a
Contracting Party that harmed the trade of another, and which 'could not
reasonably have been anticipated' by the other at the time it negotiated for
a concession. Thus, the concept of 'reasonable expectations' was introduced,
which is almost a 'contract'-type concept.[22] But even this elaboration is
ambiguous.

At the beginning of the GATT's history, disputes were generally taken
up by the diplomatic procedures. At first they were dealt with at semi-
annual meetings of the CONTRACTING PARTIES (CPs). Later they would be
brought to an 'intersessional committee' of the CPs, and even later were
delegated to a working party set up to examine either all disputes or only
the particular disputes brought to the GATT.[23]

However, around 1955 a major shift in the procedure occurred, largely
because of the influence of the then Director General, Eric Wyndham-
White.[24] It was decided that, rather than use a 'working party' composed
of nations (so that each nation could designate the person who would
represent it, subject to that government's instructions), a dispute would
be referred to a 'panel' of experts. The three or five experts would be
specifically named and were to act in their own capacities and not as
representatives of any government. This development, it can be argued,
represented a shift from primarily a 'negotiating' atmosphere of multilateral

diplomacy to a more 'arbitrational' or 'judicial' procedure, designed to arrive impartially at the truth of the facts and the best interpretation of the law. Almost all subsequent dispute procedures in the GATT (and the new WTO) have contemplated the use of a panel in this fashion.[25]

Although under GATT Article XXIII the CONTRACTING PARTIES were authorized (by majority vote) to suspend concessions (by way of retorsion, retaliation or the 're-balancing' of benefits – a term that is not and never has been clear), they have actually done so in only one case, in 1953. That instance was the result of a complaint brought by the Netherlands against the United States for the latter's use, contrary to the GATT, of import restraints on dairy products imported from the Netherlands.[26] For seven years in a row, the Netherlands was authorized to utilize restraints against importation of US grain,[27] although it never acted on that authorization. This had no effect on US action, however. There have been other moves to seek authorization to suspend obligations.[28] Also, the United States has taken 'retaliatory' measures without authorization.[29]

In 1962 an important case was brought by Uruguay, alleging that various practices of certain industrial countries were violations of the GATT obligations. The Panel grappled with the language of Article XXIII, which called for 'nullification or impairment' as the basis of a complaint, but decided to push the jurisprudence beyond the language, and determined in its report that any 'violation' of the GATT would be considered a 'prima facie nullification or impairment'[30] which required a defending Contracting Party to carry the burden of proving that nullification or impairment did *not* exist. This case, followed by many subsequent GATT dispute panels, reinforced a shift in the focus of GATT cases towards the treaty obligations of the GATT, i.e. in the direction of rule orientation. The panels still talked about the need to facilitate settlements and sometimes they acted like mediators. However, in some cases occurring much later, panels that tried too hard to 'mediate' were criticized for not developing more precise and analytical 'legal' approaches.[31]

During the Tokyo Round negotiation, some initiative was taken to improve the dispute settlement processes of the GATT. The so-called 'Group Framework Committee' of the negotiation was given this task, among others. However, partly because of the strong objection of the EC to any changes in the existing procedures, this effort did not get very far. The result was a document entitled 'Understanding Regarding Notification, Consultation, Dispute Settlement and Surveillance', which was adopted by the CONTRACTING PARTIES at their thirty-fifth Session in Geneva in November 1979.[32] Like the other 'understandings' resulting from the

Tokyo Round, the precise legal status of this Understanding is not clear. Unlike the Tokyo Round Codes and other Agreements, it is not a stand-alone treaty. It is also not a waiver under Article XXV of GATT, but presumably was adopted under the general powers of Article XXV to 'facilitate the operation and further the objectives' of the GATT. This document was, nevertheless, very interesting and was also very influential, since it (along with its annex) consisted of a detailed description of the GATT dispute settlement processes. It can be considered a 'definitive' interpretation of the GATT Agreement, binding on all parties by a decision taken by consensus. It thus formed a sort of 'constitutional framework' for these processes in the GATT after 1974 and prior to the WTO.

This Understanding described the procedures of the GATT dispute settlement, noting the requirement of consultation as the first step, and providing explicit recognition of a conciliation role for the GATT Director General (almost never utilized). If these steps did not result in a settlement, then there was provision for a panel process (on decision of the CONTRACTING PARTIES usually acting through their 'Council'). There was some ambiguity whether the complaining party had a *right* to a panel process. If the process went forward, there was provision for oral and written advocacy from the disputants, and a written report by the Panel. The Understanding reinforced the concept of the prima facie nullification or impairment and permitted the use of non-government persons for panels while stating a preference for government persons.

The procedure under the GATT was for the Panel to make its report and deliver it to the 'Council', the standing body of the GATT, which met regularly and disposed of most of the business of GATT. (This body was not provided in the GATT text, but arose through practice and decision of the CONTRACTING PARTIES.) The practice then became firmly established that if the Council approved the report by consensus it became 'binding'; if it did not approve, the report would not have a binding status. The problem was 'consensus'. In effect, the procedure which relied on consensus meant that the nation that 'lost' in the Panel, and might otherwise be obligated to follow the panel obligations, could 'block' the Council action by raising objections to the consensus. Thus, the losing party to the dispute could avoid the consequences of its loss. This 'blocking' was deemed to be the most significant defect in the GATT process.

Subsequent to the 1979 Understanding, there was continued dissatisfaction in the GATT about the dispute settlement procedures. At the 1982 Ministerial Meeting, a new attempt to improve them was made, again with modest success. The resulting resolution suggests the possibility of departing from the tradition of requiring a consensus to approve a panel report, so that the 'losing' party could not block or delay that approval,[33] but subsequent practice did not seem much improved. Later, many GATT members continued to talk of the need for improving procedures, and this subject was included in the Punta del Este Declaration, establishing the framework for the eighth round of trade negotiations.[34]

In the 1980s, as the procedures became more legally precise and juridical in nature, there developed the idea that there were two types of cases in the GATT: the violation cases (based on the prima facie concept), and certain 'non-violation cases', which were cases not involving a violation but nevertheless alleging 'nullification or impairment'. In fact, the non-violation cases have been relatively few in the history of the GATT. One group of scholars has indicated that there are only between three and eight cases of this type in the history of GATT (out of several hundred total cases).[35] Nevertheless, some of these non-violation cases have been quite important.[36]

Many of the treaty agreements resulting from the Tokyo Round negotiations included special procedures devoted to the settlement of disputes relating to a particular agreement. Some of these followed the traditional GATT procedure very closely, and unfortunately they utilized the language 'nullification or impairment'. In a few cases, special 'expert' groups were called into the process to handle highly technical problems involving such things as scientific judgments.[37]

A 1988 panel report pushed the prima facie concept one step further. The case (sometimes called the 'superfund' case) was a complaint by the European Community, Mexico and Canada against the United States for the effects of the US 1986 legislation which taxed imported petroleum products. Since the tax on imported products was admittedly higher than that for domestic products, the United States did not deny that the Article III national treatment obligation had been violated. But it then prepared to prove that the small tax had not caused nullification or impairment, by using trade flow statistics to show that no effects on the flow occurred because of the tax.[38] The Panel refused to examine this proof. It noted that

> there was no case in the history of the GATT in which a Contracting Party had successfully rebutted the presumption that a measure infringing obligations causes nullification and impairment.

It then also noted that,

although the CONTRACTING PARTIES had not explicitly decided whether the presumption ... could be rebutted, the presumption had in practice operated as an irrefutable presumption.

The Panel said that Article III:2, first sentence,

obliges the CONTRACTING PARTIES to establish certain competitive conditions for imported products in relation to domestic products. Unlike some other provisions in the General Agreement, it does not refer to trade effects ... A change in the competitive relationship contrary to that provision must consequently be regarded ipso facto as a nullification or impairment of benefits accruing under the General Agreement.

Therefore, the Panel concluded, a demonstration that a measure was inconsistent with Article III:2 first sentence has no or insignificant effects

would ... in the view of the Panel not be a sufficient demonstration that the benefits accruing under that provision had not been nullified or impaired even if such a rebuttal were in principle permitted.

When one reflects on this history of the GATT dispute settlement process, some generalizations seem both apparent and quite remarkable. With very meagre treaty language as a start, plus divergent alternative views about the policy goals of the system, the GATT, like so many human institutions, to some extent took on a life of its own. Regarding both the dispute procedures (a shift from working parties to panels), and the substantive focus of the system (a shift from general ambiguous ideas about 'nullification or impairment' to more analytical or 'legalistic' approaches to the interpretation of rules of treaty obligation), the GATT panel procedure became more rule-oriented. The oil fee case may perhaps be a high-water mark in this regard, since it arguably turns the treaty language 'on its head'; by stating that a 'prima facie case' cannot be rebutted, it makes the 'presumption' that nullification or impairment derive *ipso facto* from a violation, thus almost discarding the nullification or impairment concept in favour of a focus on whether or not a 'violation' or 'breach' of obligation exists.

The GATT jurisprudence was thus brought almost full circle by the evolutionary case-by-case process of the procedure. However, before one accepts this conclusion completely, it must be said that it is not clear that the implications of the oil fee case – non-rebuttability – will be pursued in the future. The language of the DSU,[39] copied largely from the 1979 Understanding on Dispute Settlement,[40] still states that the prima facie nullification or impairment creates a presumption so that then 'it shall be up to the Member against whom the complaint has been brought to rebut the charge'. This may lead panels to back away from some of the implications of the oil fee panel under the GATT.[41]

The GATT process still had a number of problems, mostly because of the 'birth defects' resulting from the flawed GATT origins described in Chapter 2.[42] These flaws included the following:

- The sparse language gave little detail about goals or procedures.
- The imprecise power of the Contracting Parties concerning super-vision of the dispute settlement process led to the practice of requiring consensus for many decisions, and this gave rise to two 'blocking' defects, whereby a Contracting Party unwilling to submit to the dispute procedure or unwilling to accept a panel report could block a decision by raising an objection which then prevented 'consensus'.
- The first blocking potential could occur at the time of request for a panel procedure by a complaining party; the defendant sometimes would block this decision, although by about the mid-1980s such a blocking vote became diplomatically very difficult to use.
- The second and more serious blocking problem would occur at the time the GATT Council (or a committee for one of the Tokyo Round agreement procedures) would be asked to 'adopt' a panel report. As mentioned above, the losing party could object, defeating the consensus and thus blocking the adoption of a report. During the 1980s various attempts to resolve this problem were proposed, but none succeeded.
- Because there were separate dispute settlement procedures in various Tokyo Round-specific 'Code' Agreements, dispute settlement pro-cedures were fragmented; also, some disputes would occur over which procedure to use.
- There had been several unfortunate instances of a Contracting Party government interfering with potential panel decisions by inappro-priately pressuring a particular panelist.

Not all of these problems have been resolved, of course, but the next section will explore how the Uruguay Round DSU has measurably improved the system.

Despite these various problems and defects, however, the GATT dispute settlement process was sufficiently admired that various trade policy interests sought to bring their subjects under it. This was one of the motivations that led both the intellectual property interests and the services trade interests to urge that those subjects be included in the Uruguay Round. The UR result, of course, applies the new DSU procedures to those subjects. In addition, both the US–Canada free trade agreement and the subsequent NAFTA largely adopted the GATT-type processes and language (and for certain cases established even more powerful procedures).[43]

## 4.3 The DSU and outline of procedure

The new text solves many, although not all, of the issues that have plagued the GATT dispute settlement system. It accomplishes the following:

(1) It establishes a unified dispute settlement system for all parts of the GATT/WTO system, including the new subjects of services and intellectual property. Thus, controversies over which procedure to use will not occur.
(2) It clarifies that all parts of the Uruguay Round legal text relevant to the matter in issue and argued by the parties can be considered in a particular dispute case.
(3) It reaffirms and clarifies the *right* of a complaining government to have a panel process initiated, preventing blocking at that stage.
(4) It establishes a unique new appellate procedure which will substitute for some of the former procedures of Council approval of a panel report. Thus, a panel report will effectively be deemed adopted by the new Dispute Settlement Body (DSB), unless it is appealed by one of the parties to the dispute. If appealed, the dispute will go to an appellate division. After the Appellate Body has ruled, its report will go to the DSB, but in this case it will be deemed adopted unless there is a consensus *against* adoption, and presumably that negative consensus can be defeated by any major objector. Thus, the presumption is the reverse of previous procedures, with the ultimate result that the appellate report will come into force as a matter of international law in virtually every case. The opportunity for a losing party to block the adoption of a panel report will no longer be available.

The DSU is designed to provide a single unified dispute settlement procedure for almost all the Uruguay Round texts. However, there remain some potential disparities. Many of the separate documents entitled 'agreements', including the GATT in Annex 1A and certain other texts such as the subsidies 'code' or the textiles text, have clauses in them relating to dispute settlement. But the DSU Article 1 provides that the DSU rules and procedures shall apply to all disputes concerning 'covered agreements' listed in a DSU Appendix, so presumably this trumps most of the specific dispute settlement procedures.

However, even the DSU provisions allow for some disparity. For example, parties to each of the plurilateral agreements (Annex 4) may make a decision regarding dispute settlement procedures and how the DSU shall apply (or not apply). In addition, another DSU appendix specifies exceptions for certain listed texts. Thus, the goal of uniformity of dispute settlement procedures may not be 100% achieved. Actual practice will determine to what degree this may be a problem.

The new dispute settlement system has faced certain hurdles in its first years. The first was the US–Japan controversy over automobiles, which was fortunately settled. The second was the selection of the Appellate Body itself, a very interesting process that turned out to take six months longer than expected but in the end worked out well, with the establishment and swearing in of that body in December 1995. The third hurdle was the first case that went all the way through the Appellate Body – the case against the United States on gasoline regulations (which now seems to be headed for a satisfactory resolution).[44] The fourth problem is the question of resource allocation needed for the dispute settlement process. Although there has been an encouraging amount of resources allocated to the dispute settlement process and to the Appellate Body, within a secretariat that otherwise is very short of resources, projections for the near future suggest the possibility of cases outstripping those resources.

As of May 1998, 133 complaints had been initiated under the new dispute settlement process.[45] That is two or three times the normal rate of application for dispute settlements experienced in the later years of the GATT. Perhaps this is a tribute to the new process. These complaints involved 97 discrete cases (because many complaints now have multiple complainants). Already, 28 cases seem to have been settled, which is a very encouraging aspect of the new process. Indeed, the tendency towards settlement is influenced partly by the automaticity of the system mentioned earlier.

Recently there have been dozens of cases in operation which press the limits of WTO resources for disputes. Ten appeals had been completed by May 1998. Many consultations are continuing in the other disputes. The United States has brought more than twenty-five disputes. This indicates a quite remarkable reliance on the new procedure, and would seem to represent confidence by the US government in the new system.[46] On the other hand, the United States is defending in many cases. There have already been settlements in a number of such cases, and indications from the US government are that settlements in others are expected.

The EC has brought nine cases and is defending in thirteen, and Japan has brought four, one of which has been settled, and is defending in nine. One of the most remarkable phenomena in this area is the fact that developing countries are using this process among themselves; that is, developing countries have complained against other developing, countries. This was extraordinarily rare under the GATT.[47]

Although the DSU text has clauses that arguably go both ways, if one reads the DSU through carefully and inventories the clauses that are relevant, it is easy to come to the conclusion that the DSU opts for the rule-oriented procedure.[48] After several years of appeals, and with an Appellate Body that obviously seems to lean towards that direction very strongly, this is likely to be even more definitive.[49] This will be explored further in section 4.7.

The issue of a nation-state's participation in an international dispute settlement procedure poses sovereignty questions of a different sort. If a nation has consented to a treaty and the norms it contains, why should it object to an external process which could rule on the consistency of that nation's actions with the treaty norms? It might be argued that such objections manifest a lack of intent to follow the norms, a sort of accepting of the treaty with fingers crossed behind the back. Indeed, there may be some elements of this thinking in this context. However, it could also be suggested that a nervousness about international dispute procedures reflects a government's desire to have some flexibility to resist future strict conformity to norms in certain special circumstances, particularly circumstances that could pose great danger to the essential national objectives. This is rather an 'escape clause' idea where a nation could accept norms with sincere intent to follow them except in the most severe and egregious cases of danger to the nation or its political system. (Candidly, though, it may also be noted that danger to the political fortunes of the ruling party in such a nation may take on great weight in these considerations.)

Apart from these 'escape clause' notions, however, there is an institutional concern that the dispute procedures may not be objective, may be subject to procedural irregularities, may be overreaching, or may have other important defects that even other nations would recognize, but that are not redressed by the treaty or its institutional structure. This danger, either at the outset or developing at some later time, could legitimately constrain a nation's willingness to enter into stringent commitments to a dispute settlement procedure.

Clearly, some of these considerations played a part in the US 'Great Sovereignty Debate' of 1994.[50] The objections raised to dispute procedures may thus not be objections to the substance of the rules, but objections to the nature, stringency or automaticity of the enforcement mechanisms for those rules. Since international institutions are generally less sophisticated or elaborate than most national institutions, various problems can be feared, such as the difficulty of changing treaties and treaty norms that can become seriously out of date, or the methods of filling in the details for seriously ambiguous text which is often associated with treaties drafted by many countries. The text of the WTO 'Charter' suggests some of these worries, for example the super-majority procedure included in that text for decisions on 'formal interpretations'. Similarly, the Dispute Settlement Understanding reflects a number of hedges and concerns about international dispute settlement.

The DSU continues some of the GATT dispute procedures as developed through practice over forty years, but it now includes elaborate treaty text to govern this practice, as well as a number of new features. As in the GATT, a dispute is initiated by a request for consulta-tions by a disputant (or group of complainants), and the consultation period is a prerequisite for further procedures. If no settlement is achieved, the DSU now makes it clear that the complainant is entitled to a panel procedure, and rules spell out the process for forming a panel (usually three impartial individuals). The rules correct some problems seen in the GATT by requiring stricter time limits and fall-back procedures when the parties cannot agree to certain aspects, such as the Panel's composition or its terms of reference. Much more attention is made in the rules to third-party participation, and initial experience demonstrates a great desire to use this opportunity to participate. But only 'members', i.e. nation-states or 'independent customs territories', can bring cases or participate formally. As in the GATT, the Panel receives oral and written arguments and 'testimony', and formulates a report which, after opportunities for the parties to comment and urge changes, is sent to the Dispute Settlement Body.[51]

The major change, however, is the elimination of 'blocking' when the DSB considers the report. Since the report is deemed adopted unless there is a 'consensus' against adoption (the 'reverse consensus'), and since the 'winning party' could always object, the adoption is considered to be virtually automatic. The 'quid pro quo' for this automaticity, however, is the appeal, which is now allowed for the first time. If an appeal is taken, then the report is not 'adopted'; instead, an appellate division of three individuals, drawn from a permanent roster of seven such individuals (with renewable four-year staggered terms),[52] considers the first-level report, receives arguments from the parties, and writes its own report. This report also is sent to the DSB, where the same 'reverse consensus' rule applies to adoption, again making it virtually certain to be adopted. It is this 'automaticity' that scares some diplomats and critics of the WTO system, although 'automaticity', in the sense of no opportunity to block a report, also exists in many other international tribunals.

The DSU then has a series of detailed rules regarding an 'enforcement' phase if a losing party appears unwilling to carry out the 'recommendations' of the report as adopted by the DSB. These rules provide for 'compensation' with trade measures, and for certain other pressures such as continuous monitoring to enhance the implementation of the dispute results.

In the US 1994 debate, some interests testified that the United States should include in its implementing legislation certain measures regarding dumping law, even if those would appear to be vulnerable to dispute procedure challenges at some future time.[53] Other witnesses argued against the WTO, partly because the dispute procedure was 'tougher', and no longer permitted a single nation to 'block' acceptance of a dispute report. There was criticism of the GATT panels ('decisions by three faceless bureaucrats in Geneva'), and thus of the likely form of the WTO process. Criticism was also targeted at the secrecy of the procedures, the lack of opportunity of private groups (non-government organizations, etc.) to offer views and evidence, the possible conflict of interest of the panellists, the possibility that WTO secretariat lawyers would be biased and would have too much influence on the panels and appeals, and so on. Indeed, although there have been important efforts to 'open up' the WTO procedures (even those relating to decision-making discussed above), many constructive critics of the WTO feel that there is much more to be done.[54]

A very important consideration affecting a nation's willingness to accept the WTO dispute procedures is that nation's view of the role that the treaty and its institutions should play in its international economic diplomacy. The United States (as well as many other nations) has often expressed the view that the GATT and now WTO treaty texts are vitally important to improving a 'rule-oriented' international economic system, which should enhance the predictability and stability of the circumstances of international commerce, which in turn should allow private entrepreneurs to plan better for longer-term investment and other decisions. In short, a basic goal is to reduce the 'risk premium' associated with commerce between nations with vastly differing governmental and cultural structures.[55] If a nation wishes to benefit from these policies, then it becomes difficult to oppose dispute procedures when they impinge on it. There is a 'reciprocity' element in these conditions, and this must be taken into account in reflecting on the weight to be given 'sovereignty objections'.

The United States has explicitly made these considerations part of its diplomacy and has often expressed the view that the rules of the GATT and the WTO are vital for US commerce, particularly US exports.[56] The United States was the most frequent initiator of dispute settlement procedures in the GATT and continues in the WTO with the same approach. It learned very early in the WTO history that to appear to 'thumb its nose' at the dispute procedures posed very serious diplomatic risks to its status in the WTO and therefore to the potential usefulness of the WTO to the United States.[57]

How does all this fit the 'sovereignty objections'? Again, it is abundantly clear that 'sovereignty' is not a unitary concept, but rather a series of particular considerations centred around the problem of allocation of power. Thus, when objection is made to the United States accepting the WTO because of the WTO dispute settlement procedures, the specific ('decomposed') issues of that objection are substantially different from those regarding the problem of treaty norm application, or the institutional structure of decision-making. In addition, the sovereignty objection could really be a series of specific objections about the nature or details of the dispute procedure. These in turn must be considered in the aggregate (unless there were options which allowed a nation to accept some details but not others), and that aggregate weighed against the policy advantages of belonging. 'Sovereignty' thus is not a magical wand that one waves to ward off any 'entanglement' in the international system, but rather a policy-weighing process. The policies most often regard the question of allocation of power: should this nation accept the obligation to allow certain decisions affecting it (or its view of international economic relations) to be made by an international institution, rather than retaining that power in the national government?

As 'heroic' as they may appear, the dispute procedures of the WTO have a number of features that are obviously designed to 'protect sovereignty' of the WTO members, and to prevent too much power being allocated to the dispute process. Many different illustrations could be described here, including (1) the obligation to comply with a dispute ruling; (2) the legal precedent effect of a dispute report; (3) the standard of review by which the WTO panels examine national government actions; and (4) the broad question of 'judicial activism' or worries about panels stretching interpretations to achieve certain policy results which they favour.

Of course, part of the background for these subjects is the detailed procedures and the *persons* who sit on Appellate Body divisions in appeals. The credibility of the procedures, and thus the likely willingness over time of members to accept the results of these procedures, is affected by the procedures and the personnel. Of the seven roster members, for example, three were chosen from large trading powers (United States, European Union and Japan), while at present four are from smaller or less powerful members (Philippines, New Zealand, Egypt, Uruguay).[58] Since policy perceptions about 'sovereignty' might sometimes differ between large and small nations, this majority could create some concerns (at least until practice suggests these are not troublesome) for larger members (who are the most frequent participants in the procedures). In the following sections we explore some of these subjects more deeply.

The DSU provides some of the procedures for appeals. In particular it specifies that appeals will be considered by appellate divisions of three of the seven Appellate Body members, which shall be limited to issues of law covered in the first-level panel report and legal interpretations developed by the initial panel in the case; that the appellate division shall consider only issues that are appealed; and that the appeal may 'uphold, modify or reverse the legal findings and conclusions of the panel'. Opinions expressed in the appellate report shall be anonymous, and the proceedings shall be confidential.[59]

The DSU also provides for 'appropriate administrative and legal support',[60] and this was set up in mid-1995. For various reasons, a separate secretariat (currently four lawyers plus secretarial and administrative staff) was established for the Appellate Body (arguably separate from the WTO Secretariat as such, and certainly separate and separated from the WTO general legal staff). Part of the reasoning here was to make the appeal as impartial and uninfluenced by the proceedings prior to appeal as possible.

Regarding procedures, DSU Article 17:9 explicitly empowers the Appellate Body to draw up 'working procedures' in consultation with the chairman of the DSB and the director-general, communicated to the WTO members for their information. One of the first tasks of the legal staff and the newly appointed Appellate Body members[61] was to draft and approve these procedures.[62] Obviously, many judgments were necessary to flesh out the sparse DSU text regarding appellate procedures. This power of the Appellate Body to establish working procedures is in contrast to the relative silence in the DSU about procedures for the first stages of dispute settlement, and there has been some criticism of the WTO dispute settlement process for lack of such established procedures. The panels at this first stage each have the authority to establish their own procedures, but of course there is considerable continuity in those procedures through advice from the general legal staff of the WTO Secretariat. Still, it is probably unfortunate that there is not a clear explicit authority to establish a set of procedural rules, although there is a strong argument that the DSB (consisting of all WTO members) has that authority if it were willing to exercise it. A nervousness of some WTO members about the dispute settlement process has apparently inhibited the use of such authority, and some might argue that such rules would have to be adopted by consensus, which is often difficult to get.

The appellate experience so far reveals other interesting facets to some of these treaty principles and working procedures. For example, the process of designating which three of the seven Appellate Body members will sit on a particular appeal has purposely been kept very secret. The process appears partly random, but is influenced in some way to share the case load burden roughly evenly. It clearly is not just a rotation basis. A major objective appears to be to prevent anyone (even the Appellate Body members or their secretariat) from predicting who is likely to decide a particular appeal. Interesting also is the fact that, while the DSU provides that for first-stage panels no person who is a citizen of a disputing government may sit on such panel (unless parties all agree otherwise), no such rule exists for the Appellate Body divisions. In part, this may be because in certain cases it would eliminate so many of the Appellate Body that it could be difficult to constitute an appropriate division. But also there may be a sense, stressed in some of the speeches and discussions about the procedures, that the Appellate Body members feel they should not be identified with any particular nation-state member, but rather give importance to their role as an international impartial judicial-type official.

A potentially significant practice for the appeals work that has developed is sometimes described as the 'collegiality principle'. While only three Appellate Body members sit on any division, all the other four members are kept informed, receive the relevant documents, and at a certain point in the proceedings gather together in Geneva to discuss the case. By this means, the appeal division members receive the advice and judgments of the combined wisdom of other Appellate Body members. This process can also be important not only to developing a spirit of valuing high-quality legal work but also to promoting an important sense of consistency and continuity among appellate members for future cases.

At the outset and continuing at present, the Appellate Body members are 'part-time', and work when called upon for appeals and other collegiality or governance (rule-making) meetings. But appellate members often must spend thirty or more days in Geneva for each process they sit on, and with an increasing number of appeals the workload of these members begins to approach full-time. Thus, questions are being asked as to whether the members should be full-time, exclude other occupations, and probably reside in Geneva. The fact that the WTO officials assigned a separate office to each of the seven members suggests that this problem may have been foreseen at the outset. Time will tell whether full-time status and compensation will really occur.

There are many other significant procedural issues arising, as one can see from the early appeal reports. To mention only a few, one can notice in the first appeal report the strong sense of the appellate division to follow rather strictly the DSU language and the rules of the working procedures. For example, appeal report language suggests that the appellate division members should confine themselves to issues that were appealed. On the other hand, since the DSU does not provide the possibility of remand (which could be awkward anyway, since the first-stage panels are ad hoc and tend to disperse after they finish their report), the appellate division clearly felt some necessity to 'complete the case'. Since in the first case they disagreed with one step in the first-stage reasoning, it became logically necessary to address an issue relatively untouched at the first stage, in order to come to a final judgment. The lack of a remand possibility will probably need to be rethought in any review of the dispute settlement procedures.[63]

Similarly, the DSU requirement that appeals be on issues of law will sometimes prove difficult (but is not an unknown difficulty in national legal system). The line between 'fact' and 'law' is often very murky, especially in cases where a judgment is applying the 'law' to a set of complex 'facts', such as in anti-dumping cases, or in certain potential nullification or impairment cases.

Another procedural problem is how to handle 'preliminary objections' in a case. Such objections could include an argument that the WTO or its dispute settlement process does not have jurisdiction; or that improper parties are present; or that the allegations clearly do not make out any case at all. At present there seems no clear way to handle such objections without proceeding to set up a panel at the first stage. Then some party might feel it necessary to appeal against a ruling, so recourse to an appeal could be in hand. But should all of this be mixed with the full substance of the case, so that a whole procedure occurs which in the end may be nullified by a ruling on a preliminary objection? Again, more thought will be needed.

### 4.4 The legal effect and meaning of a WTO/GATT dispute settlement report

What is the international law or other legal effect of a WTO dispute panel or appellate report? First, a brief look at the GATT practice will supply useful background.[64] What can be said about the international legal effects of the result of the GATT dispute procedure?[65] GATT Article XXIII itself is not very revealing. It does say that, if disputing parties cannot reach a satisfactory adjustment between them, they can refer the matter to the CONTRACTING PARTIES, who

> shall promptly investigate any matter so referred to them and shall make appropriate recommendations to the Contracting Parties which they consider to be concerned, or give a ruling on the matter, as appropriate.

The Article also provides explicit authority for the CONTRACTING PARTIES to 'authorize the suspension of concessions or other obligations under the agreement to offending Contracting Parties'. But the Article does not explicitly say that there is an international law obligation to carry out the results of the dispute settlement process. Indeed, the Article does not even provide for such process, except by referral to the CONTRACTING PARTIES. As we have seen earlier in this chapter, a fairly elaborate dispute settlement procedure has evolved, with a process of written and oral advocacy before panels leading to a panel report. We also have seen that the panel report was not considered binding until the CONTRACTING

PARTIES (acting through the Council under current procedures) either 'adopted' it or modified it and adopted it. Thus, an unadopted report under that practice did not have binding force (although it could have persuasive force as the opinion of experts).

Assuming that the process resulted in an adopted panel report, however, what was its legal effect? Several possibilities come to mind:

(1) merely a recommendation, possibly implying that failure to follow it could result in the CONTRACTING PARTIES' authorization of suspension of concessions;
(2) an obligation to obey, with some notion of precedent operating, so that the report has a legal and moral obligation on other non-participating CONTRACTING PARTIES;
(3) an obligation under international law for the disputants to obey in the case in question but with no precedential effect;
(4) the possibility that the adoption by the CONTRACTING PARTIES (or their Council) of a panel report is the equivalent of a 'definitive' resolution by the CONTRACTING PARTIES (as a governing body) interpreting the GATT, pursuant to authority of GATT Article XXV;
(5) 'practice' under the treaty and the institution, such as to provide a basis for arguing for a particular interpretation consistent with the practice, as suggested by Article 31 of the Vienna Convention on the Law of Treaties.[66]

A brief exploration of each of these possibilities will shed some light. Basically, one can argue that the most likely interpretation of the legal effect of the GATT panel report that is adopted is a combination of alternatives (3) and (5) above.

(1) *Mere recommendation* Sometimes it has been argued, referring to the structure of Article XXIII of the GATT, that there is no obligation under the GATT to obey the results of the dispute settlement process, or even the 'findings' of the GATT Contracting Parties. The argument supports this by reference to the possibility under Article XXIII of the Contracting Parties' authorization of the suspension of concessions. Thus, the legal impact of the dispute settlement process is in the form of a contingency: it can result in the authorization of a suspension of concessions, but, in so far as it does not, there is no further legal exposure to the losing party. The problem with this interpretation is the extensive practice in the GATT, which seems generally to confirm the view of the

CONTRACTING PARTIES that there is an obligation to carry out a dispute settlement result.[67]

(2) *Precedent* Some might argue not only that GATT practice suggests an interpretation that there is an obligation to obey the results of the dispute settlement process, but that an adopted panel report would have a 'precedent effect', and thus would operate with a legal and moral obligation on non-disputant Contracting Parties. There are several problems with this idea, however. First, under international law gener-ally, it is considered that dispute settlement procedures or tribunal opinions or decisions do not have a '*stare decisis*' effect.[68] In addition, there are several specific instances in the GATT jurisprudence where panels have consciously decided to depart from the results of a prior panel, and the panel seems to think that it is within its power to do so. This reinforces the notion that a strict 'precedent effect' or *stare decisis* is not operating, even though panels often do cite prior panel reports to support their conclusions. However, there clearly is a de facto prece-dential effect operating, albeit not strictly. (Early WTO appellate reports confirm this approach.)

(3) *Obligating disputants only* It can be argued that the general effect of a GATT-adopted dispute settlement panel report has by practice (and possibly by implications of the GATT language) the effect of providing an international legal obligation for the disputants to obey the results and adopt the report of the panel (sometimes as modified by the Council) for the facts of the particular case being reviewed. Arguably, there was no precedential effect for any future cases, including future cases between the same parties, although it would appear that a future panel could be strongly influenced by the result of the prior panel. There is considerable practice in the GATT to support this approach, although the next alternative suggests a possible different conclusion.

(4) *Definitive interpretation* It can be argued that the Council adop-tion of a panel report was the equivalent of a resolution or decision by the CONTRACTING PARTIES (as the GATT governing body) definitively inter-preting the GATT. As we have seen, Article XXV of the GATT treaty provides very broad authority for the CONTRACTING PARTIES to act jointly.[69] This language would appear to support the notion that the CONTRACTING PARTIES had the power to make a definitive interpretation by decision or resolution (adopted by majority vote, under one-nation–one-vote procedures also established in Article XXV). A definitive interpretation is intended to mean a binding secondary treaty action which obligates all CONTRACTING PARTIES to the GATT pursuant to their advance

delegation of this authority under Article XXV. This concept of the adoption of a panel report would provide its strongest legal impact. In this case, the impact is stronger even than *stare decisis*. It is virtually as strong as the treaty language itself.

That the CONTRACTING PARTIES had the authority to act in this manner seems supported by the practice in GATT. From time to time the CONTRACTING PARTIES adopted 'interpretations' of the GATT. Some-times these were in the form of a chairman's ruling made without objection.[70] At other times the CONTRACTING PARTIES adopted elaborate 'understandings' concerning the implications of the GATT language. We have considered one such understanding adopted in 1979 at the end of the Tokyo Round, with many pages describing the procedures traditionally followed in disputes.[71]

However, even if the CONTRACTING PARTIES did have the authority to make a definitive interpretation,[72] it is not clear that they *intended* their adoption of a *panel* report to have that effect. Indeed, it seems that their intention was quite the contrary. If delegates were asked, when they voted to adopt a panel report, whether they intended to make it binding as a matter of treaty law on all CONTRACTING PARTIES, it is very doubtful that they would have answered in the affirmative. Statements from time to time, as well as the practice evidenced in some panel reports of Contracting Parties departing from prior panel reports, seem to confirm that the GATT CONTRACTING PARTIES did not view their adoption of a panel report as a 'definitive interpretation pursuant to authority of Article XXV'.

There was an advantage to the GATT dispute settlement system in not taking this alternative approach to the legal effect of a panel ruling, but rather following the third approach mentioned. The advantage is that the CONTRACTING PARTIES, in accepting a dispute settlement report, did not have to view it as locking in concrete all the reasoning and conclusions of the report. This left open the possibility in the future for the Council itself to take action (perhaps actually intending a definitive interpretation) that might be different from a previously adopted panel report. It also, of course, left open the possibility of future panels departing from prior panel reports, which is more consistent with general international law practice.

(5) *Practice of states* Apart from the various approaches mentioned above, if a panel report were adopted, and resulted in the disputing parties conforming their practice to the conclusions and findings of the report, this would be one piece of evidence of 'practice under the agreement', as mentioned in the Vienna Convention on the law of treaties as a ground for interpretation. The Vienna Convention Article 31 states that, in interpreting a treaty,

There shall be taken into account, together with the context... any subsequent practice in the application of the treaty which establishes the agreement of the parties regarding its interpretation. ...

Thus, there can be some controversy about whether the practice has gone far enough to establish this 'agreement of the parties'. If later panels follow prior panels, this would add to the evidence of practice, and if there were no considered counter-examples in practice among the Contracting Parties, it is likely to be argued that the practice confirms the particular interpretation of the GATT treaty that has been set forth in the adopted panel reports. This is a more fluid approach than the alternatives mentioned above, and also one that has considerable conceptual difficulties, particularly in what constitutes the 'sufficient practice'. Nevertheless, it can be a useful adjunct to the points made in alternative (3) above.

Now in turning to the new WTO procedures, we can see that these problems are part of the broader question of the legal effect of a final ruling of the dispute settlement process (that is, a report of a dispute settlement panel, or the appellate division which judges an appeal from the first-level dispute settlement report).[73] There is some controversy about the legal status of such a report when adopted (as it will almost automatically be, under the new WTO procedures). The specific question here is whether the international law obligation deriving from such a report gives the option either to compensate with trade or other measures, or alternatively to fulfil the recommendation of the report which mandates that the member bring its practices or law into consistency with the international law treaty texts of the annexes to the WTO. In other words, does it give the choice to 'compensate' or obey? There has been some confusion about this, and some important leaders of major trading entities of the WTO have made statements that indicate this confusion, that are misleading, and that in some cases are flatly wrong.[74]

The alternative interpretation to those mentioned above is that an adopted dispute settlement report establishes an international law obligation upon the member to which the findings are directed to change its practice so as to make it consistent with the treaty text obligations of the WTO and annexed agreements. In this view, the 'compensation' (or retaliation) approach is only a fall-back in the event of non-compliance. This latter approach to the question seems correct.

Some may question whether there is much 'real' differenc; that is, whether a report can really be 'enforced'. International law, however, has very important real effects. In particular, the difference between the two approaches to the legal effect of a dispute settlement process in the WTO can have some important impacts. In some cases the legal obligation may actually have a 'direct application', or at least have fairly direct effects on the legal system. It is true that in other major jurisdictions, including the United States and the Commonwealth countries, this effect is very different. Arguably, in these latter places there is no 'direct application' or 'self-executing' effect, but nevertheless, under long-established US court precedents,[75] a court has the obligation to utilize international law obligations in its interpretation of national law (statutes, etc.). Similarly, if there is an international legal obligation upon a member state and such member state refuses to comply with it, this has a number of 'diplomatic ripples'. There are various responses, albeit often inadequate, permitted under international law. In addition, there are informal pressures that can apply. The United States, for example, found in the 1970s, when it refused to follow the results of the GATT DISC (Domestic International Sales Corporation related to the subsidy rules) case, that it was having trouble capturing meaningful attention from other major trading entities with regard to their own subsidy rules, which the United States felt were quite remiss. Other trading entities would simply note that the United States was not complying with US obligations, so why should they take seriously US complaints against them? This matter was finally resolved with an uneasy, complex and somewhat contradictory settlement, but nevertheless the point had been made to the United States.[76] In another context, the European Union Court of Justice (Luxembourg) has struggled with different questions concerning the GATT and its domestic application. If one concludes that under the WTO the result of a dispute settlement is not 'binding', this is likely to have an important effect on the jurisprudence of that court.

We explored above the GATT practice and jurisprudence (which is 'guidance' for the WTO).[77] Despite various possible views, by the last two decades of GATT history, it seemed quite clear to virtually any perceptive and close observer of GATT practice that the GATT CONTRACTING PARTIES were treating the results of an adopted panel report as legally binding. These reports often 'recommended' that a nation bring its practice into conformity with its legal obligations under the GATT. Indeed, the Tokyo Round Understanding on the dispute settlement process makes this reasonably clear.[78] When adopted, the panel report was treated as binding. A basic problem with the GATT procedure was the opportunity of nations to 'block' a consensus vote on adoption, and thus keep a panel report in 'legal limbo'. It was generally agreed that an *unadopted* report did not have the legal binding effect. The GATT practice was quite strong in this regard, and of course it is well known that under both customary international law and the Vienna Convention on the Law of Treaties, 'practice under the agreement' is important interpretive material.[79]

What can we say about the new DSU? Unfortunately, the language of the DSU does not solidly 'nail down' this issue. For example and contrast, Article 94 of the UN Charter states:

Each Member of the United Nations undertakes to comply with the decision of the International Court of Justice in any case to which it is a party.

Similarly, the statute of the International Court of Justice (ICJ), Article 59, implies such obligation, stating:

The decision of the Court has no binding force except between the parties and in respect of that particular case.

Some sort of comparable language for the WTO[80] and/or the DSU would have been welcome. Oddly enough, some diplomats who assisted in the negotiation of the DSU have said in a private communication that in their view they thought they *had* nailed it down. But one does not find language of the ICJ type in the DSU.

It is also true that the DSU for the first time establishes an explicit treaty text implementing procedure for the result of panel reports. This procedure includes measures for possible 'compensation' or retaliation. Thus, some people have argued that this is an option available to members as an alternative to obeying the mandate of the panel report. As indicated before, however, several arguments point to a contrary view.

So what does the DSU language itself say? We can examine a number of clauses, and the overall gist of those clauses, in the light of GATT practice, and perhaps with some assistance from the preparatory work of the negotiators (unfortunately not well documented). The clauses and the practice strongly suggest that the legal effect of an adopted panel report[81] is the international law obligation to perform the recommendation of the panel report.

At least eleven of the DSU clauses are relevant.[82] In particular, it should be noted that the DSU clauses provide, *inter alia*, the following:

> The first objective of the dispute settlement mechanism is usually to secure the withdrawal of the measures concerned ... compensation shall be resorted to only if immediate withdrawal ... is impracticable ... (DSU Article 3:7)

> When a panel or the Appellate Body concludes that a measure is inconsistent with a covered agreement it shall recommend that the member concerned bring the measure into conformity with that agreement. (19:1)

> Prompt compliance with recommendations or rulings of the DSB is essential in order to ensure effective resolution of disputes to the benefit of all members. (21:6)

> Compensation and the suspension of concessions or other obligations are temporary measures available in the event that the recommendations and rulings are not implemented within a reasonable period of time. However neither compensation nor the suspension of concessions or other obligations is preferred to full implementation of a recommendation to bring a measure into conformity with the covered agreements. (22:1)

> The suspension of concessions or other obligations shall be temporary ... the DSB shall continue to keep under surveillance the implementation of adopted recommendations or rulings ... [while] the recommendations to bring a measure into conformity with the covered agreements have not been implemented. (22:8)

For 'non-violations complaints', the DSU specifies:

> where a measure has been found to nullify or impair benefits under, or impede the obtainment of objectives, of the relevant covered agreement without violation thereof, there is no obligation to withdraw the measure. (26(b))

Thus, the DSU clearly establishes a preference for an *obligation to perform* the recommendation, notes that the matter be kept under surveillance until performance has occurred, indicates compensation shall be resorted to only if the *immediate* withdrawal of the measure is impracticable, and provides that in *non-violation* cases, there is *no* obligation to withdraw an offending measure, which strongly implies that for *violation* cases, there *is* an obligation to conform.

It is true that, once the 'binding' international law obligation to follow a dispute report recommendation has been established, international law has a variety of ways of dealing with a breach of such obligation, and that, understandably, those methods available to the international law system are not always very effective.[83] However, that is a different issue from the question of whether the 'WTO rules are ... binding in the traditional sense'. Certainly they are binding in the traditional *international law* sense. In fact, for many national legal systems, they are also binding in the 'traditional sense' domestically, although not always in a 'statute-like' sense. In the United States it can be argued that the WTO rules, and certainly therefore the results of a dispute settlement report, do not *ipso facto* become part of the domestic jurisprudence that courts are bound to follow as a matter of judicial notice, etc. However, the international law 'binding-ness' of a report certainly can and should have an important effect in domestic US jurisprudence, as in the jurisprudence of many other nation-states.

### 4.5  The role of the dispute settlement bodies:  deference, judicial activism, creativity

There are a number of interesting 'jurisprudential' subjects involved in the new WTO dispute settlement procedure, a few of which are discussed below and in the next section.

*WTO jurisprudence relation to general international law*
The first Appellate Body report[84] is an extraordinarily interesting one, even apart from the substance of what it was addressing, (i.e. the environmental protection matters of US regulation and how they related to at least three different clauses in the GATT, most particularly Article XX). The flavour of that report is significant. Among other things, the report definitely says that this process, and the GATT and WTO generally, are a part of 'international law' as such. There has been some dispute as to whether it was a 'separate regime', sort of sealed off from normal concepts of international law, but the Appellate Body explicitly states that the WTO is part of international law, and it goes on to engage international law principles of treaty interpretation very deeply, referring to the 'Vienna Convention on the Law of Treaties'.[85] Arguably, this suggests an endorsement of the rule-oriented concept.

*The standard of review*
A second important issue is that of the standard of review. This section does not address the standard of review of the Appellate Body when it

reviews the first-level report. Instead, it addresses the degree to which the WTO dispute settlement process as a whole, both panel and appellate levels, should second-guess national government administrative decisions that relate to treaty clauses in the Uruguay Round.

National governments will inevitably be interpreting some of these broad clauses themselves; they will have to, because there is ambiguity as mentioned earlier. To what degree, then, should the international dispute settlement bodies give deference to those national decisions on interpretation? This is the 'standard of review' question. An article in the April 1996 *American Journal of International Law*[86] discusses this question, noting some of the efforts by certain negotiators, mostly those of the United States, who tried to achieve a very restricted standard of review treaty obligation in the Uruguay Round, especially in the context of the anti-dumping measures. The US negotiators tried to translate the domestic US jurisprudence of the 'Chevron Case' into the international obligation in the treaties, but they did not succeed in doing so. There is, however, some very curious language in the anti-dumping text about the degree of deference that a panel or appeal should give to national governments.[87] Basically, it says that if an analysis, according to normal interpretation procedures under international law, results in ambiguity, and if a government has chosen one of the 'permissible options' for interpretation, then the international body should allow the government to continue with that option. There are numerous other problems with that approach, but without going into these it can be noted that the particular language of DSU Article 17:6 of the anti-dumping text applies only to anti-dumping decisions.[88] It does not apply to the rest of the dispute settlement process, and therefore, regardless of what it means in the other areas, perhaps a different approach can be expected.

The DSU text and other provisions in the Uruguay Round text, and resolutions of the Marrakesh meeting, provide for several possibilities that the anti-dumping standard of review text will apply more broadly than to anti-dumping decisions. For one thing, a Marrakesh decision notes, but does not require, the possibility that countervailing duty decisions should be consistent and similar to anti-dumping decisions. In addition, a Marrakesh resolution provides for a review of this anti-dumping Article 17:6 language at the end of five years.[89]

Nevertheless, this issue is an important one. It seems clear there should be *some* measure of deference, at the international dispute settlement level in the dispute settlement process, to national government decisions. There is support for that in other areas of international law, for example in the European Convention of Human Rights.[90] At the very end of the 1996 first Appellate Body report, on the US gasoline case, the report includes this language:

> WTO members have a large measure of autonomy to determine their own policies on the environment, including its relationship with trade.[91]

This appears to be a declaration of intention by the first Appellate Body report to give some measure of latitude to national governments in this respect. That raises a host of other issues. For example, how far should this go? What issues are more appropriately decided at the national level instead of the international level? Europeans sometimes call this a 'subsidiarity' principle.

*Judicial restraint or activism*
Another 'fundamental principle of WTO jurisprudence' is the question of how much 'judicial activism', or 'judicial restraint', should be exercised by the international system. This question obviously relates to the standard of review, but there are other concepts and ideas involved, including how far an international body should 'push the envelope' of interpreting ambiguous clauses to suit certain policy preferences – possibly preferences of the panel or appeal body alone, or policy preferences that the negotiators, or currently the governments, are detected to have. Again, the dispute settlement understanding has some interesting clauses on this. DSU Article 3:2 says:

> Recommendations and rulings of the DSB cannot add to or diminish the rights and obligations provided in the covered agreements.

What does this mean? Arguably, it resonates in the direction of a caution to the panels and appeal divisions to use 'judicial restraint', and not to be too activist. Of course, the US Congress feels quite strongly about that, and in the US Dole Commission proposal,[92] the language 'rights or obligations' is picked up again. It is also included, incidentally, in the WTO Charter. So this notion of restraining changes in the rights and obligations of the nation states is quite prevalent in the system.

The United States arguably would be one of the most jealous about that, and yet it seems to want to push the borderlines in some of the disputes it is bringing. For example, with reference to the so-called 'non-violation cases', almost uniquely in the WTO/GATT system, there is an opportunity to bring a case that does not involve any violation of treaty obligations. Instead, the case may involve what is called 'nullification or impairment', which, as we have seen, is a very ambiguous phrase,[93] and such 'non-violation' cases could seem to urge 'changing rights and obligations', as below.

*Examination of facts*

By and large, the GATT dispute settlement process was not able and did not try to explore facts to any degree. Indeed, it was generally assumed that the facts would be brought to the attention of the international panel by written and oral arguments of the representatives of the disputing nations.

In the WTO procedure, this may also continue. Indeed, in the anti-dumping 'standard of review' text of Section 17.6, it is largely contemplated that the facts will be determined at the national level. However, this text applies only to the anti-dumping cases (so far), and may be difficult to sustain. Certain kinds of issues, such as environmental, financial services and other service issues, as well as intellectual property, may require some greater attention to facts.

It has been noted that competition policy decisions in national legal systems tend to be very fact-oriented, with massive hearings and records to contend with. Indeed, in the potential dispute between the United States and Japan concerning film (Kodak and Fuji), the two private firms that are perhaps the major contenders in the dispute have produced very extensive fact accounts (most of which can be found on the Internet). A serious and prolonged fact-type hearing could easily bankrupt the resource allocation to the WTO dispute settlement system. For example, in a personal communication one party gave an account of a hearing on environmental matters in Canada that lasted nearly 120 days! This would exceed all the hearing days of all the procedures in a typical GATT dispute settlement year, and would probably involve budgetary allocation exceeding all the normal procedures combined for a year.

Clearly, some care will have to be taken about where the dividing line should be drawn between an essential examination of facts in order to determine how the law applies, and more extensive fact records.

*Non-violation cases*

One potentially very troublesome issue concerns the unique special attention given to 'non-violation' cases. Under the GATT, this attention developed through practice by the language in the GATT text, including the phrase 'nullification or impairment' (as discussed above.) This language has been carried into the WTO, and for the first time, a separate type of procedure under the DSU has been designed,[94] as the route to take when a non-violation case is pursued. One problem with non-violation cases is the generality of the language 'nullification or impairment', which creates great ambiguity about what would be an appropriate way to analyse these cases and to determine when one nation had some sort of right of relief from another nation. It is interesting that in the DSU rules for non-violation cases there are no clauses similar to those in the violation cases that would suggest an obligation actually to perform recommendations, that is, to bring one's law into consistency with the international rule. The relief allowed under the DSU is merely 'negotiation for appropriate compensation'. This makes sense, since the basis of a non-violation case is *not* the alleged inconsistency of national laws or practices with an international rule.

One can hope that nations and the responding WTO institutions will be cautious about entertaining non-violation cases for new types of issue for which there are not adequate or adequately precise rules contained in the Uruguay Round treaty texts. This is a matter that has been discussed in connection with so-called 'competition policy'. Competition policy is not centrally or explicitly taken up in the Uruguay Round and GATT treaty texts. Indeed, the fact that such policy was contained in the 1948 ITO Charter, which failed to come into force, led the GATT itself to be very cautious about taking up such policy issues. On the other hand, there are a number of clauses in the new treaty texts for services and intellectual property, etc., which do relate to competition policy. When the United States, say, brings a case that does not involve a violation, but targets something like competition policy, or the Japanese Keiretsu, or something else that is not included within the current treaty texts, it is likely to ask a panel to change the 'rights and obligations'; in other words, it is saying to a panel: 'We want you to interpret nullification or impair-ment to embrace some of these results that for policy reasons we would like to see in this case'. That is risky – it is almost doing with one hand what the other hand is trying to prevent. Obviously, this has longer-term fundamental implications.

*Resource implications*
An important issue for any institution, particularly a new one, is the allocation and adequacy of resources. The 'judicialization' of the WTO procedures does not necessarily come cheap. Already, there is a considerably enhanced budget for dispute settlement compared with that

of the GATT. However, under the GATT, dispute settlement was almost always a 'part-time affair', with virtually no specific allocated resources, except some secretariat lawyers to assist panels. Now there is an Appellate Body with significant staff and other resources, including retainers and per diems, as well as travel and support funds for staying in Geneva. There is a new legal staff devoted to the Appellate Body consisting of a director and three staff lawyers, as well as some non-professional staff. Considerable and, one must say, very admirable space has been allocated for this effort in the secretariat building of the WTO on the shores of Lake Geneva. The regular legal staff continues from its former embodiment, but is finding its work greatly increased, partly because of the large number of disputes that have been initiated.

*Treaty interpretation and preparatory work*

The use of treaty negotiation preparatory work in interpretating treaty clauses, an analogy to 'legislative history' for statutory interpretation, is an issue that is often perplexing. Clearly, different cultures and legal systems have different approaches to using such historical evidence of the 'draftspersons'' intent. In the United States lawyers and courts are accustomed (too easily, some would say) to dredging the record of parliamentary (or diplomatic) negotiations and discussions to glean ideas about what the draftspersons had in mind. Yet in many if not most other countries, generally including European legal systems, there is a reluctance to do this.[95]

The general principle often stated for international law activity in treaty interpretation is largely embodied in the Vienna Convention on the Law of Treaties, particularly Articles 31 and 32.[96] Some commentary on these articles suggests that they establish the principle that preparatory work is a subsidiary or fall-back technique for treaty interpretation, to be utilized only when the other principles of interpretation fail. Article 31 embodies these other principles; Article 32 discusses the use of preparatory work, stating that:

> Recourse may be had to supplementary means of interpretation, including the preparatory work of the treaty and the circumstances of its conclusion, in order to confirm the meaning resulting from the application of Article 31, or to determine the meaning when the interpretation according to Article 31:
> (a) leaves the meaning ambiguous or obscure; or
> (b) leads to a result which is manifestly absurd or unreasonable.

In some GATT dispute reports, panels have made reference to these rules, and in at least one case have even quoted the above Vienna Convention language. Thus, the potential WTO approach is obviously very interesting, and in some cases could be significant in determining or tilting an outcome.

What, then, can we see so far regarding WTO dispute practice? Probably the best evidence we have is the language and approaches we see in some of the Appellate Body reports. In its first two reports this issue was addressed.[97] These reports indicated that WTO law was part of general international law; the Vienna Convention on the law of treaties was deemed particularly relevant, and in one case the provisions of Articles 31 and 32 were quoted. This might suggest a hesitation to use preparatory work. On the other hand both of these early reports readily utilized preparatory work without discussion of the so-called Article 32 prerequisites quoted above. In one case the appellate report noted that the principles of Article 31 call for interpretation in the light of a treaty's 'object and purpose', and seemed to say that, in order to ascertain the purpose, the Panel or Appeal should look at what the draftspersons had in mind. A preliminary and tentative conclusion can thus be made that the WTO dispute bodies will rather easily utilize preparatory work, perhaps without explicitly saying so. Indeed, some would argue that this is in reality the most common practice in international discourse over treaty interpretation.[98]

## 4.6 Implementation and compensation

Early in this chapter it was noted that, under GATT Article XXIII, the Contracting Parties could 'authorize a contracting party or parties to suspend' GATT obligations as sort of a 'sanction' provision. This could even be used in a punitive manner with suspensions much larger than the damage of an offending measure. But in fact the GATT formally authorized suspension in only one early case.[99] The authorization apparently had no realistic effect. In later years the United States and perhaps other nations took trade action without the formal authorization contemplated (almost certainly such action constituting a GATT violation),[100] and there were a few cases where a Contracting Party was contemplating going to the GATT for authority.

All in all, however, effective 'sanctions' were not a realistic part of the practice under the GATT, and yet the conclusion of some academic analyses[101] was that on the whole the record of compliance to the dispute report results of GATT panels was very good. Obviously, the reasons why this was so are intriguing. They relate to more general views about why nations often carry out their international obligations,[102] including ideas about notions of 'reciprocity' whereby nations perceive an importance to their 'good behaviour' so as to be able to demand compliance from other nations.[103]

The DSU, in contrast, has a series of clauses relating explicitly to enforcement and implementation.[104] With blocking no longer possible so that adoption of reports is virtually automatic, the enforcement provisions could prove quite significant. It remains to be seen whether these provisions really enhance the implementation practice in the WTO dispute proceedings, or whether in the end many of the attitudes and policies that made GATT work without real enforcement techniques will be the real force for rule implementation. Certainly informal and anecdotal discussions suggest that governments are realizing the important diplomatic pressures that currently exist to avoid violation of the WTO legal norms,[105] and this realization is considerably strengthened under the WTO as compared with the GATT. Maybe the DSU treaty text has some '*in terrorem*' and reputation effect.

As we have seen in a previous section of this chapter, the DSU calls for nations to carry out the findings and recommendations of the dispute settlement system. One question that is not yet entirely clear is how much time should be given to a WTO member to conform to the dispute report recommendations. In the case of Japan's measures regarding alcoholic beverages, which was ruled inconsistent with the WTO,[106] a special arbitrator ruled that implementation should occur within fifteen months, as suggested by DSU Article 21:3(c). In what cases a longer period will be judged adequate, we do not yet know.

When a member fails to carry out a dispute report, DSU Article 22 calls for compensation and the suspension of concessions or other obligations as temporary measures. This text is more explicit and more elaborate than the brief phrases of GATT Article XXIII, and even provides for arbitration concerning the amount of compensation. However, the DSU has somewhat narrowed the GATT rules on compensation, allowing only suspension of concessions or obligations 'equivalent to the level of the nullification or impairment'.[107] This builds into the WTO a considerable asymmetry of compensatory/suspension activity among different members. A small member will notice that its activity of this type is not likely to have much effect on a large member. This again suggests that it is important to recognize an international treaty obligation to perform (and not just to compensate or endure suspension) and to understand the importance of less formal pressures like those effective in the GATT.

As noted above, however, an interesting measure in the DSU provides a separate track for so-called 'non-violation' cases, and provides in such cases that there is no obligation to 'conform', but only an obligation to negotiate for appropriate compensation to redress the 'nullification or impairment'.[108]

Another question of importance is the time all this takes until the day of reckoning by concrete action against an offending member. It could take two to three years for the whole process. When compared with many national domestic court procedures, this may look quite speedy and efficient, and indeed some participants in these processes have suggested that the WTO proceedings are superior to some national procedures.[109] However, the WTO procedure does not have provisions for 'interim measures' or redress for damage caused during the delay. Thus, an offending nation can be somewhat cynical in promising ultimately to obey whatever comes out of the dispute process, knowing that during the time required for the procedure billions of dollars' worth of damage can be incurred by private businesses located in the complaining country, bringing pressure on that country to settle on terms relatively favourable to the offending nation.

## 4.7 Conclusions and the issue of rule orientation in the new dispute settlement procedure

What conclusions and perceptions can we make about the new dispute settlement procedures and the experience so far? Perhaps two tentative conclusions can be put forth. First, it seems reasonably clear at this point that the new procedures tend rather strongly towards a rule-oriented approach. Second, the new procedure clearly has some impact on the 'sovereignty' issue, but the matter is complex.

Regarding rule orientation, there are two ways to analyse the WTO dispute settlement process: by the implication of the DSU rules, and through the actual practice and the cases.

The language of the DSU is a bit equivocal. On the one hand, there is language that arguably emphasizes the rules, such as Article 3:2, which states:

The dispute settlement system of the WTO is a central element in providing security and predictability to the multilateral trading system. The Members recognize that it serves to preserve the rights and obligations of Members under the covered agreements, and to clarify the existing provisions of public international law.

The discussion in Section 4.4 above emphasizing the 'obligation to perform' can also be seen as evidence of a rule approach, as can the procedures that now prevent blocking and the general thrust of the appellate process and opportunity. The experiences of the first-stage panels and appellate divisions also seem to emphasize a more 'judicial' approach to disputes. The prima facie nullification or impairment principles are restated in the DSU.[110]

On the other hand, some of the old language of the GATT suggesting 'negotiation' and diplomacy approaches might be read as perpetuating some of the GATT's opposing earlier views. DSU Article 3:4 says, 'Recommendations or rulings made by the DSB shall be aimed at achieving a satisfactory settlement of the matter ...', but it does go on to say '... in accordance with the rights and obligations ...' of the DSU and the covered agreements. The DSU also requires settlements to be consistent with the agreements, and to be reported to the relevant WTO bodies.[111]

Turning to the actual practice so far, here too one can detect a pretty strong rule-oriented approach. The appeal case reports so far read much more like a judicial opinion of a national court than did some of the much earlier GATT cases. Indeed, several appellate reports[112] emphasize the general international law nature of these cases, and indicate an attempt by the appellate divisions to address carefully and precisely the legal issues, including some of the procedural issues covered in the Appellate Body's own 'working procedures'.

There is also some interesting additional evidence[113] that the first-stage panels are concerned more with the possible views of the Appellate Body and the risk of being overturned on appeal than they are with a possible vote by the DSB to which dispute reports are formally submitted. Since the DSB virtually cannot overturn the report, this seems natural. But an additional phenomenon has been noticed: this 'rule orientation' emphasis seems to be influencing the selection of panellists for first-stage proceedings, since it is said that the disputing governments wish to have panellists who perform their duties without being overruled on appeal, or who can at least write a legal report that can help persuade the appeal division they are correct. Similarly, the participating governments are finding that the process requires them to be much more 'legalistic' in their advocacy, to the extent of feeling the need to seek non-government expertise to assist them in cases.

To some extent, one can also perceive an important shift in the attitudes of diplomats and officials who are participating in the WTO/ GATT system, often in negotiations for rule formulation or for settlement of disputes. It seems to some observers[114] that the diplomats find it useful or necessary to take much greater account of the dispute settlement procedures in their negotiations. A threat to bring a dispute settlement process is deemed a worthwhile 'bargaining chip', as news reports note.[115] To some extent this is unsettling to traditional diplomats, who worry that their power to defend their country's interests has been diminished or put into the hands of lawyers rather than diplomats or politicians.

As to issues of sovereignty, it is important not to view this subject as one all-embracing issue, but rather to desegregate certain features of the dispute settlement process, as noted in Section 4.3 above. One can perceive different attributes of the system having different approaches, some of which may lead in opposing directions. Issues such as those discussed as 'jurisprudential' can have importance for the issues of 'sovereignty', weakening the international system and thereby yielding more to national 'sovereignty', or on the contrary leading to a strengthening of the international system. Some of the following are relevant in this regard:

- the type of persons selected as panellists and their prior experiences;
- the lack of interim measures in the WTO dispute procedures (weakening the international system);
- the DSU language that admonishes against 'changing the rights and obligations' of members;
- an obligation to perform rather than merely compensate;
- the relative lack of remedies such as monetary compensation, refunds of improper duties, etc.

Finally, one can ponder what the future will bring regarding these important questions. It seems likely that, as time goes on, the WTO dispute settlement system will face more and more 'jurisprudential' issues, many of which have often been faced in national legal systems. Thus, we may see concepts expressed in terms used by the US Supreme Court, or the European Court of Justice – such as 'standing', or 'justiciability', or 'ripeness' or 'mootness' – playing roles in various proceedings.

As we will note in the next chapter, the evolution of the practice of the dispute settlement procedures can be very important, and could, as has often been the case with major national and international tribunals, lead to results not easily anticipated by the original draftspersons of the treaty clauses or by governments that accepted them. But that, after all, is a phenomenon that coexists with the human spirit. The direction of these developments will also be strongly influenced by how well the new institutions perform their role in the world economic system. If they do well, they will gain greater credibility and thus are likely to gain greater leeway to exercise more power in a responsible way not necessarily fully contemplated by the treaty language itself.

# Chapter 5

# Reflections on and implications of the WTO constitution

It now seems increasingly clear that the WTO, although still very young, is becoming one of the most significant multilateral international organizations in existence, and perhaps *the* most significant for economic affairs. With a clearer and much improved 'constitution'[1] compared with its predecessor, the WTO also has an extraordinarily broad mandate and appears ever more significant to economic diplomacy and discourse in an increasingly globalized world. Its dispute settlement procedures may be its most important feature, and clearly nations are utilizing this feature to the point of straining the Organization's resources. Diplomats and governments are adjusting to the new situation created by the WTO's institutions and its dispute settlement procedures, in some cases with trepidation and worry about its impact on more traditional ways of conducting inter-national economic affairs.

In recent decades, economists and other scholars have joined lawyers in recognizing and emphasizing the importance of human institutions to economic development and the effective functioning of markets. Nobel Prize winner Douglas North has noted:

> That institutions affect the performance of economics is hardly controversial. … Institutions reduce uncertainty by providing a structure to everyday life. … Institutions affect the performance of the economy by their effect on the costs of exchange and production.[2]

Sometime earlier Ronald Coase, also a Nobel Prize winner, stated:

It is evident that, for their operation, markets ... require the establishment of legal rules governing the rights and duties of those
carrying out transactions ... To realize all the gains from trade, ...
there has to be a legal system and political order ... Economic
policy consists of choosing those legal rules, procedures and administrative structures which will maximize the value of production... .[3]

The WTO can be considered a part of the world's institutional structure
that is essential for the satisfactory operation of world markets, which
experience and theory have shown can be so important to world welfare.
Thus, the 'constitution' of the WTO will clearly shape world economics
for decades to come, and can also have important influences on many
non-economic goals, including the vital issues of maintaining peace in
the world.

What, then, are the implications and important attributes of the WTO
Charter, or, to embrace a broader concept, its 'constitution', as discussed
in the previous chapters?

Clearly, the Charter has a more carefully constructed architecture than
its predecessor, as we have seen in Chapter 2. This reflects the fact that
much attention has been given to important questions of allocation of
power concerning delicate issues of statecraft and 'sovereignty'. As we
have seen in Chapter 3, many constraints against the international abuse
of power are built into the language of the treaty text; but also, the dispute
settlement procedure, discussed in Chapter 4, is designed at least in part
to prevent member nation-states from abusing their national powers
when those would damage the operation of world markets. Here we see a
*vertical* allocation of power, but in addition the WTO provides interaction between its various parts – its governing bodies and councils,
dispute settlement processes, etc. – which we might characterize as
*horizontal* allocations of power.

One important conclusion we can make from the history of GATT
institutions, as seen in Chapter 2 and also in the later chapters (especially
in Section 4.2, concerning the history of the dispute settlement
procedures) is that the GATT had a remarkable evolution despite its
meagre treaty text. The lesson here is that such evolution occurred, and is
likely to continue to occur in the WTO through day-to-day practice that
accumulates over time and often reflects fairly ad hoc solutions to
perceived problems. It seems unlikely that this will be cease to be the
case for the WTO after some years of its activity at the centre of world
economic affairs.

One issue that does arise, however, is whether the constraints built into the WTO Charter are too confining, making it difficult for the institution to adjust to the rapidly changing landscape of economic activity in the world. Only time will tell how evolution through practice will influence the ability of the WTO to continue to cope effectively. Already one can see various 'accommodations' to the reality of economics, although the language of the WTO Charter is not always clear about how to implement important negotiated agreements such as the formidable and ambitious agreement on telecommunications.[4]

As broad and complex as the WTO mandate is, it is clear that there is potentially much more that could be encompassed. Indeed, many member states have indicated a desire to pull new issues into the WTO competence, to the concern of some who fear that this might overload the ability of the WTO to function as an institution. Indeed, the Uruguay Round texts themselves have an extensive built-in agenda of activities and issues for resolution by WTO processes and negotiations.[5] Among the subjects specified by the existing treaty for WTO attention are institutional matters such as dispute settlement procedures, further elaboration of rules concerning subsidies, agriculture and services (including four sector negotiations,[6] government procurement procedures) and so on. Among subjects mentioned for future attention are competition policy (anti-trust and monopoly rules), environment and trade,[7] and investment rules.[8]

In addition, there are a number of puzzling 'link' issues that will inevitably require the attention of the new organization, such as links to environmental rules (mentioned already), links to human rights practices and democratic institutions, links to monetary policy, questions of trade in armaments and globalization effects on the cultural values of particular societies.

Many of the traditional rules and practices of the GATT, carried over into the WTO, are also being questioned and will thus demand ongoing attention. For example important questions are being raised about the most favoured nation principle and whether it adequately protects against undue free-riding and /or creates a rigidity in the system because it makes it harder to get consensus or other agreement when the institution has so many different 'players'. Closely related to this is the challenge of 'regionalism' and the worries that regional arrangements will undercut some of the principles of non-discrimination that have been central to the trade system in the past. Questions similarly arise about the older concepts of 'reciprocity' and whether they will be adequate to the need for a more rule-based institutional framework for world trade in a much more complex world economy. National treatment rules are often the source of dispute, and raise significant questions of product standards and how scientific evidence should be handled and judgments about risk decided.[9]

Most of these issues are subjects for future research and scholarship, and indeed, many of them will merit an entire book on their own. In many respects, however, most of them have a very broad question in common. This is the problem of how international economic activity that crosses governmental borders will be regulated.[10] As an ever increasing percentage of economic activity in the world does involve cross-border activity, national and sub-federal governments are finding it increasingly difficult to regulate such activity effectively enough to protect the efficiency and integrity of markets. In most such situations, governments realize that some type of international cooperation is the only effective way to proceed; yet there is fear and mistrust of international institutions, sometimes justified, sometimes not, because national or local officials are motivated by goals that are not compatible with more desirable policy objectives. The challenge that the new WTO faces is to reconcile some of these justified worries with the needs of international cooperation, while diminishing the opportunity for success of those who pursue undesirable goals.

In a sense, two perceptive observations by eminent persons sum this up. The first is by former Speaker of the US House of Representatives Tip O'Neill, who said 'all politics is local'.[11] The second is by the renowned economics and business writer/consultant Peter F. Drucker, who notes that 'all economics is international'.[12] The reconciliation of these two propositions is the great challenge for future international economic relations and institutions.

# Notes

## Chapter 1: The Uruguay Round and the WTO: the new organization and its antecedents

1. See John H. Jackson, 'The World Trade Organization: Watershed Innovation or Cautious Small Step Forward?', *The World Economy*, 18 (1995): 11–30. See also Jackson, 'The Uruguay Round and the Launch of the WTO: Significance and Challenges', ch. 1 in Terence P. Stewart (ed.), *World Trade Organization* (Washington, DC: American Bar Association, 1996); Jackson, 'Managing the Trading System: The World Trade Organization and the Post-Uruguay Round GATT Agenda', in Peter B. Kenen (ed.), *Managing The World Economy: Fifty Years After Bretton Woods* (Washington, DC: Institute for International Economics, 1994), p. 131.
2. Leonard Bierman, Donald R. Fraser and James W. Koari, 'The General Agreement on Tariffs and Trade from a Market Perspective', *University of Pennsylvania Journal of International Economic Law*, 17 (1996): 845.
3. Based on interviews with WTO officials and Uruguay Round negotiations.
4. Fact File, *WTO Focus* (January/February 1995): 4,5.
5. 'Final Act Embodying the Results of the Uruguay Round of Multilateral Trade Negotiations, April 15, 1994, Legal Instruments', *Results of the Uruguay Round of Multilateral Trade Negotiations*, 1 (GATT Secretariat, 1994): 33; ILM 1140–1272 (1994). See also H.R. Doc. no. 103–316 (1994).
6. See Jackson, *The World Trading System*, 2nd edn (Cambridge, MA: MIT Press, 1997).
7. See Appendix G below which contains the text of the Ministerial Declaration of the Uruguay Round (Punta del Este, 20 September 1986).

8. See n. 5, 'Final Act', which includes General Agreement on Trade in Services (GATS), Geneva (1994), and 'Agreement on Trade-Related Aspects of Intellectual Property Rights, 15 April 1994, Marrakesh Agreement Establishing the World Trade Organization (hereinafter 'WTO Agreement'), Annex 1c, Legal Instruments'; *Results of the Uruguay Round,* 31; 33 ILM 81 (1994) (hereinafter 'TRIPS Agreement'). See e.g. Jackson, William J. Davey and Alan O. Sykes, Jr, Document Supplement to *Legal Problems of International Economic Relations*, 3rd edn (St Paul, MN: West Publishing, 1995).

9. See e.g. GATT Uruguay Round Document MTN.GNS/W/120, of 10 July 1991, including a Services Sectoral Classification list of approximately 122 or more sectors. See also Jude Kearney, Deputy Assistant Secretary for Service Industries and Finance Bureau, US Department of Commerce, 'Benefits to Service Industries of the General Agreement on Trade in Services' (1994) at p. 2. The document reports there are about 150 service sectors and sub-sectors.

10. See Edwin Vermulst, Paul Waer and Jacques Bourgeois, *Rules of Origin in International Trade: A Comparative Study* (Ann Arbor, MI: University of Michigan Press, 1994); Joseph A. LaNasa III, 'Rules of Origin and the Uruguay Round's Effectiveness in Harmonizing and Regulating Them', *American Journal of International Law* 90 (1996): 625; LaNasa, 'Symposium on the North Atlantic Free Trade Agreement: Rules of Origin under the NAFTA: A Substantial Transition into Objectively Transparent Protectionism', *Harvard Journal of International Law* 43 (1993): 381; and Wolfgang W. Leirer, 'Rules of Origin under the Caribbean Basin Initiative and the ACP-EEC LOME IV Convention and their Compatibility with the GATT Uruguay Round Agreement on Rules of Origin', *University of Pennsylvania Journal of International Business Law* 16 (1995): 483.

11. See e.g. Jackson, Davey and Sykes, n. 8, *Legal Problems of International Economic Relations:* para. 3, p. 80.

12. Commonly called the 'Dunkel Text' after the then GATT Director-General Arthur Dunkel; see 'Multilateral Trade Negotiations in the Uruguay Round', MTN.TNC/W/FA, 20 December 1991.

13. This short book, commissioned by the RIIA, is intended to be the core of a considerably longer book on the 'constitutional' aspects of the WTO which will be published by Oxford University Press with the approval of RIIA and Pinter.

14. See e.g. Jackson, n. 6, *The World Trading System*; Jackson, Davey and Sykes, *Legal Problems of International Economic Relations*; see also Appendices A–G below.

15. See Jackson, *Restructuring the GATT System* (London: Royal Institute of International Affairs/Pinter, 1990). As many people close to the UR

negotiation know, this book had some influence on negotiators in shaping proposals for a new organization. Thus, the title of the present book could well be (as a friend suggested) 'The WTO: GATT Restructured', although such a title probably would not do justice to the many fundamental and innovative aspects of the new organization, compared with the GATT.

16. See ibid., in which some are outlined.

17. See description in ch. 2.

18. 'Marrakesh Agreement Establishing the World Trade Organization, Annex 1A', in *Results of the Uruguay Round of Multilateral Trade Negotiations,* 31 (GATT Secretariat 1994) – n. 5 above. See also n. 8, Jackson, Davey and Sykes, *Legal Problems of International Economic Relations,* Supplement; 'Message from the President of the United States Transmitting the Uruguay Round Trade Agreements', *Texts of Agreements Implementing Bill, Statement of Administrative Action and Required Supporting Statements,* H.R. Doc. no. 103–316, vol. 1 (27 September 1994).

19. See n. 15.

20. Particularly important and useful are the following GATT documents: *Analytical Index* (2 vols, 1995), BISD series. The total documents of GATT (mostly available on microfiche from the GATT and now the WTO Publications Office) number many thousands of pages, for dozens of document series, the most important of which are part of the 'L' series; see e.g. Jackson, Davey, and Sykes, n. 8, for bibliography of GATT documentation. Note UN series for preparatory work. See also, Jackson, *World Trade and the Law of GATT* (Indianapolis, IN: Bobbs-Merrill Company, December 1969).

21. See n. 5, WTO Agreement (VI: 4); 'Understanding regarding Notification, Consultation, Dispute Settlement and Surveillance', 26th Supp. BISD 210 (1980) (VIII:9).

22. See Appendix C, below.

23. The second Ministerial Meeting in May 1998 included a celebration of the 50th anniversary of GATT, the predecessor organization; see WT/MIN (98)/INF/1 of 8 July 1997.

24. See http://www.wto.org/wto/services/tel.htm

25. See e.g. *Journal of International Economic Law*, vol. 1 (Oxford University Press, 1998); Pieter VerLoren van Themaat, *The Changing Structure of International Economic Law* (The Hague: Martinus Nijhoff, 1981). See also Jackson, *Economic Law, International* (1985); *Encyclopedia of Public International Law* (Amsterdam: North-Holland, 1985); Dominique Carreau, Patrick Juillard and Thiebaud Flory, *Droit international écono-mique,* 3rd edn (Paris: Librairie générale de droit de jurisprudence, EJA,

1990); Paolo Picone and Giorgio Sacerdoti, *Diritto Internazionale Dell'economia* (Milan: Franco Angeli, 1982); Jackson, 'International Economic Law: Reflections on the "Boiler Room" of International Relations', *American University Journal of International Law*, 10 (1995): 595.

26. Concerning a 'GATT for Investment', see Charles Poor Kindleberger and Paul M. Goldberg, 'Toward a GATT for Investment: A Proposal for Supervision of the International Corporation' (1970), reprinted in Charles Poor Kindleberger, *Multinational Excursions* (Cambridge, MA: MIT Press, 1984), pp. 202–31; Kindleberger, 'A GATT for International Direct Investment: Further Reflections', reprinted in Kindleberger, *Multinational Excursions*, pp. 247–65.

27. See e.g. Louis Henkin, *How Nations Behave: Law and Foreign Policy*, 2nd edn (New York: Council on Foreign Relations, 1979), pp. 269–78; Harold G. Maier, et al., 'Appraisals of the ICJ's Decision: Nicaragua *v.* United States (Merits)', *American Journal of International Law* 81 (1987): 77.

28. See Henkin, n. 25, *How Nations Behave*, at pp. 26–42; Roger Fisher, *Improving Compliance with International Law* (Charlottesville, VA: University Press of Virginia, 1981), pp. 12–16.

29. See e.g. Douglas North, *Institutions, Institutional Change and Economic Performance* (Cambridge: Cambridge University Press, 1990); Anne-Marie Slaughter Burley, 'International Law and International Relations Theory: A Dual Agenda', *American Journal of International Law* 87 (1993): 205; C.A.E. Goodhart, 'Economics and the Law: Too Much One-Way Traffic?', *Modern Law Review*, 60 (January 1997): 1.

## Chapter 2:  Bretton Woods, the ITO, the GATT and the WTO

1. Portions of this chapter are adapted from John H. Jackson, *Restructuring the GATT System* (London: Royal Institute of International Affairs/Pinter, 1990). See also Jackson, *The World Trading System: Law and Policy of International Economic Relations*, 2nd edn (Cambridge, MA: MIT Press, 1997); Jackson and Alan O. Sykes, Jr, 'Implementing The Uruguay Round' (Oxford: Clarendon Press, 1997).

2. Protocol of Provisional Application to the General Agreement on Tariffs and Trade, 30 October 1947, 61 Stat. A-2051, TIAS no. 1700, 55 UNTS 308 [hereinafter 'GATT'].

3. See GATT Document GATT/LEG/1 and Supplements.

4. Other of my works relating to this subject include: Jackson, *World Trade and the Law of GATT* (Indianapolis, IN: Bobbs-Merrill, 1969), which is a treatise on a legal analysis of the GATT; Jackson, William J. Davey, and

Alan O. Sykes, *Legal Problems of International Economic Relations,* 3rd edn (St Paul, MN: West Publishing, 1995); Jackson, Jean-Victor Louis and Mitsuo Matsushita, 'Implementing the Tokyo Round: National Constitutions and International Economic Rules' (Ann Arbor, MI: University of Michigan Press, 1984); Jackson, n. 1, *The World Trading System*; Jackson, 'Governmental Disputes in International Trade Relations: A Proposal in The Context of GATT', *Journal of World Trade Law,* 13 (1979): 1. Readers may also be interested in the following works related to this study: Robert Hudec, *The GATT Legal System and World Trade Diplomacy* (New York: Praeger, 1975); Kenneth Dam, *The GATT: Law and International Economic Organization* (Chicago, IL: University of Chicago Press, 1970); Edmond McGovern, *International Trade Regulation*, 2nd edn (Exeter: Globefield Press, 1986); Gerard Curzon, *Multilateral Commercial Diplomacy* (London: Michael Joseph, 1965); Thiebaut Flory, *GATT, Droit international et commerce mondial* (Paris: Librairie Générale du Droit et Jurisprudence, 1968); Meinhard Hilf, Francis G. Jacobs and Ernst-Ulrich Petersmann (eds), *The European Community and GATT* (Deventer, Netherlands: Kluwer, 1986).

5. See Jackson, n. 1, *Restructuring the GATT System.*
6. See Jackson, n. 4, *World Trade and the Law of GATT*; Jackson, n. 1, *The World Trading System.*
7. See R. N. Cooper, 'Trade Policy as Foreign Policy', in R. M. Stern (ed.), *US Trade Policies in a Changing World Economy* (Cambridge, MA: MIT Press, 1987), pp. 291–336.
8. See United Nations Monetary and Financial Conference (Bretton Woods, NH, 1–22 July 1944), Proceedings and Documents 941 (US Department of State Publication no. 2866, 1948).
9. See Act to extend the Authority of the President under sec. 350 of The Tariff Act of 1930 as amended, and for other purposes, 5 July 1945, Pub. L. 79–130, 59 Stat. 410.
10. 1 UN ECOSOC Res. 13, UN Doc. E/22 (1946).
11. For example, if a tariff commitment for a maximum 10% tariff charge were made, a country might nevertheless decide to use a quantitative restriction to prevent imports and thus would evade the trade-liberalizing effect of the tariff commitment.
12. See GATT, art. XXV; see also Jackson, n. 4, *World Trade and the Law of GATT*, Sec. 5.1, p. 121.
13. 'Most favoured nation' (MFN) refers to an obligation found in a number of trade and other commercial treaties during the past several centuries. In GATT article I, this is worded as follows: 'With respect to customs duties and charges of any kind ... and with respect to the method of levying such

duties and charges, and with respect to all rules and formalities in connection with importation and exportation ... any advantage, favour, privilege or immunity granted by any contracting party to any product originating in or destined for any other country shall be accorded immediately and unconditionally to the like product originating in or destined for the territories of all other contracting parties'. The meaning of this clause can be summarized by saying that every country shall grant to a beneficiary of its MFN obligation, treatment or privileges at least as good as those which it grants to any other country. In short, it is a non-discrimination clause. See also Jackson n. 1, *The World Trading System*, 2nd edn, ch. 6; Jackson, n. 4, *World Trade and the Law of GATT*, ch. 11; 'Equality and Discrimination in International Economic Law (XI): The General Agreement on Tariffs and Trade', in *The British Yearbook of World Affairs* (1983), p. 224. Thus, a GATT Contracting Party that limits its tariff on an item exported to it by another country must also so limit its tariffs on the same item imported from any GATT country.

14. See GATT, art. XXIX; Jackson, n. 4, *World Trade and the Law of GATT,* Sec. 2.4.

15. Jackson, n. 4, *World Trade and the Law of GATT,* Sec. 2.2. See also S. A. Aaronson, *Trade and the American Dream: A Social History of Postwar Trade Policy* (Lexington, KY: University Press of Kentucky, 1996).

16. See Jackson, n. 1, *The World Trading System*, p. 34; Jackson, 'United States of America', in Francis G. Jacobs and Shelley Roberts (eds), *The Effect of Treaties in Domestic Law* (London: Sweet & Maxwell, 1987), vol. 7, pp. 141–70. See e.g. M. Laeffer (ed.), *International Treaties on Intellectual Property* (Washington, DC: Bureau of National Affairs, 1990).

17. See n. 9. The act expired on 12 June 1948.

18. See UN Doc. EPCT/TAC/4, 8 (1947).

19. See n. 2.

20. See Jackson, n. 4, *World Trade and the Law of GATT*, p. 154.

21. Ibid., Ch. 6.

22. GATT, BISD 14 Supp. 17 (1966).

23. See e.g. Jackson, n. 4, *World Trade and the Law of GATT*.

24. See Jackson, n. 1, *The World Trading System*, Sec. 2.5.

25. For more substantive detail, see e.g. Jackson, n. 1, *The World Trading System;* Jackson, Davey and Sykes, n. 4, *Legal Problems of International Economic Relations*.

26. Adapted from Jackson, Davey and Sykes, n. 4, *Legal Problems of International Economic Relations,* pp. 290–91.

27. Jackson, n. 1, *The World Trading System*, sec. 12.3; 'A Compendium of

the agreements, including the Paris and the Berne Convention', in Laeffer, n. 16, *International Treaties on Intellectual Property.*

28. Partly adapted from Jackson, n. 1, *Restructuring the GATT System*, Ch. 4. See e.g. Ernest H. Preeg, *Traders in A Brave New World: The Uruguay Round and the Future of the International Trading System* (Chicago, IL: University of Chicago Press, 1995), p. 113; Hugo Paemen, Preeg and Alexandra Bensch, *From the GATT to the WTO: The European Community in the Uruguay Round* (Leuven, Belgium: Leuven University Press, 1995); Jackson, 'The Uruguay Round and the Launch of the WTO: Significance and Challenges', in *American Bar Association Book on the Uruguay Round* (American Bar Association, 1996), p. 76; Julio A. LaCarte Muró, *Ronda Uruguay del GATT: La Globalización del Comercio Mundial* (Montevideo, Uruguay: Fundación de Cultura Universitaria, 1994); John Croome, *Reshaping the World Trading System: A History of the Uruguay Round* (Geneva: World Trade Organization, 1995); Terence P. Stewart (ed.), *Multilateral Trade Framework for the 21st Century* (Washington, DC: American Bar Association, 1996).

29. Ibid.

30. See Appendix G below: Ministerial Declaration on the Uruguay Round, Declaration of 20 September 1986.

31. GATT Document GATT/1405 lists the decisions of January 1987 setting up the negotiating group structure, which included the following: Group on Negotiating Goods (GNG); Tariffs; Non-tariff measures; Natural resource-based products; Textile and clothing; Agriculture; Tropical products; GATT articles; MTN agreements and arrangements; Safeguards; Subsidies and countervailing measures; Trade-related aspects of intellectual property rights including trade in counterfeit goods; Trade-related investment measures; Dispute settlement; Functioning of the GATT system; Group of Negotiations on Services (GNS).

32. See e.g. *GATT Newsletter*, no. 61 (May 1987).

33. A manuscript by myself was noted and there were further discussions in the autumn, based partly on some of the ideas contained therein. That manuscript became Jackson, n. 1, *Restructuring the GATT System*. Canadian government officials and negotiators began work on a more specific and detailed proposal for a new organization, using myself as one of several consultants. See Amelia Porges (US and GATT trade official), 'The Marrakesh Agreement Establishing the World Trade Organization', in Stewart, n. 28, *Multilateral Framework for the 21st Century.*

34. 'Canada Proposes Post-GATT Trade Agency', *Journal of Commerce*, 12 April 1990; 'Canada Signals Proposal to Make GATT a World Trade Organization',

*Sosland Publishing Company Milling & Banking News*, 69/7 (17 April 1990): 50.

35. This group often met (and still meets) separately and developed some common positions on trade policy.

36. See Ernest H. Preeg, *Traders in a Brave New World: The Uruguay Round and the Future of the International Trading System* (Chicago, IL, University of Chicago Press, 1995), p. 116–26, and fn. 36. See also: for new highlights, GATT, 'USTR Hills Says Chances of Success Impossible to Predict', *International Trade Reporter*, 7/50 (19 December 1990): 1912. For general developments, see GATT. 'US Lacked "Diplomatic Competence" at GATT Talks, French Minister Says', *International Trade Reporter*, 8/1 (2 January 1991): 23. For new highlights, see GATT, 'US, Others Blame EC for Failure in Brussels to Agree on New Rules to Govern World Trade' *International Trade Reporter*, 7/49 (12 December 1990): 1876.

37. See Jackson, Davey and Sykes, n. 4, *Legal Problems of International Economic Relations*, p. 142.

38. See the Omnibus Trade and Competitiveness Act of 1988, Pub. L. no. 100–418, 102 Stat. 445, Sec. 1103: Implementation of Trade Agreements; David W. Leebron, 'Implementation of the Uruguay Round Results in the United States', in Jackson and Sykes, n. 1, *Implementing the Uruguay Round*, pp. 175–242.

39. See e.g. Draft Final Act Embodying the Results of the Uruguay Round of Multilateral Trade Negotiations, 20 December 1991, MTN.TNC/W/FA, in 'The Dunkel Draft' from *The GATT Secretariat Arthur Dunkel* (Buffalo, NY: William S. Hein, 1992). A footnote to 'The Dunkel Draft' provided that 'Participants have addressed institutional issues relating to the implementations of the results of the Uruguay Round and work has been proceeding on the Articles of Agreement of a proposed MTO. The MTO text represents the stage reached in this work. Further elaboration of this text will be required to ensure a proper relation to the other results of the Uruguay Round' MTN.TNC/W/FA, 20 December 1991, p. 103, in Porges, n. 33, 'The Marrakesh Agreement', p. 77, fn. 49.

40. For the North Atlantic Free Trade Agreement Implementation Act and its legislative history, see the Act, 20 November 1993, Pub. L. no. 103–182, 1993 US *Code Congressional and Administrative News* (US CCAN) (107 Stat. 2057), 2552.

41. See Trade Act of 1974, Pub. L. no. 93–618 (as amended at 19 USC §§ 2101–487, 88 Stat. 1978), sec. 103(e)(i) and the Omnibus Trade and Competitiveness Act of 1988, n. 38, sec. 1103(b). See e.g. Jackson, Davey,

and Sykes, n. 4, Document Supplement to *Legal Problems of International Economic Relations.*

42. Based on interviews with negotiators. See also n. 43.

43. Final Act Embodying the Results of the Uruguay Round of Multilateral Trade Negotiations, Version of 15 December 1993, Corrigendum. GATT Doc. MTN/FA/Corr. 1, 15 December 1993.

44. See n. 34.

45. See, generally, Preeg, n. 28, *Traders in a Brave New World*; Paemen, Preeg and Bensch, n. 28, *From the GATT to the WTO*; Jackson, n. 28, 'The Uruguay Round and the Launch of the WTO'; LaCarte, n. 28; Croome, n. 28; La Carte Muró, n. 28, *Rond a Uruguay del GATT*; Croome, n. 28, *Reshaping the World Trading System.*

46. Information supplied by the GATT Secretariat, June 1994.

47. Jackson and Sykes, n. 1, *Implementing the Uruguay Round.*

48. Information supplied by the GATT Secretariat, June 1994, indicated that about 21 signatories at Marrakesh were 'definite' acceptances.

49. See ch. 3, and Appendix C.

50. Ibid.

51. See e.g. Hilf, Jacobs and Petersmann, n. 4, *The European Community and GATT*; Leebron, n. 38, 'Implementation of the Uruguay Round Results'.

52. See e.g. Jackson, 'The Great 1994 Sovereignty Debate: United States Acceptance and Implementation of the Uruguay Round Results', in *Essays in Honor of Louis Henkin* (Deventer, Netherlands: Kluwer, forthcoming) and *Columbia Journal of Transnational Law* (November 1997); Jackson, Davey and Sykes, n. 4, *Legal Problems of International Economic Relations.*

53. See the Uruguay Round Agreements Act, 8 December 1994, Pub. L. no. 103–465, 108 Stat. 4954. The votes for this Statute were: House 288 for, 146 against; Senate 76 for, 24 against.

54. See Agreement on Implementation of Article VI of the GATT 1994 (Antidumping Code) in Jackson, Davey and Sykes, n. 4, (part of Uruguay Round Results), Document Supplement to *Legal Problems of International Economic Relations*, pp. 174–97; President's Message to Congress Transmitting the Uruguay Round Trade Agreements, Texts of Agreements Implementing Bill, Statement of Administrative Action, and Required Supporting Statements, pp. 656–708 in House Document 103–316, Vol. 1, 103rd Congress, 2nd Session (27 September 1994).

55. Peter L. H. Van den Bossche, 'The European Community and the Uruguay Round Agreements', in Jackson and Sykes, n. 1, *Implementing the Uruguay Round*, pp. 23–102.

56. See e.g. Hilf, 'Negotiating and Implementing the Uruguay Round: The Role of EC Member States – The Case of Germany', in Jackson and Sykes, n. 1, *Implementing the Uruguay Round,* pp. 121–36.
57. Van den Bossche, n. 55, 'The European Community and the Uruguay Round Agreements'; Hilf, n. 56, 'Negotiations and Implementing the Uruguay Round'.
58. Eric Stein, *Thoughts from the Bridge: Collective Writings on New Europe and American Federalism* (Ann Arbor, MI: University of Michigan Press, forthcoming), introduction to Ch. IV; Piet Eeckhout, 'The Domestic Legal Status of the WTO Agreement: Interconnecting Legal Systems', 34 *Common Market Law Review,* 11 (1997): 24–32. On European Community practice generally, see, Stein, 'External Relations of the European Community: Structure and Process', in *Collected Courses of the Academy of European Law,* Vol. 1, Book 1 (Deventer, Netherlands: Kluwer, 1991), pp. 115, 168–77.
59. See Hilf, 'New Frontiers in International Trade: The Role of National Courts in International Trade Relations', 18 *Michigan Journal of International Law* 321 (Winter 1997): fn. 48.
60. Yuji Iwasawa, 'Constitutional Problems Involved in Implementing the Uruguay Round in Japan', in Jackson and Sykes, n. 1, *Implementing the Uruguay Round*, pp. 137–74.
61. Ibid. at Sec. 5.
62. Jackson, n. 52, 'The Great Sovereignty Debate'.
63. Ibid.
64. See e.g. Daniel C. Esty, *Greening the GATT: Trade, Environment and the Future* (Washington, DC: Institute for International Economics, 1994).

## Chapter 3: The WTO – Charter and organization

1. GATT, BISD Vol. I) at 75–83 (1955). See e.g. John H Jackson, *World Trade and the Law of GATT* (Indianapolis, IN: Bobbs-Merrill, 1969), p. 51.
2. Ibid., pp. 42–51.
3. Often to achieve consensus on a draft developed by large numbers of negotiators, it is necessary to make text less explicit so that different negotiators can agree on the words, if not their meaning.
4. See discussion in ch. 2.
5. See especially sec. 3.4.
6. See WTO 'Charter', Appendix A, below.
7. See sec. 1.2 above.
8. See GATT, *Analytical Index*, Art. 34. See generally GATT, *Status of Legal*

*Instruments*, Supp., 15 December 1993.

9. See Jackson and Alan O. Sykes Jr, *Implementing the Uruguay Round,* (Oxford: Clarendon Press, 1997); Jackson, Jean-Victor Louis and Mitsuo Matsushita, *Implementing the Tokyo Round: National Constitutions and International Economic Rules* (Ann Arbor, MI: University of Michigan Press, 1984).

10. See ch. 2, and Appendix A.

11. See list in Appendix E below.

12. See ch. 4 below.

13. World Trade Organization (WTO), *Final Act Embodying the Results of the Uruguay Round of Multilateral Trade Negotiations* (Marrakesh, 1994); 33 ILM 1140 (1994); see also H.R. Doc. no. 316, 103rd Cong., 2nd Sess. (1994).

14. See sec. 3.4.

15. See Appendix E.

16. The Trade Policy Review Mechanism (TPRM) was originally established by the GATT in April 1989; see Decision of 12 April 1989, GATT Doc. L/ 6490, BISD 36 Supp., p. 403. The WTO Agreement Annex 3 is now the governing text.

17. See Appendices A and D.

18. See Appendix A.

19. GATT, BISD 31 Supp. viii (1985). Hong Kong became the 91st party in 1986.

20. GATT, BISD (Vol. II), 11 (1952). Also see Jackson, 'The Legal Meaning of a GATT Dispute Settlement Report: Some Reflections' in Niels Blokker and Sam Muller (eds.), *Towards More Effective Supervision by International Organizations: Essays in Honour of Henry G. Schermers*, Vol. I, (Deventer, Netherlands: Kluwer, 1994), pp. 149–64.

21. See GATT, BISD (Vol. II), 12 (1952) (Ruling by the Chairman on 24 August 1948).

22. WTO Art. XVI:3.

23. WTO Art. IX:2.

24. WTO Art. IX:4.

25. e.g. GATT Doc. L/403, 7 September 1955.

26. See WTO Art. IX:3.

27. WTO Art. III:2.

28. WTO Arts IX:5, X:10, X:9.

29. WTO Art. IX has a fn. 1 which reads: '1. The body concerned shall be deemed to have decided by consensus on a matter submitted for its consideration, if no Member, present at the meeting when the decision is taken, formally objects to the proposed decision.'

30. See WTO Articles XI and XII.
31. See generally Jackson, n. 1, *World Trade and the Law of GATT*, sec. 4.6. It was felt that it would be unreasonable to force a nation to accept an agreement with another nation when it may have compelling political reasons not to enter into such a relationship with another country. The WTO Art. XIII continues this approach. Most invocations have been withdrawn.
32. See Jackson, n. 1, *World Trade and the Law of GATT*, p. 101, and see GATT, *Analytical Index 1995*, Art. 39.
33. See Jackson, n. 1, *World Trade and the Law of GATT*, pp. 98–102.
34. All but three of the 1979 MTN arrangements had measures permitting non-application of the rights and obligations between signatories. The three that contained no such waiver provision were the Arrangement Regarding Bovine Meat (GATT, BISD 26 Supp. 84 (1980)), the International Dairy Arrangement (GATT, BISD 26 Supp. 91 (1980)), and the Agreement on the Implementation of Art. VII (GATT, BISD 26 Supp. 116 (1980)).
35 The WTO clarifies an ambiguity in the previous GATT, as to the time when notice of the opt-out must be made: Art. XIII: 2.
36. WTO Art. XIII:5.
37. See Jean Groux and Philippe Manin, *The European Communities in the International Order*, (Brussels: European Commission, 1985), pt 2, ch. 1; see also E.U. Petersmann, 'Participation of the European Communities in GATT: International Law and Community Law Aspects', in David O'Keeffe and Henry Schermers (eds.), *Mixed Agreements* (Deventer, Netherlands; Boston, MA: Kluwer Law and Taxation Publisher, 1983), pp. 167–98; Petersmann, 'The EEC as a GATT Member: Legal Conflicts between GATT Law and European Community Law', in Meinhard Hilf, Francis Jacobs and Ernst-Ulrich Petersmann (eds.), *The European Community and GATT* (Deventer, Netherlands: Kluwer, 1986), pp. 23–71.
38. See WTO Art. IX:1.
39. See Li Chung-chou, 'Resumption of China's GATT Membership', *Journal of World Trade Law*, 21 (1987): 25; Robert E. Herzstein, 'China and GATT: Legal and Policy Issues raised by China's Participation in the General Agreement on Tariffs and Trade', *Law and Policy in International Business*, 18 (1986): 371. See sec. 3.2.
40. China became a signatory to the GATT MFA on 15 December 1983, the agreement taking effect on 18 January 1984 (*GATT Status of Legal Instruments.*)
41. Francis Williams and Nancy Dunne, 'China: Hopes High for WTO Bid', *Financial Times* (London), 5 August 1997.
42. For example, Hong Kong once brought an action before a GATT panel,

although the request for the establishment of the panel was placed by the UK (see GATT, BISD 30 Supp. 129 (1984)).

43. See GATT/1384, 24 April 1986.
44. WT/L/218, 3 June 1997.
45. DSU Arts 13 and 14.
46. The agreements between the United Nations and the IMF and World Bank can be found at UN Treaty Series references as follows: 16 UNTS 321 (1948), 16 UNTS 341 (1949), 33 UNTS 261 (1949). *The Statesman's Yearbook* (133rd edition, 1996, also describes these matters, at p. 18.
47. Jackson, n. 1, *World Trade and the Law of GATT*, p. 49.
48. WTO Art. VI. See e.g. WTO Documents WT/L/223 (1 July 1997) regarding 'Conditions of Service Applicable to the Staff of the WTO Secretariat'.
49. Interviews with WTO officials. See also WTO Documents, WT/L/223.
50. See e.g. WTO documents WT/PC/R para. 54 (1994), WT/GC/M/5 (1995) and exchange of letters between the United Nations and the WTO reproduced in WT/GC/W/10 (1995).
51 See e.g. observing status of IGOs, the following WTO documents: G/L/140 of 15 January 1997, WT/GC/W/51/REV.3 of 18 July 1997, IP/C/W/52/ADD.1 of 23 May 1997.
52. GATT Arts XIV and XV.
53 WTO Documents WT/L/194 and WT/L/195 of 18 November 1996.
54. The Dispute Settlement Understanding Art. 13, 'Right to Seek Information' (right for panels to seek information) could be the basis for such a 'presumption'.
55. The WTO has not yet made any provision for formal recognition of NGOs; however, it has taken some measures to try to accommodate some NGO interest. For example, with respect to environmental NGOs, the WTO secretariat has organized 'under its own responsibility' symposia with non-government organizations; see press/TE019 of 14 August 1997 describing a symposium in May 1997. In addition, the WTO made arrangements for the presence of NGOs at the first WTO ministerial meeting in Singapore in December 1996, and appeared similarly to be making arrangements for NGOs for the second ministerial meeting in May 1998. One of the concerns of NGOs and other private parties is documents. The WTO has taken considerable measures to try to open documents to the public, and to avoid derestricting documents unnecessarily. See e.g. WTO document WT/L/160/REV.1 of 26 July 1996, 'Procedures of the Circulation and Derestriction of WTO Documents – Decisions Adopted by the General Council on 18 July 1996'. The WTO has an important web site at

www.wto.org, with many documents which can be printed or downloaded. One of the questions often raised by NGOs is the disputes element procedures. This is the subject of the next chapter, but it can be mentioned here that NGOs have several times already produced memoranda or other documents relating to specific disputes and have submitted those to interested persons and even, in at least one case, to the legal staff of the WTO itself (for example, motion to submit amicus brief from the Center for Marine Conservation to the panel on United States – Import Prohibition of Certain Shrimp and Shrimp Products). It is unknown what effect, if any, these submissions have, since there is currently no provision for receiving them officially.

56. See Jagdish Bhagwati, et al., *The Dangerous Drift to Preferential Trade Agreements* (Washington, DC: AEI Press, 1995); Jackson, n. 1, *World Trade and the Law of GATT*, ch. 24; Jackson, *The World Trading System: Law and Policy of International Economic Relations*, 2nd edn (Cambridge, MA: MIT Press, 1997), sec. 6.3; Jackson, 'Regional Trade Blocs and GATT' *The World Economy*, 16/2 (1993): 121–31; Kenneth W. Dam, 'Regional Economic Arrangements and the GATT: The Legacy of a Misconception', *University of Chicago Law Review*, 30 (1963): 615; *Reflections on Regionalism: Report of the Study Group on International Trade* (Pittsburgh, PA: Carnegie Endowment for International Peace, 1997).

57. Art. XXIV of GATT, particularly XXIV:8, which provides that a 'customs union' is understood to mean the 'substitution of a single customs territory for two or more customs territories, so that ... duties and other restrictive regulations ... are eliminated with respect to substantially all the trade between the constituent territories, ... and substantially the same duties and other regulations of commerce are applied by each of the members of the union to the trade of territories not included in the union'. With respect to the 'free trade area', the definition in para. 8 of Art. XXIV reads that it shall be understood to mean 'a group of two or more customs territories in which the duties and other restrictive regulations of commerce ... are eliminated on substantially all the trade between the constituent territories in products originating in such territories'.

58. See GATT, n. 15, *Analytical Index*, Art. XXIV; see also n. 35; Edmond McGovern, *International Trade Regulation*, 2nd edn (Exeter: Globefield Press, 1986), p. 262.

59. See Jackson, William J. Davey and Alan O. Sykes Jr, *Legal Problems of International Economic Relations*, 3rd edn (St Paul, MN: West Publishing, 1995), Documents Supplement, p. 90; part of the Uruguay Round Final

Act, n. 13.

60. See Unpublished GATT Panel Report, 'EC: Import Regime for Bananas', DS38/R.11, February 1994, available in LEXIS ITRADE Library, GTTWTO File. See also Unpublished GATT Panel Report, 'EEC: Member States' Import Regime for Bananas', DS32/R, 3 June 1993.

61. Jackson, n. 56, *The World Trading System*, ch. 4.

62. See Edwin Vermulst, Paul Waer and Jacques Bourgeois (eds), *Rules of Origin in International Trade: A Comparative Study* (Ann Arbor, MI: University of Michigan Press, 1994).

63. See US–Canada Free Trade Agreement, 22 December 1987–2 January 1988, Art. 1902, H.R. Doc. no. 216, 100th Cong., 2nd Sess. 297 (entered into force 1 January 1989), reprinted in *International Legal Material*, 27, 1988): 281. Note however that the agreement also contemplates the two countries negotiating a substitute system of rules in both countries for anti-dumping and countervailing duties as applied to their bilateral trade. See US–Canada Free Trade Agreement, Art. 1906–1907. See also US–Israel Free Trade Agreement, 2 April 1985, TIAS, reprinted in *International Legal Materials*, 24 (1985): 653.

64. See e.g. 'Conference Explores Issues, Obstacles, and Support for NAFTA Agreement', *IMF Survey*, 3 August 1992: 242.

65. See the interesting article by Joel P. Trachtman, 'International Regulatory Competition, Externalization and Jurisdiction', 34 *Harvard International Law Journal*, 47 (1993).

## Chapter 4: Dispute settlement and procedures

1. *WTO Focus*, newsletter (August/September 1996): 7.

2. See Singapore Ministerial Declaration, *WTO Focus* (December 1996).

3. See the web site <http://www.ustr.gov> (US Trade Representative); see 'Testimony Before the House Ways and Means Trade Subcommittee' by Ambassador Michael Kantor, 13 March 1996.

4. See e.g. Douglas North, *Institutions, Institutional Change and Economic Performance* (Cambridge: Cambridge University Press, 1990).

5. Claus-Dieter Ehlermann, 'The European Community, its Law and Lawyers', the Second Wilberforce Lecture, London, 9 October 1991, printed in *Common Market Law Review*, 29 (1992): 213–27. Reproduced with the kind permission of Kluwer Law International.

6. See sec. 2.2 above.

7. See generally Leo Gross (ed.), *The Future of the International Court of Justice* (Dobbs Ferry, NY: Oceana, 1976); Daniel G. Partan, 'Increasing

the Effectiveness of the International Court', *Harvard International Law Journal,* 18 (1977): 559.

8. John H. Jackson, *The World Trading System,* 2nd edn (Cambridge, MA: MIT Press, 1997), ch. 4.

9. See Oliver Long, *Law and its Limitations in the GATT Multilateral Trade System* (Boston, MA: Kluwer, 1985). GATT is at the same time a legal framework and a forum for negotiation. See also Robert Hudec, 'GATT or GABB?', *Yale Law Journal,* 80 (1971): 1299.

10. See Long, n. 9, *Law and its Limitations,* p. 71, citing Kenneth Dam, *The GATT: Law and International Economic Organization* (Chicago, IL: University of Chicago Press, 1970), pp. 335–6.

11. Statement of Harry Hawkins, representing the United States, speaking about the proposed ITO Charter at the London meeting of the Preparatory Committee of the UN Conference on Trade and Employment, UN Doc. EPCT/C.II/PV.2,9 (1946).

12. See Charter of the ITO, ch. VIII, arts. 92–7; UN, Final Act and Related Documents, UN Conference on Trade and Employment, held at Havana, Cuba, 21 November 1947–24 March 1948; Interim Commission for the International Trade Organization, Lake Success, NY, April 1948, UN Doc. E/Conf. 2/78. See also Clair Wilcox, *A Charter For World Trade* (New York: Macmillan, 1949), pp. 159, 305–8.

13. See Wilcox, n. 12, *A Charter for World Trade,* p. 159.

14. Ibid., p. 160.

15. Jackson, *World Trade and the Law of GATT* (Indianapolis, IN: Bobbs-Merrill, 1969), pp. 167–71.

16. Ibid. Generally on the GATT dispute settlement procedure, see William J. Davey, 'Dispute settlement in GATT', *Fordham International Law Journal,* 11 (1987): 51; Rosine Plank, 'An Unofficial Description of How a GATT Panel Works and Does Not', *Swiss Review of International Competition Law,* 29 (1987): 81.

17. Jackson, n. 15, *World Trade and the Law of GATT,* pp. 164–6.

18. Ibid., p. 175.

19. See generally GATT, *Analytical Index* (1995), Article XXIII.

20. An action may also be brought under Article XXIII when the attainment of any objective of the agreement is being impeded.

21. *Australian Ammonium Sulphate,* GATT, BISD (Vol. II) at 188 (1952). This case is sometimes called the 'Marbury *v.* Madison' of GATT. See Hudec, 'Retaliation against Unreasonable Foreign Trade Practices', *Minnesota Law Review,* 59 (1975): 46; Hudec, *The GATT Legal System and World Trade Diplomacy* (New York: Praeger, 1975), pp. 144–53; Hudec, n. 9, 'GATT

or GABB?', p. 1341.

22. The *Australian Subsidy on Ammonium Sulphate* case and the *German Duty on Sardines* case (GATT, BISD 1 Supp. 53 (1953)) both endorsed the view that the GATT should be construed to protect 'reasonable expectations' of the Contracting Parties. See Hudec, n. 21, *The GATT Legal System*, pp. 144–53; and Hudec, n. 9, 'GATT or GABB?' p. 1341. On the notion of protecting reasonable expectations generally, see Edward Allen Farnsworth, *Contracts* (Boston, MA: Little Brown, 1982), p. 19.

23. See Hudec, n. 21, *The GATT Legal System and World Trade,* pp. 66–96.

24. Some of this information is developed from private conversations with senior GATT officials closely associated with the early development of the GATT.

25. *Understanding regarding Notification, Consultation, Dispute Settlement and Surveillance*, GATT, BISD 26 Supp. 210 (1980), especially paras. 10–21.

26. *Netherlands Measures of Suspension of Obligations to the United States*, GATT, BISD 1 Supp. 32 (1953). This was one fallout result of the US Congress's enactment of sec. 22 of the Agriculture Act in 1951. See Jackson, William J. Davey and Alan O. Sykes, *Legal Problems of International Economic Relations*, 3rd edn (St Paul, MN: West Publishing, 1995), p. 1162, fn. 9.

27. The Netherlands never enforced the quota, arguably because of its ineffectiveness in removing the US quota on dairy products. See Hudec, 'Retaliation against Unreasonable Foreign Trade Practices: The New Sec. 301 and GATT Nullification and Impairment', *Minnesota Law Review*, 59 (1975): 57.

28. As a result of the panel decision in the so-called Superfund case (GATT, BISD 34 Supp. 136 (1988)), the EC requested that the CONTRACTING PARTIES authorize retaliation: *International Trade Reporter*, 5 (1988): 681 and 1303–40.

29. For example, in the Citrus case the United States took retaliatory action as a result of the failure of the EC to accept the findings of a 1985 GATT panel (*International Trade Reporter,* 2/50 (6 November 1985): 1389). However, in the light of continuing discussion between the EC and the USA, the President issued Proclamation 5363 of 15 August 1985 (*Federal Register,* 50 (1985): 337110) suspending the application of the duty until 1 November 1985. The duties became effective until 21 August 1986, when the President revoked the increased rates of duty owing to a settlement of the Citrus case (*Federal Register*, 51 (1986): 30146). However, it must be noted that trade in pasta between the USA and the EC was itself a problem, and so retaliation against a problematic product may have had a certain added attraction. See Jackson, Davey and Sykes, n. 26, *Legal Problems of International Economic Relations*, sec. 17.2.

30. The *prima facie* concept was also applied in situations involving quotas or domestic subsidies on products subject to agreed upon tariff limitations (i.e. tariffs bound under Article II; see generally, Jackson, n. 15, *World Trade and the Law of GATT*, p. 182.

31. See Jackson, n. 8, *The World Trading System*, p. 118.

32. See 1979 Understanding on Dispute Settlement; GATT, BISD 26 Supp. 216 (1979).

33. GATT, BISD 29 Supp. 13 (1983).

34. See Ministerial Declaration, GATT, BISD 33 Supp. 19, 25 (1987), and Decision of 28 January 1987 (GATT, BISD 33 Supp. 31, 44–5(1987)). See also, e.g., Clayton Yeutter, 'The GATT Must Be Repaired – and Fast!', *The International Economy* (March/April 1988): 44–8; address by Lamb (US Department of State, *Current Policy*, no. 585 (1984)). Improvement of the dispute settlement procedures of the GATT is also listed in the 1988 Trade Act (Omnibus Trade and Competitiveness Act of 1988, Pub. L. 100–418, sec. 1101(b)(1), 102 Stat. 1121) as a US objective under the Uruguay Round.

35. Jackson, Davey and Sykes, n. 26, *Legal Problems of International Economic Relations*, p. 362.

36. GATT Case, 'EEC – Payments and Subsidies Paid to Processors and Producers of Oilseeds and Related Animal-Feed Proteins', Panel Report adopted 25 January 1990, GATT, 37, BISD 86 (1991); Jackson, Davey and Sykes, n. 26, *Legal Problems of International Economic Relations,* p. 357.

37 'Agreement on Technical Barriers to Trade': GATT, BISD 26 Supp. 8 (1980).

38. 'United States: Taxes on Petroleum and Certain Imported Substances', GATT, BISD 34 Supp. 136 (1988), Panel Report adopted 17 June 1987. The superfund tax was 8.2 cents/barrel imposed on domestic petroleum products, compared with 11.7 cents/barrel on imported products.

39. Annex 2, 'Understanding on Rules and Procedures Governing the Settlement of Disputes', Art. 3, para. 8 (from Jackson, Davey and Sykes, n. 26, *Legal Problems of International Economic Relations*, Doc. Supp., p. 368) states: 'In cases where there is an infringement of the obligations assumed under a covered agreement, the action is considered *prima facie* to constitute a case of nullification or impairment. This means that there is normally a presumption that a breach of the rules has an adverse impact on other Members' parties to that covered agreement, and in such cases, it shall be up to the Member against whom the complaint has been brought to rebut the charge.'

40. See 1979 'Understanding on Dispute Settlement', n. 25.

41. GATT case, n. 36, EEC: Payments and Subsidies Paid to Processors and

Producers of Oilseeds and Related Animal-Feed Proteins, n. 36.

42. See ch. 2, sec. 2.2.

43. See chapter 19 of the US–Canada Free Trade Agreement, 27 ILM 281 (1988) (entered into force 1 January 1989). See also chapter 19 of the North American Free Trade Agreement (entered into force 1 January 1994).

44. Early Appellate Body reports include:

*United States*: Standards for Reformulated and Conventional Gasoline, Appellate Body Report and Panel Report, WTO Document WT/DS2/9 of 20 May 1996. US action to conform: see article by John Maggs, 'White House Alters Rules on Imported Gasoline', *Journal of Commerce*, 21 August 1997: 3A.

*Japan*: Taxes on Alcoholic Beverages, Report of the Appellate Body, World Trade Organization, WT/DS8,10,11/AB/R, 4 October 1996.

*United States*: Restrictions on Imports of Cotton and Man-Made Fibre Underwear, Complaint by Costa Rica (WTO Doc. WT/DS24, Appellate Report of 10 February 1997, adopted by the Dispute Settlement Body on 25 February 1997.

*Brazil* : Measures affecting Desiccated Coconut, Complaint by the Philippines (WT/DS22), Appellate Report adopted on 20 March 1997.

*United States*: Measures affecting Imports of Woven Wool Shirts and Blouses, Complaint by India (WT/DS33), Appellate Report adopted 23 May 1997.

*Canada*: Certain Measures concerning Periodicals, Complaint by the United States (WT/DS31), Appellate Report adopted 30 July 1997.

*European Communities*: Regime for the Importation, Sale and Distribution of Bananas, Complaints by Ecuador, Guatemala, Honduras, Mexico and the United States (WT/DS27), Appellate Body adopted 25 September 1997.

See WTO, *Overview of State-of-Play of WTO Disputes*, 26 September 1997.

45. WTO, *Overview of the State-of-Play of WTO Disputes*, <http:// www.wto.org/wto/dispute/bulletin.htm>. See also Frances Williams, 'WTO Sets up Panel to Probe US Shrimp Row', *Financial Times* (London), 26 February 1997; and *WTO Focus*.

46. See Ambassador Michael Kantor, n. 2, Testimony Before the House Ways and Means Trade Subcommittee.

47. See WTO, n. 44, *Overview of the State-of-Play of WTO Disputes*.

48. See e.g. DSU Article 3:2, which in part reads: '3.2 The dispute settlement system of the WTO is a central element in providing security and predictability to the multilateral trading system'. Also see speech of King Hassan II for the host government of the April 1994 Marrakesh ministerial

meeting to conclude the Uruguay Round, where he said, 'By bringing into being the World Trade Organization today, we are enshrining the rule of law in international economic and trade relations, thus setting universal rules and disciplines over the temptations of unilateralism and the law of the jungle.'

49. See US Gasoline case, discussing applicability of Vienna Convention on Law of Treaties for interpretative purposes. 'That general rule of interpretation has attained the status of a rule of customary or general international law. As such, it forms part of the customary rules of interpretation of public international law which the Appellate Body has been directed, by Article 3(2) of the DSU, to apply in seeking to clarify the provisions of the General Agreement ... That direction reflects a measure of recognition that the General Agreement is not to be read in clinical isolation from public international law.' WTO Document WT/DS2/9 p. 17, n. 44. See also Japan Alcoholic Beverages case: 'WTO rules are reliable, comprehensible and enforceable ... They will serve the multilateral trading system best if they are interpreted with that in mind. In that way, we will achieve the "security and predictability" sought for the multilateral trading system by the Members of the WTO through the establishment of the dispute settlement system.' WTO Document WT/DS8, 10, 11/AB/R p. 22, n. 44.

50. See generally Jackson, 'The Great 1994 Sovereignty Debate: United States Acceptance and Implementation of the Uruguay Round Results' in *Essays in Honor of Louis Henkin* (Boston, MA: Kluwer, 1998), also published in the *Columbia Journal of Transnational Law*, 36 (1997): 157–88.

51. DSU Articles 11–16. The DSB has the same members as the WTO General Council, but a different chairman.

52. DSU Article 17.

53. *Hearings* (23 March 1994, testimony of Steven R. Appleton, on behalf of the Semiconductor Industry Association (SIA)). *The World Trade Organization and US Sovereignty: Hearings before the Senate Committee on Foreign Relations*, 103rd Congress (14 June 1994), Statements by Rufus Yerxa (Deputy USTR) and John H. Jackson (Hessel E. Yntema Professor of Law, University of Michigan).

54. I share many, but not all, the concerns expressed. See Jackson, 'World Trade Rules and Environmental Policies: Congruence or Conflict?', *Washington and Lee Law Review*, 49 (1992): 1227.

55. See e.g. North, n. 4, *Institutions, Institutional Change and Economic Performance*.

56. *Hearings*, Senate Foreign Relations Committee, 14 June 1994, testimony of Ambassador Rufus Yerxa. See also Statement by USTR, 'Identification of

Trade Expansion Priorities (Super 301) pursuant to Executive Order 12901' (1 October 1996), <http://www.ustr.gov/reports/12901report.html>.

57. Jackson, 'US Threat to New World Trade Order', *Financial Times*, 23 May 1995: 13; B. Wildavsky, 'The Big Deal', *National Journal* (24 June 1995): 1650; Jagdish Bhagwati, 'The US–Japan Car Dispute: A Monumental Mistake', *International Affairs*, 72 (1996): 261.

58. Appellate Body Secretariat includes: James Bacchus (US); Debra Steger (Switzerland); Christopher D. Beeby (New Zealand); Claus-Dieter Ehlermann (Italy); Said El-Naggar (Egypt); Florentino P. Feliciano (Philippines); Mitsuo Matsushita (Japan); Julio Lacarte-Muro (Uruguay).

59. DSU Article 17: 4, 6, 10, 11, 12, 13.

60. DSU Article 17.7.

61. Announced 29 November 1995, *WTO Focus* (October/November, 1995): 1, 8.

62. WTO Appellate procedures found on the WTO web pages at <http://www.wto.org/wto>.

63. See US Standards for Reformulated and Conventional Gasoline, n. 44.

64. Jackson, 'The Legal Meaning of a GATT Dispute Settlement Report', in Niels Blokker and Sam Muller (eds), *Towards More Effective Supervision by International Organizations: Essays in Honour of Henry G. Schermers*, Vol. I (Boston, MA: Kluwer Academic Publishers, 1994), pp. 149–64.

65. Jackson, n. 64, 'The Legal Meaning of a GATT Dispute Settlement Report', pp. 149–64.

66. Vienna Convention on the Law of Treaties, signed 23 May 1969, 1155 UNTS 331.

67. Jackson, n. 8, *The World Trading System*, ch. 4.

68. Ian Brownlie, *Principles of Public International Law* (4th edn), (Oxford: Clarendon Press, 1990) p. 21; Art. 59, Statute of the ICJ signed 26 June 1945, 59 Stat. 1055, TS 993.

69. See ch. 2, sec. 3.2.

70. Jackson, n. 15, *World Trade and the Law of GATT*, p. 411; GATT Doc. L/3149 (1968).

71. Understanding regarding Notification Consultation Dispute Settlement and Surveillance, adopted 28 November 1979, GATT Doc. L/4907, BISD 26 Supp. 210, Annex on Agreed Description of the Customary Practice of the GATT in the Field of Dispute Settlement (art. XXIII:2) BISD 26 Supp. 215.

72. See Jackson, n. 8, *The World Trading System*, ch. 4.

73. Jackson (editorial comment), 'The WTO Dispute Settlement Understanding: Misunderstandings on the Nature of Legal Obligation', *American Journal of International Law*, 90 (1997): 60; Jackson, n. 64, 'The Legal Meaning of a GATT Dispute Settlement Report', pp. 149–64.

74. See e.g. *Hearings*, n. 56.
75. See American Law Institute, *Restatement of the Foreign Relations Law of the United States*, 3rd edn (1986), ch. 2, esp. sec. 114 (citing later, *inter alia*, Charming Betsy Case).
76. GATT, BISD 28 Supp. 114 (1982); Jackson, Davey and Sykes, *Legal Problems of International Economic Relations*, p. 777.
77. WTO Agreement Article XVI:1.
78. GATT, n. 71, Understanding regarding Notification, Consultation, Dispute Settlement and Surveillance, esp. paras. 16, 21, and 22, and Annex para. 5.
79. Vienna Convention on the Law of Treaties (1969), n. 66, art. 31: 3(b).
80. The WTO Agreement includes the following language which could be relevant: 'Article XVI: 4: Each member shall ensure the conformity of its laws, regulations and administrative procedures with its obligations as provided in the Annexed agreements.' However, this appears to beg the question, since it depends on a determination as to what *are* the obligations provided.
81. Remember that under the new procedures there can be no blocking and therefore adoption is virtually automatic. Also remember that the report will almost always specify an obligation to bring the national practices and law into consistency with the international treaty clauses.
82. See particularly the following articles and paragraphs of the Dispute Settlement Understanding text (Annex 2 to the WTO): DSU Article 3:4, 3:5, 3:7, 11, 19:1, 21:1, 21:6, 22:1, 22:2, 22:8, 26:1(b).
83. I do not here address another interesting legal question of the WTO and the DSU, namely whether the new text of the DSU imposes an obligation on states to refrain from all other international law remedies for redress of a complaint, except those provided in the DSU.
84. See n. 44, United States: Standards on Reformulated and Conventional Gasoline.
85. Vienna Convention on the Law of Treaties (1969), entered into force 1980, art. 31: 3(b). The Vienna Convention is deemed to express the general rules of international customary law, even for many nations which have not technically accepted the Vienna Convention itself. The convention clearly notes the obligation of *pacta sunt servanda*, namely, the treaties will be fulfilled. It also sets up a series of principles for interpreting treaties (art. 31), most notably the question of 'preparatory work', in a way that is often different from such treatment in national legal systems. In the case of all of these principles, the Appellate Body's statement that GATT/WTO law is part of international law means that these general principles of international law apply to its work and that of the WTO generally. This could have the most significance with respect to principles of interpretation of treaties.

Some GATT dispute reports had also taken this approach. See e.g. United States – restrictions on Imports of Tuna, Report of the Panel, GATT Document DS29/R (16 June 1994), para. 6.3; also *International Legal Materials*, v. 33, p. 839 (1994).

86. Jackson and Steven P. Croley, 'WTO Dispute Procedures, Standard of Review, and Deference to National Governments', *American Journal of International Law*, 90 (1996): 193–213.

87. Jackson, Davey and Sykes, n. 26, *Legal Problems of International Economic Law*, 1995 Documents Supplement, p. 194 (Text on Antidumping):

17.6 In examining the matter referred to in paragraph 5:

(i) in its assessment of the facts of the matter, the panel shall determine whether the authorities' establishment of the facts was proper and whether their evaluation of those facts was unbiased and objective. If the establishment of the facts was proper and the evaluation was unbiased and objective, even though the panel might have reached a different conclusion, the evaluation shall not be overturned;

(ii) the panel shall interpret the relevant provisions of the Agreement in accordance with customary rules of interpretation of public international law. Where the panel finds that a relevant provision of the Agreement admits of more than one permissible interpretation, the panel shall find the authorities' measure to be in conformity with the Agreement if it rests upon one of those permissible interpretations.

88. Ibid.

89. Decisions at Marrakesh: Decision on Review of Article 17.6 of the Agreement on Implementation of Article VI of the GATT, 1994 (Anti–dumping text); Declaration on Dispute Settlement pursuant to the Agreement on Implementation of Article VI of the GATT, 1994, or Part V of the Agreement on Subsidies and Countervailing Measures (Subsidies text). See Jackson, Davey and Sykes, *Legal Problems of International Economic Relations*, Doc. Supp. p. 435.

90. R. St J. Macdonald, F. Matscher and H. Petzold, *The European System for the Protection of Human Rights* (Amsterdam: Martinus Nijhoff, 1993), ch. 6, p. 83: Macdonald, 'The Margin of Appreciation'.

91. WTO Case, n. 44: United States: Standards for Reformulated and Conventional Gasoline, Appellate Body Report and Panel Report, page 30.

92. This proposal was part of a compromise agreement between Senator Dole and President Clinton, just before the Senate vote which was on 1 December 1994. The Agreement and the later Bill introduced by Senator Dole (but not yet passed as of this writing) called for a special commission

of US federal judges to review the panel report results of every WTO dispute settlement proceeding affecting the United States. The commission would give its advice to the Congress on the appropriateness of such report, in the light of four specified criteria in the Dole proposal. A description of the proposal is contained at 104th Congress, 1st Session, S.1438, 4 December 1995.

93. See n. 20.

94. DSU Article 26.

95. I am indebted to my European colleague Professor Meinhard Hilf for supplying information to me about this, referring to European Court of Justice cases ECR 1961 at 539 and 562; ECR 1973 at 575, 583, and to the following article: U. Everling, 'Probleme atypischer Rechts- und Handlungsformen bei der Auslegung des europäischen Gemein-schaftsrechts', in Bieber/Ress (eds), *The Dynamics of EC Law* (Baden-Baden: Nomos, 1987), pp. 417ff (with a summary in English).

96. See n. 66.

97. See e.g. Brownlie, n. 68, *Principles of Public International Law*, p. 628.

98. See n. 44.

99. Jackson, n. 15, *World Trade and the Law of GATT*, p. 185.

100. See n. 29 above. See also Henkin et al., *International Law Cases and Materials* (St Paul, MN: West Publishing, 1993), p. 570 (sec. 7, 'Countermeasures and Self-Help'). See also general discussion of US Section 301 in Jackson, Davey and Sykes, n. 26, *Legal Problems of International Economic Relations*, ch. 17.

101. Hudec, *Enforcing International Trade Law: The Evolution of the Modern GATT Legal System* (London: Butterworth, 1993).

102. See Henkin, *How Nations Behave: Law and Foreign Policy* (New York: Council on Foreign Relations, 1968).

103. See Jackson, *The World Trading System*, n. 8, p. 136.

104. DSU Articles 21, 22 and 26.

105. Based on author's discussions with diplomats.

106. See n. 44, *Japan: Taxes on Alcoholic Beverages*.

107. DSU Article 22: 4, etc.

108. DSU Article 26.

109. Author's private discussion with practitioners.

110. DSU Article 3:8.

111. DSU Article 3:5 and 3:6. Also see the following DSU Articles that could be relevant to this issue: 3:1, 3:2, 3:3, 3:4, 3:5,3:6, 6:1, 8:2, 8:9, 11.

112. See n. 44, first two Appellate Body Reports.

113. Based on author's discussions with participant officials and panellists in

the first-stage proceedings.

114. Author's discussions with officials and diplomats.

115. In just one issue of the weekly news publication *Inside US Trade* (Washington, DC), 1 August 1996, there were at least three articles which mention the use by diplomats of a warning or threat to bring a WTO dispute case in controversies being discussed; see articles at pp. 6 ('EU ban on animal parts' and 'EU Fur Ban') and 8 ('US Poultry Ban').

## Chapter 5: Reflections on and implications of the WTO constitution

1. The term 'constitution' is obviously here being used in a broad sense, not confined just to one or several documents or even to writing, but referring generally to the practice as well as to documents that define the structure of a particular system of governing rules.

2. Douglas C. North, *Institutions, Institutional Change and Economic Performance* (Cambridge: Cambridge University Press, 1990).

3. Ronald Coase, *The Firm, the Market and the Law* (Chicago, IL: University of Chicago Press, 1988), ch. 5 (reprint of 1960 article). See also C.A.E. Goodhart, 'Economics and the Law: Too Much One-Way Traffic?', *The Modern Law Review*, 60 (1997): 1.

4. See e.g. *Journal of Commerce* and *New York Times* articles in early February 1997, such as 'Historical Pact Opens Phone Market', *Journal of Commerce*, 19 February 1997, p. 1A, and 'Senators Challenge Administration to Review International Telecom Deal', *Journal of Commerce*, 7 February 1997, p. 2A.

5. See WTO Document WT/L/151, 1 June 1996, 'Summary of Built-in Agenda Issues for the Singapore Ministerial Conference', communication from ASEAN countries.

6. Four service sectors sometimes mentioned as early priority activities for WTO Service negotiations include telecommunications, financial services, accountancy services and maritime services.

7. See the WTO document series 'Press/TE...', e.g. Press/TE019 of 14 August 1997. Also see description of activity at the Marrakesh Minsterial Meeting of April 1994 (finalizing the Final Act of the Uruguay Round Negotiations), at *GATT Focus*, no. 107, Special Issue, May 1994.

8. See Singapore Ministerial Declaration, concluded 13 December 1996 at the First WTO Minsterial Meeting, *WTO Focus*, No. 15, January 1997. The OECD has been sponsoring a major negotiation to develop a MAI (Multilateral Agreement on Investment), and it is not entirely clear as this is written how these two organizations will cooperate on this subject.

9. John H. Jackson, 'Dolphins & Hormones: GATT and the Legal Environment for International Trade after the Uruguay Round', *University of Arkansas at Little Rock Law Journal*, 14 (1992): 429–54; 'Why the Beef Over Hormones?', *Time Magazine*, 16 January 1989: 44; WTO Panel Report, 'European Communities: Measures affecting Meat and Meat Products (Hormones)', WT/DS26 Report of 18 August 1997.

10. Jackson, *The Uruguay Round, World Trade Organization, and the Problem of Regulating International Economic Behaviour*, The Hyman Soloway Lecture, May 1994 (Ottawa: Centre for Trade Policy and Law, 1995); Jackson, 'Reflections on Constitutional Changes to the Global Trading System', *Chicago Kent Law Review*, 72 (1996): 511–20.

11. See Jackson, n. 10, 'Soloway Lecture'.

12. Ibid.

*Appendices*

# Appendix A
# The WTO Agreement

Final Act embodying the results of the Uruguay Round of Multilateral Trade Negotiations. Done at Marrakesh, April 15, 1994. Entered into force January 1, 1995.

The Parties to this Agreement,

Recognizing that their relations in the field of trade and economic endeavour should be conducted with a view to raising standards of living, ensuring full employment and a large and steadily growing volume of real income and effective demand, and expanding the production of and trade in goods and services, while allowing for the optimal use of the world's resources in accordance with the objective of sustainable development, seeking both to protect and preserve the environment and to enhance the means for doing so in a manner consistent with their respective needs and concerns at different levels of economic development,

Recognizing further that there is need for positive efforts designed to ensure that developing countries, and especially the least developed among them, secure a share in the growth in international trade commensurate with the needs of their economic development,

Being desirous of contributing to these objectives by entering into reciprocal and mutually advantageous arrangements directed to the substantial reduction of tariffs and other barriers to trade and to the elimination of discriminatory treatment in international trade relations,

Resolved, therefore, to develop an integrated, more viable and durable multilateral trading system encompassing the General Agreement on Tariffs and Trade, the results of past trade liberalization efforts, and all of the results of the Uruguay Round of Multilateral Trade Negotiations,

Determined to preserve the basic principles and to further the objectives underlying this multilateral trading system,

Agree as follows.

## Article I
### Establishment of the Organization

The World Trade Organization (hereinafter referred to as 'the WTO') is hereby established.

133

## Article II
### Scope of the WTO

1. The WTO shall provide the common institutional framework for the conduct of trade relations among its Members in matters related to the agreements and associated legal instruments included in the Annexes to this Agreement.
2. The agreements and associated legal instruments included in Annexes 1, 2 and 3 (hereinafter referred to as 'Multilateral Trade Agreements') are integral parts of this Agreement, binding on all Members.
3. The agreements and associated legal instruments included in Annex 4 (hereinafter referred to as 'Plurilateral Trade Agreements') are also part of this Agreement for those Members that have accepted them, and are binding on those Members. The Plurilateral Trade Agreements do not create either obligations or rights for Members that have not accepted them.
4. The General Agreement on Tariffs and Trade 1994 as specified in Annex 1A (hereinafter referred to as 'GATT 1994') is legally distinct from the General Agreement on Tariffs and Trade, dated 30 October 1947, annexed to the Final Act Adopted at the Conclusion of the Second Session of the Preparatory Committee of the United Nations Conference on Trade and Employment, as subsequently rectified, amended or modified (hereinafter referred to as 'GATT 1947').

## Article III
### Functions of the WTO

1. The WTO shall facilitate the implementation, administration and operation, and further the objectives, of this Agreement and of the Multilateral Trade Agreements, and shall also provide the framework for the implementation, administration and operation of the Plurilateral Trade Agreements.
2. The WTO shall provide the forum for negotiations among its Members concerning their multilateral trade relations in matters dealt with under the agreements in the Annexes to this Agreement. The WTO may also provide a forum for further negotiations among its Members concerning their multilateral trade relations, and a framework for the implementation of the results of such negotiations, as may be decided by the Ministerial Conference.
3. The WTO shall administer the Understanding on Rules and Procedures Governing the Settlement of Disputes (hereinafter referred to as the 'Dispute Settlement Understanding' or 'DSU') in Annex 2 to this Agreement.
4. The WTO shall administer the Trade Policy Review Mechanism (hereinafter referred to as the 'TPRM') provided for in Annex 3 to this Agreement.
5. With a view to achieving greater coherence in global economic policy-making, the WTO shall cooperate, as appropriate, with the International Monetary Fund and with the International Bank for Reconstruction and Development and its affiliated agencies.

## Article IV
## Structure of the WTO

1. There shall be a Ministerial Conference composed of representatives of all the Members, which shall meet at least once every two years. The Ministerial Conference shall carry out the functions of the WTO and take actions necessary to this effect. The Ministerial Conference shall have the authority to take decisions on all matters under any of the Multilateral Trade Agreements, if so requested by a Member, in accordance with the specific requirements for decision-making in this Agreement and in the relevant Multilateral Trade Agreement.

2. There shall be a General Council composed of representatives of all the Members, which shall meet as appropriate. In the intervals between meetings of the Ministerial Conference, its functions shall be conducted by the General Council. The General Council shall also carry out the functions assigned to it by this Agreement. The General Council shall establish its rules of procedure and approve the rules of procedure for the Committees provided for in paragraph 7.

3. The General Council shall convene as appropriate to discharge the responsibilities of the Dispute Settlement Body provided for in the Dispute Settlement Understanding. The Dispute Settlement Body may have its own chairman and shall establish such rules of procedure as it deems necessary for the fulfilment of those responsibilities.

4. The General Council shall convene as appropriate to discharge the responsibilities of the Trade Policy Review Body provided for in the TPRM. The Trade Policy Review Body may have its own chairman and shall establish such rules of procedure as it deems necessary for the fulfilment of those responsibilities.

5. There shall be a Council for Trade in Goods, a Council for Trade in Services and a Council for Trade-Related Aspects of Intellectual Property Rights (hereinafter referred to as the 'Council for TRIPS'), which shall operate under the general guidance of the General Council. The Council for Trade in Goods shall oversee the functioning of the Multilateral Trade Agreements in Annex 1A. The Council for Trade in Services shall oversee the functioning of the General Agreement on Trade in Services (hereinafter referred to as 'GATS'). The Council for TRIPS shall oversee the functioning of the Agreement on Trade-Related Aspects of Intellectual Property Rights (hereinafter referred to as the 'Agreement on TRIPS'). These Councils shall carry out the functions assigned to them by their respective agreements and by the General Council. They shall establish their respective rules of procedure subject to the approval of the General Council. Membership in these Councils shall be open to representatives of all Members. These Councils shall meet as necessary to carry out their functions.

6. The Council for Trade in Goods, the Council for Trade in Services and the Council for TRIPS shall establish subsidiary bodies as required. These subsidiary bodies shall establish their respective rules of procedure subject to the approval of their respective Councils.

7. The Ministerial Conference shall establish a Committee on Trade and Development, a Committee on Balance-of-Payments Restrictions and a Committee on

Budget, Finance and Administration, which shall carry out the functions assigned to them by this Agreement and by the Multilateral Trade Agreements, and any additional functions assigned to them by the General Council, and may establish such additional Committees with such functions as it may deem appropriate. As part of its functions, the Committee on Trade and Development shall periodically review the special provisions in the Multilateral Trade Agreements in favour of the least-developed country Members and report to the General Council for appropriate action. Membership in these Committees shall be open to representatives of all Members.

8. The bodies provided for under the Plurilateral Trade Agreements shall carry out the functions assigned to them under those Agreements and shall operate within the institutional framework of the WTO. These bodies shall keep the General Council informed of their activities on a regular basis.

### Article V
### Relations with other Organizations

1. The General Council shall make appropriate arrangements for effective cooperation with other intergovernmental organizations that have responsibilities related to those of the WTO.

2. The General Council may make appropriate arrangements for consultation and cooperation with non-governmental organizations concerned with matters related to those of the WTO.

### Article VI
### The Secretariat

1. There shall be a Secretariat of the WTO (hereinafter referred to as 'the Secretariat') headed by a Director-General.

2. The Ministerial Conference shall appoint the Director-General and adopt regulations setting out the powers, duties, conditions of service and term of office of the Director-General.

3. The Director-General shall appoint the members of the staff of the Secretariat and determine their duties and conditions of service in accordance with regulations adopted by the Ministerial Conference.

4. The responsibilities of the Director-General and of the staff of the Secretariat shall be exclusively international in character. In the discharge of their duties, the Director-General and the staff of the Secretariat shall not seek or accept instructions from any government or any other authority external to the WTO. They shall refrain from any action which might adversely reflect on their position as international officials. The Members of the WTO shall respect the international character of the responsibilities of the Director-General and of the staff of the Secretariat and shall not seek to influence them in the discharge of their duties.

### Article VII
### Budget and Contributions

1. The Director-General shall present to the Committee on Budget, Finance and Administration the annual budget estimate and financial statement of the WTO. The Committee on Budget, Finance and Administration shall review the annual budget estimate and the financial statement presented by the Director-General and make recommendations thereon to the General Council. The annual budget estimate shall be subject to approval by the General Council.

2. The Committee on Budget, Finance and Administration shall propose to the General Council financial regulations which shall include provisions setting out:

(a) the scale of contributions apportioning the expenses of the WTO among its Members; and

(b) the measures to be taken in respect of Members in arrears.

The financial regulations shall be based, as far as practicable, on the regulations and practices of GATT 1947.

3. The General Council shall adopt the financial regulations and the annual budget estimate by a two-thirds majority comprising more than half of the Members of the WTO.

4. Each Member shall promptly contribute to the WTO its share in the expenses of the WTO in accordance with the financial regulations adopted by the General Council.

### Article VIII
### Status of the WTO

1. The WTO shall have legal personality, and shall be accorded by each of its Members such legal capacity as may be necessary for the exercise of its functions.

2. The WTO shall be accorded by each of its Members such privileges and immunities as are necessary for the exercise of its functions.

3. The officials of the WTO and the representatives of the Members shall similarly be accorded by each of its Members such privileges and immunities as are necessary for the independent exercise of their functions in connection with the WTO.

4. The privileges and immunities to be accorded by a Member to the WTO, its officials, and the representatives of its Members shall be similar to the privileges and immunities stipulated in the Convention on the Privileges and Immunities of the Specialized Agencies, approved by the General Assembly of the United Nations on 21 November 1947.

5. The WTO may conclude a headquarters agreement.

### Article IX
### Decision-making

1. The WTO shall continue the practice of decision-making by consensus followed under GATT 1947. Except as otherwise provided, where a decision cannot be arrived at by consensus, the matter at issue shall be decided by voting.

At meetings of the Ministerial Conference and the General Council, each Member of the WTO shall have one vote. Where the European Communities exercise their right to vote, they shall have a number of votes equal to the number of their member States which are Members of the WTO. Decisions of the Ministerial Conference and the General Council shall be taken by a majority of the votes cast, unless otherwise provided in this Agreement or in the relevant Multilateral Trade Agreement.

2. The Ministerial Conference and the General Council shall have the exclusive authority to adopt interpretations of this Agreement and of the Multilateral Trade Agreements. In the case of an interpretation of a Multilateral Trade Agreement in Annex 1, they shall exercise their authority on the basis of a recommendation by the Council overseeing the functioning of that Agreement. The decision to adopt an interpretation shall be taken by a three-fourths majority of the Members. This paragraph shall not be used in a manner that would undermine the amendment provisions in Article X.

3. In exceptional circumstances, the Ministerial Conference may decide to waive an obligation imposed on a Member by this Agreement or any of the Multilateral Trade Agreements, provided that any such decision shall be taken by three fourths of the Members unless otherwise provided for in this paragraph.

(a) A request for a waiver concerning this Agreement shall be submitted to the Ministerial Conference for consideration pursuant to the practice of decision-making by consensus. The Ministerial Conference shall establish a time-period, which shall not exceed 90 days, to consider the request. If consensus is not reached during the time-period, any decision to grant a waiver shall be taken by three fourths of the Members.

(b) A request for a waiver concerning the Multilateral Trade Agreements in Annexes 1A or 1B or 1C and their annexes shall be submitted initially to the Council for Trade in Goods, the Council for Trade in Services or the Council for TRIPS, respectively, for consideration during a time-period which shall not exceed 90 days. At the end of the time-period, the relevant Council shall submit a report to the Ministerial Conference.

4. A decision by the Ministerial Conference granting a waiver shall state the exceptional circumstances justifying the decision, the terms and conditions governing the application of the waiver, and the date on which the waiver shall terminate. Any waiver granted for a period of more than one year shall be reviewed by the Ministerial Conference not later than one year after it is granted, and thereafter annually until the waiver terminates. In each review, the Ministerial Conference shall examine whether the exceptional circumstances justifying the waiver still exist and whether the terms and conditions attached to the waiver have been met. The Ministerial Conference, on the basis of the annual review, may extend, modify or terminate the waiver.

5. Decisions under a Plurilateral Trade Agreement, including any decisions on interpretations and waivers, shall be governed by the provisions of that Agreement.

## Article X
## Amendments

1. Any Member of the WTO may initiate a proposal to amend the provisions of this Agreement or the Multilateral Trade Agreements in Annex 1 by submitting such proposal to the Ministerial Conference. The Councils listed in paragraph 5 of Article IV may also submit to the Ministerial Conference proposals to amend the provisions of the corresponding Multilateral Trade Agreements in Annex 1 the functioning of which they oversee. Unless the Ministerial Conference decides on a longer period, for a period of 90 days after the proposal has been tabled formally at the Ministerial Conference any decision by the Ministerial Conference to submit the proposed amendment to the Members for acceptance shall be taken by consensus. Unless the provisions of paragraphs 2, 5 or 6 apply, that decision shall specify whether the provisions of paragraphs 3 or 4 shall apply. If consensus is reached, the Ministerial Conference shall forthwith submit the proposed amendment to the Members for acceptance. If consensus is not reached at a meeting of the Ministerial Conference within the established period, the Ministerial Conference shall decide by a two-thirds majority of the Members whether to submit the proposed amendment to the Members for acceptance. Except as provided in paragraphs 2, 5 and 6, the provisions of paragraph 3 shall apply to the proposed amendment, unless the Ministerial Conference decides by a three-fourths majority of the Members that the provisions of paragraph 4 shall apply.

2. Amendments to the provisions of this Article and to the provisions of the following Articles shall take effect only upon acceptance by all Members:

Article IX of this Agreement
Articles I and II of GATT 1994
Article II:1 of GATS
Article 4 of the Agreement on TRIPS

3. Amendments to provisions of this Agreement, or of the Multilateral Trade Agreements in Annexes 1A and 1C, other than those listed in paragraphs 2 and 6, of a nature that would alter the rights and obligations of the Members, shall take effect for the Members that have accepted them upon acceptance by two thirds of the Members and thereafter for each other Member upon acceptance by it. The Ministerial Conference may decide by a three-fourths majority of the Members that any amendment made effective under this paragraph is of such a nature that any Member which has not accepted it within a period specified by the Ministerial Conference in each case shall be free to withdraw from the WTO or to remain a Member with the consent of the Ministerial Conference.

4. Amendments to provisions of this Agreement or of the Multilateral Trade Agreements in Annexes 1A and 1C, other than those listed in paragraphs 2 and 6, of a nature that would not alter the rights and obligations of the Members, shall take effect for all Members upon acceptance by two thirds of the Members.

5. Except as provided in paragraph 2 above, amendments to Parts I, II and III of GATS and the respective annexes shall take effect for the Members that have

accepted them upon acceptance by two thirds of the Members and thereafter for each Member upon acceptance by it. The Ministerial Conference may decide by a three-fourths majority of the Members that any amendment made effective under the preceding provision is of such a nature that any Member which has not accepted it within a period specified by the Ministerial Conference in each case shall be free to withdraw from the WTO or to remain a Member with the consent of the Ministerial Conference. Amendments to Parts IV, V and VI of GATS and the respective annexes shall take effect for all Members upon acceptance by two thirds of the Members.

6. Notwithstanding the other provisions of this Article, amendments to the Agreement on TRIPS meeting the requirements of paragraph 2 of Article 71 thereof may be adopted by the Ministerial Conference without further formal acceptance process.

7. Any Member accepting an amendment to this Agreement or to a Multilateral Trade Agreement in Annex 1 shall deposit an instrument of acceptance with the Director-General of the WTO within the period of acceptance specified by the Ministerial Conference.

8. Any Member of the WTO may initiate a proposal to amend the provisions of the Multilateral Trade Agreements in Annexes 2 and 3 by submitting such proposal to the Ministerial Conference. The decision to approve amendments to the Multilateral Trade Agreement in Annex 2 shall be made by consensus and these amendments shall take effect for all Members upon approval by the Ministerial Conference. Decisions to approve amendments to the Multilateral Trade Agreement in Annex 3 shall take effect for all Members upon approval by the Ministerial Conference.

9. The Ministerial Conference, upon the request of the Members parties to a trade agreement, may decide exclusively by consensus to add that agreement to Annex 4. The Ministerial Conference, upon the request of the Members parties to a Plurilateral Trade Agreement, may decide to delete that Agreement from Annex 4.

10. Amendments to a Plurilateral Trade Agreement shall be governed by the provisions of that Agreement.

### Article XI
### Original Membership

1. The contracting parties to GATT 1947 as of the date of entry into force of this Agreement, and the European Communities, which accept this Agreement and the Multilateral Trade Agreements and for which Schedules of Concessions and Commitments are annexed to GATT 1994 and for which Schedules of Specific Commitments are annexed to GATS shall become original Members of the WTO.

2. The least-developed countries recognized as such by the United Nations will only be required to undertake commitments and concessions to the extent consistent with their individual development, financial and trade needs or their administrative and institutional capabilities.

### Article XII
### Accession

1. Any State or separate customs territory possessing full autonomy in the conduct of its external commercial relations and of the other matters provided for in this Agreement and the Multilateral Trade Agreements may accede to this Agreement, on terms to be agreed between it and the WTO. Such accession shall apply to this Agreement and the Multilateral Trade Agreements annexed thereto.
2. Decisions on accession shall be taken by the Ministerial Conference. The Ministerial Conference shall approve the agreement on the terms of accession by a two-thirds majority of the Members of the WTO.
3. Accession to a Plurilateral Trade Agreement shall be governed by the provisions of that Agreement.

### Article XIII
### Non-Application of Multilateral Trade Agreements between Particular Members

1. This Agreement and the Multilateral Trade Agreements in Annexes 1 and 2 shall not apply as between any Member and any other Member if either of the Members, at the time either becomes a Member, does not consent to such application.
2. Paragraph 1 may be invoked between original Members of the WTO which were contracting parties to GATT 1947 only where Article XXXV of that Agreement had been invoked earlier and was effective as between those contracting parties at the time of entry into force for them of this Agreement.
3. Paragraph 1 shall apply between a Member and another Member which has acceded under Article XII only if the Member not consenting to the application has so notified the Ministerial Conference before the approval of the agreement on the terms of accession by the Ministerial Conference.
4. The Ministerial Conference may review the operation of this Article in particular cases at the request of any Member and make appropriate recommendations.
5. Non-application of a Plurilateral Trade Agreement between parties to that Agreement shall be governed by the provisions of that Agreement.

### Article XIV
### Acceptance, Entry into Force and Deposit

1. This Agreement shall be open for acceptance, by signature or otherwise, by contracting parties to GATT 1947, and the European Communities, which are eligible to become original Members of the WTO in accordance with Article XI of this Agreement. Such acceptance shall apply to this Agreement and the Multilateral Trade Agreements annexed hereto. This Agreement and the Multilateral Trade Agreements annexed hereto shall enter into force on the date determined by Ministers in accordance with paragraph 3 of the Final Act Embodying the Results of the Uruguay Round of Multilateral Trade Negotiations and shall remain open for acceptance for a period of two years following that date unless the Ministers decide otherwise. An acceptance following the entry into

force of this Agreement shall enter into force on the 30th day following the date of such acceptance.

2. A Member which accepts this Agreement after its entry into force shall implement those concessions and obligations in the Multilateral Trade Agreements that are to be implemented over a period of time starting with the entry into force of this Agreement as if it had accepted this Agreement on the date of its entry into force.

3. Until the entry into force of this Agreement, the text of this Agreement and the Multilateral Trade Agreements shall be deposited with the Director-General to the CONTRACTING PARTIES to GATT 1947. The Director-General shall promptly furnish a certified true copy of this Agreement and the Multilateral Trade Agreements, and a notification of each acceptance thereof, to each government and the European Communities having accepted this Agreement. This Agreement and the Multilateral Trade Agreements, and any amendments thereto, shall, upon the entry into force of this Agreement, be deposited with the Director-General of the WTO.

4. The acceptance and entry into force of a Plurilateral Trade Agreement shall be governed by the provisions of that Agreement. Such Agreements shall be deposited with the Director-General to the CONTRACTING PARTIES to GATT 1947. Upon the entry into force of this Agreement, such Agreements shall be deposited with the Director-General of the WTO.

## Article XV
### Withdrawal

1. Any Member may withdraw from this Agreement. Such withdrawal shall apply both to this Agreement and the Multilateral Trade Agreements and shall take effect upon the expiration of six months from the date on which written notice of withdrawal is received by the Director-General of the WTO.

2. Withdrawal from a Plurilateral Trade Agreement shall be governed by the provisions of that Agreement.

## Article XVI
### Miscellaneous Provisions

1. Except as otherwise provided under this Agreement or the Multilateral Trade Agreements, the WTO shall be guided by the decisions, procedures and customary practices followed by the CONTRACTING PARTIES to GATT 1947 and the bodies established in the framework of GATT 1947.

2. To the extent practicable, the Secretariat of GATT 1947 shall become the Secretariat of the WTO, and the Director-General to the CONTRACTING PARTIES to GATT 1947, until such time as the Ministerial Conference has appointed a Director-General in accordance with paragraph 2 of Article VI of this Agreement, shall serve as Director-General of the WTO.

3. In the event of a conflict between a provision of this Agreement and a provision of any of the Multilateral Trade Agreements, the provision of this Agreement shall prevail to the extent of the conflict.

4. Each Member shall ensure the conformity of its laws, regulations and administrative procedures with its obligations as provided in the annexed Agreements.

5. No reservations may be made in respect of any provision of this Agreement. Reservations in respect of any of the provisions of the Multilateral Trade Agreements may only be made to the extent provided for in those Agreements. Reservations in respect of a provision of a Plurilateral Trade Agreement shall be governed by the provisions of that Agreement.

6 This Agreement shall be registered in accordance with the provisions of Article 102 of the Charter of the United Nations.

DONE at Marrakesh this fifteenth day of April one thousand nine hundred and ninety-four, in a single copy, in the English, French and Spanish languages, each text being authentic.

*Explanatory Notes*: The terms 'country' or 'countries' as used in this Agreement and the Multilateral Trade Agreements are to be understood to include any separate customs territory Member of the WTO.

In the case of a separate customs territory Member of the WTO, where an expression in this Agreement and the Multilateral Trade Agreements is qualified by the term 'national', such expression shall be read as pertaining to that customs territory, unless otherwise specified.

**List of Annexes**

ANNEX 1

    ANNEX 1A: Multilateral Agreements on Trade in Goods
       General Agreement on Tariffs and Trade 1994
       Agreement on Agriculture
       Agreement on the Application of Sanitary and Phytosanitary Measures
       Agreement on Textiles and Clothing
       Agreement on Technical Barriers to Trade
       Agreement on Trade-Related Investment Measures
       Agreement on Implementation of Article VI of the General Agreement on Tariffs and Trade 1994
       Agreement on Implementation of Article VII of the General Agreement on Tariffs and Trade 1994
       Agreement on Preshipment Inspection
       Agreement on Rules of Origin
       Agreement on Import Licensing Procedures
       Agreement on Subsidies and Countervailing Measures
       Agreement on Safeguards

*Appendix A*

ANNEX 1B: General Agreement on Trade in Services and Annexes

ANNEX 1C: Agreement on Trade-Related Aspects of Intellectual Property Rights

ANNEX 2
Understanding on Rules and Procedures Governing the Settlement of Disputes

ANNEX 3
Trade Policy Review Mechanism

ANNEX 4
Plurilateral Trade Agreements
Agreement on Trade in Civil Aircraft
Agreement on Government Procurement
International Dairy Agreement
International Bovine Meat Agreement

# Appendix B

# Understanding on Rules and Procedures Governing the Settlement of Disputes

Annex 2 to the Final Act embodying the results of the Uruguay Round of Multilateral Trade Negotiations. Done at Marrakesh, April 15, 1994. Entered into force January 1, 1995.

*Members* hereby *agree* as follows:

### Article 1
### Coverage and Application

1. The rules and procedures of this Understanding shall apply to disputes brought pursuant to the consultation and dispute settlement provisions of the agreements listed in Appendix 1 to this Understanding (referred to in this Understanding as the 'covered agreements'). The rules and procedures of this Understanding shall also apply to consultations and the settlement of disputes between Members concerning their rights and obligations under the provisions of the Agreement Establishing the World Trade Organization (referred to in this Understanding as the 'WTO Agreement') and of this Understanding taken in isolation or in combination with any other covered agreement.

2. The rules and procedures of this Understanding shall apply subject to such special or additional rules and procedures on dispute settlement contained in the covered agreements as are identified in Appendix 2 to this Understanding. To the extent that there is a difference between the rules and procedures of this Understanding and the special or additional rules and procedures set forth in Appendix 2, the special or additional rules and procedures in Appendix 2 shall prevail. In disputes involving rules and procedures under more than one covered agreement, if there is a conflict between special or additional rules and procedures of such agreements under review, and where the parties to the dispute cannot agree on rules and procedures within 20 days of the establishment of the panel, the Chairman of the Dispute Settlement Body provided for in paragraph 1 of Article 2 (referred to in this Understanding as the 'DSB'), in consultation with the parties to the dispute, shall determine the rules and procedures to be followed within 10 days after a request by either Member. The Chairman shall be guided by the principle that special or additional rules and procedures should be used where possible, and the rules and procedures set out in this Understanding should be used to the extent necessary to avoid conflict.

## Article 2
## Administration

1. The Dispute Settlement Body is hereby established to administer these rules and procedures and, except as otherwise provided in a covered agreement, the consultation and dispute settlement provisions of the covered agreements. Accordingly, the DSB shall have the authority to establish panels, adopt panel and Appellate Body reports, maintain surveillance of implementation of rulings and recommendations, and authorize suspension of concessions and other obligations under the covered agreements. With respect to disputes arising under a covered agreement which is a Plurilateral Trade Agreement, the term 'Member' as used herein shall refer only to those Members that are parties to the relevant Plurilateral Trade Agreement. Where the DSB administers the dispute settlement provisions of a Plurilateral Trade Agreement, only those Members that are parties to that Agreement may participate in decisions or actions taken by the DSB with respect to that dispute.
2. The DSB shall inform the relevant WTO Councils and Committees of any developments in disputes related to provisions of the respective covered agreements.
3. The DSB shall meet as often as necessary to carry out its functions within the time-frames provided in this Understanding.
4. Where the rules and procedures of this Understanding provide for the DSB to take a decision, it shall do so by consensus.[1]

## Article 3
## General Provisions

1. Members affirm their adherence to the principles for the management of disputes heretofore applied under Articles XXII and XXIII of GATT 1947, and the rules and procedures as further elaborated and modified herein.
2. The dispute settlement system of the WTO is a central element in providing security and predictability to the multilateral trading system. The Members recognize that it serves to preserve the rights and obligations of Members under the covered agreements, and to clarify the existing provisions of those agreements in accordance with customary rules of interpretation of public international law. Recommendations and rulings of the DSB cannot add to or diminish the rights and obligations provided in the covered agreements.
3. The prompt settlement of situations in which a Member considers that any benefits accruing to it directly or indirectly under the covered agreements are being impaired by measures taken by another Member is essential to the effective functioning of the WTO and the maintenance of a proper balance between the rights and obligations of Members.
4. Recommendations or rulings made by the DSB shall be aimed at achieving a satisfactory settlement of the matter in accordance with the rights and obligations under this Understanding and under the covered agreements.
5. All solutions to matters formally raised under the consultation and dispute

settlement provisions of the covered agreements, including arbitration awards, shall be consistent with those agreements and shall not nullify or impair benefits accruing to any Member under those agreements, nor impede the attainment of any objective of those agreements.

6. Mutually agreed solutions to matters formally raised under the consultation and dispute settlement provisions of the covered agreements shall be notified to the DSB and the relevant Councils and Committees, where any Member may raise any point relating thereto.

7. Before bringing a case, a Member shall exercise its judgement as to whether action under these procedures would be fruitful. The aim of the dispute settlement mechanism is to secure a positive solution to a dispute. A solution mutually acceptable to the parties to a dispute and consistent with the covered agreements is clearly to be preferred. In the absence of a mutually agreed solution, the first objective of the dispute settlement mechanism is usually to secure the withdrawal of the measures concerned if these are found to be inconsistent with the provisions of any of the covered agreements. The provision of compensation should be resorted to only if the immediate withdrawal of the measure is impracticable and as a temporary measure pending the withdrawal of the measure which is inconsistent with a covered agreement. The last resort which this Understanding provides to the Member invoking the dispute settlement procedures is the possibility of suspending the application of concessions or other obligations under the covered agreements on a discriminatory basis vis-à-vis the other Member, subject to authorization by the DSB of such measures.

8. In cases where there is an infringement of the obligations assumed under a covered agreement, the action is considered *prima facie* to constitute a case of nullification or impairment. This means that there is normally a presumption that a breach of the rules has an adverse impact on other Members parties to that covered agreement, and in such cases, it shall be up to the Member against whom the complaint has been brought to rebut the charge.

9. The provisions of this Understanding are without prejudice to the rights of Members to seek authoritative interpretation of provisions of a covered agreement through decision-making under the WTO Agreement or a covered agreement which is a Plurilateral Trade Agreement.

10. It is understood that requests for conciliation and the use of the dispute settlement procedures should not be intended or considered as contentious acts and that, if a dispute arises, all Members will engage in these procedures in good faith in an effort to resolve the dispute. It is also understood that complaints and counter-complaints in regard to distinct matters should not be linked.

11. This Understanding shall be applied only with respect to new requests for consultations under the consultation provisions of the covered agreements made on or after the date of entry into force of the WTO Agreement. With respect to disputes for which the request for consultations was made under GATT 1947 or under any other predecessor agreement to the covered agreements before the date of entry into force of the WTO Agreement, the relevant dispute settlement rules

and procedures in effect immediately prior to the date of entry into force of the WTO Agreement shall continue to apply.[2]

12. Notwithstanding paragraph 11, if a complaint based on any of the covered agreements is brought by a developing country Member against a developed country Member, the complaining party shall have the right to invoke, as an alternative to the provisions contained in Articles 4, 5, 6 and 12 of this Understanding, the corresponding provisions of the Decision of 5 April 1966 (BISD 14S/18), except that where the Panel considers that the time-frame provided for in paragraph 7 of that Decision is insufficient to provide its report and with the agreement of the complaining party, that time-frame may be extended. To the extent that there is a difference between the rules and procedures of Articles 4, 5, 6 and 12 and the corresponding rules and procedures of the Decision, the latter shall prevail.

## Article 4
### Consultations

1. Members affirm their resolve to strengthen and improve the effectiveness of the consultation procedures employed by Members.

2. Each Member undertakes to accord sympathetic consideration to and afford adequate opportunity for consultation regarding any representations made by another Member concerning measures affecting the operation of any covered agreement taken within the territory of the former.[3]

3. If a request for consultations is made pursuant to a covered agreement, the Member to which the request is made shall, unless otherwise mutually agreed, reply to the request within 10 days after the date of its receipt and shall enter into consultations in good faith within a period of no more than 30 days after the date of receipt of the request, with a view to reaching a mutually satisfactory solution. If the Member does not respond within 10 days after the date of receipt of the request, or does not enter into consultations within a period of no more than 30 days, or a period otherwise mutually agreed, after the date of receipt of the request, then the Member that requested the holding of consultations may proceed directly to request the establishment of a panel.

4. All such requests for consultations shall be notified to the DSB and the relevant Councils and Committees by the Member which requests consultations. Any request for consultations shall be submitted in writing and shall give the reasons for the request, including identification of the measures at issue and an indication of the legal basis for the complaint.

5. In the course of consultations in accordance with the provisions of a covered agreement, before resorting to further action under this Understanding, Members should attempt to obtain satisfactory adjustment of the matter.

6. Consultations shall be confidential, and without prejudice to the rights of any Member in any further proceedings.

7. If the consultations fail to settle a dispute within 60 days after the date of receipt of the request for consultations, the complaining party may request the

establishment of a panel. The complaining party may request a panel during the 60-day period if the consulting parties jointly consider that consultations have failed to settle the dispute.

8. In cases of urgency, including those which concern perishable goods, Members shall enter into consultations within a period of no more than 10 days after the date of receipt of the request. If the consultations have failed to settle the dispute within a period of 20 days after the date of receipt of the request, the complaining party may request the establishment of a panel.

9. In cases of urgency, including those which concern perishable goods, the parties to the dispute, panels and the Appellate Body shall make every effort to accelerate the proceedings to the greatest extent possible.

10. During consultations Members should give special attention to the particular problems and interests of developing country Members.

11. Whenever a Member other than the consulting Members considers that it has a substantial trade interest in consultations being held pursuant to paragraph 1 of Article XXII of GATT 1994, paragraph 1 of Article XXII of GATS, or the corresponding provisions in other covered agreements,[4] such Member may notify the consulting Members and the DSB, within 10 days after the date of the circulation of the request for consultations under said Article, of its desire to be joined in the consultations. Such Member shall be joined in the consultations, provided that the Member to which the request for consultations was addressed agrees that the claim of substantial interest is well-founded. In that event they shall so inform the DSB. If the request to be joined in the consultations is not accepted, the applicant Member shall be free to request consultations under paragraph 1 of Article XXII or paragraph 1 of Article XXIII of GATT 1994, paragraph 1 of Article XXII or paragraph 1 of Article XXIII of GATS, or the corresponding provisions in other covered agreements.

## Article 5
### Good Offices, Conciliation and Mediation

1. Good offices, conciliation and mediation are procedures that are undertaken voluntarily if the parties to the dispute so agree.

2. Proceedings involving good offices, conciliation and mediation, and in particular positions taken by the parties to the dispute during these proceedings, shall be confidential, and without prejudice to the rights of either party in any further proceedings under these procedures.

3. Good offices, conciliation or mediation may be requested at any time by any party to a dispute. They may begin at any time and be terminated at any time. Once procedures for good offices, conciliation or mediation are terminated, a complaining party may then proceed with a request for the establishment of a panel.

4. When good offices, conciliation or mediation are entered into within 60 days after the date of receipt of a request for consultations, the complaining party must allow a period of 60 days after the date of receipt of the request for consultations before requesting the establishment of a panel. The complaining party may

request the establishment of a panel during the 60-day period if the parties to the dispute jointly consider that the good offices, conciliation or mediation process has failed to settle the dispute.

5. If the parties to a dispute agree, procedures for good offices, conciliation or mediation may continue while the panel process proceeds.

6. The Director-General may, acting in an *ex officio* capacity, offer good offices, conciliation or mediation with the view to assisting Members to settle a dispute.

### Article 6
### Establishment of Panels

1. If the complaining party so requests, a panel shall be established at the latest at the DSB meeting following that at which the request first appears as an item on the DSB's agenda, unless at that meeting the DSB decides by consensus not to establish a panel.[5]

2. The request for the establishment of a panel shall be made in writing. It shall indicate whether consultations were held, identify the specific measures at issue and provide a brief summary of the legal basis of the complaint sufficient to present the problem clearly. In case the applicant requests the establishment of a panel with other than standard terms of reference, the written request shall include the proposed text of special terms of reference.

### Article 7
### Terms of Reference of Panels

1. Panels shall have the following terms of reference unless the parties to the dispute agree otherwise within 20 days from the establishment of the panel:

To examine, in the light of the relevant provisions in (name of the covered agreement(s) cited by the parties to the dispute), the matter referred to the DSB by (name of party) in document ... and to make such findings as will assist the DSB in making the recommendations or in giving the rulings provided for in that/those agreement(s).

2. Panels shall address the relevant provisions in any covered agreement or agreements cited by the parties to the dispute.

3. In establishing a panel, the DSB may authorize its Chairman to draw up the terms of reference of the panel in consultation with the parties to the dispute, subject to the provisions of paragraph 1. The terms of reference thus drawn up shall be circulated to all Members. If other than standard terms of reference are agreed upon, any Member may raise any point relating thereto in the DSB.

### Article 8
### Composition of Panels

1. Panels shall be composed of well-qualified governmental and/or non-governmental individuals, including persons who have served on or presented a case to a panel, served as a representative of a Member or of a contracting party to GATT 1947 or as a representative to the Council or Committee of any covered agreement

or its predecessor agreement, or in the Secretariat, taught or published on international trade law or policy, or served as a senior trade policy official of a Member.

2. Panel members should be selected with a view to ensuring the independence of the members, a sufficiently diverse background and a wide spectrum of experience.

3. Citizens of Members whose governments[6] are parties to the dispute or third parties as defined in paragraph 2 of Article 10 shall not serve on a panel concerned with that dispute, unless the parties to the dispute agree otherwise.

4. To assist in the selection of panelists, the Secretariat shall maintain an indicative list of governmental and non-governmental individuals possessing the qualifications outlined in paragraph 1, from which panelists may be drawn as appropriate. That list shall include the roster of non-governmental panelists established on 30 November 1984 (BISD 31S/9), and other rosters and indicative lists established under any of the covered agreements, and shall retain the names of persons on those rosters and indicative lists at the time of entry into force of the WTO Agreement. Members may periodically suggest names of governmental and non-governmental individuals for inclusion on the indicative list, providing relevant information on their knowledge of international trade and of the sectors or subject matter of the covered agreements, and those names shall be added to the list upon approval by the DSB. For each of the individuals on the list, the list shall indicate specific areas of experience or expertise of the individuals in the sectors or subject matter of the covered agreements.

5. Panels shall be composed of three panelists unless the parties to the dispute agree, within 10 days from the establishment of the panel, to a panel composed of five panelists. Members shall be informed promptly of the composition of the panel.

6. The Secretariat shall propose nominations for the panel to the parties to the dispute. The parties to the dispute shall not oppose nominations except for compelling reasons.

7. If there is no agreement on the panelists within 20 days after the date of the establishment of a panel, at the request of either party, the Director-General, in consultation with the Chairman of the DSB and the Chairman of the relevant Council or Committee, shall determine the composition of the panel by appointing the panelists whom the Director-General considers most appropriate in accordance with any relevant special or additional rules or procedures of the covered agreement or covered agreements which are at issue in the dispute, after consulting with the parties to the dispute. The Chairman of the DSB shall inform the Members of the composition of the panel thus formed no later than 10 days after the date the Chairman receives such a request.

8. Members shall undertake, as a general rule, to permit their officials to serve as panelists.

9. Panelists shall serve in their individual capacities and not as government representatives, nor as representatives of any organization. Members shall therefore not give them instructions nor seek to influence them as individuals with regard to matters before a panel.

10. When a dispute is between a developing country Member and a developed country Member the panel shall, if the developing country Member so requests,

include at least one panelist from a developing country Member.

11. Panelists' expenses, including travel and subsistence allowance, shall be met from the WTO budget in accordance with criteria to be adopted by the General Council, based on recommendations of the Committee on Budget, Finance and Administration.

## Article 9
### Procedures for Multiple Complainants

1. Where more than one Member requests the establishment of a panel related to the same matter, a single panel may be established to examine these complaints taking into account the rights of all Members concerned. A single panel should be established to examine such complaints whenever feasible.

2. The single panel shall organize its examination and present its findings to the DSB in such a manner that the rights which the parties to the dispute would have enjoyed had separate panels examined the complaints are in no way impaired. If one of the parties to the dispute so requests, the panel shall submit separate reports on the dispute concerned. The written submissions by each of the complainants shall be made available to the other complainants, and each complainant shall have the right to be present when any one of the other complainants presents its views to the panel.

3. If more than one panel is established to examine the complaints related to the same matter, to the greatest extent possible the same persons shall serve as panelists on each of the separate panels and the timetable for the panel process in such disputes shall be harmonized.

## Article 10
### Third Parties

1. The interests of the parties to a dispute and those of other Members under a covered agreement at issue in the dispute shall be fully taken into account during the panel process.

2. Any Member having a substantial interest in a matter before a panel and having notified its interest to the DSB (referred to in this Understanding as a 'third party') shall have an opportunity to be heard by the panel and to make written submissions to the panel. These submissions shall also be given to the parties to the dispute and shall be reflected in the panel report.

3. Third parties shall receive the submissions of the parties to the dispute to the first meeting of the panel.

4. If a third party considers that a measure already the subject of a panel proceeding nullifies or impairs benefits accruing to it under any covered agreement, that Member may have recourse to normal dispute settlement procedures under this Understanding. Such a dispute shall be referred to the original panel wherever possible.

### Article 11
### Function of Panels

The function of panels is to assist the DSB in discharging its responsibilities under this Understanding and the covered agreements. Accordingly, a panel should make an objective assessment of the matter before it, including an objective assessment of the facts of the case and the applicability of and conformity with the relevant covered agreements, and make such other findings as will assist the DSB in making the recommendations or in giving the rulings provided for in the covered agreements. Panels should consult regularly with the parties to the dispute and give them adequate opportunity to develop a mutually satisfactory solution.

### Article 12
### Panel Procedures

1. Panels shall follow the Working Procedures in Appendix 3 unless the panel decides otherwise after consulting the parties to the dispute.
2. Panel procedures should provide sufficient flexibility so as to ensure high-quality panel reports, while not unduly delaying the panel process.
3. After consulting the parties to the dispute, the panelists shall, as soon as practicable and whenever possible within one week after the composition and terms of reference of the panel have been agreed upon, fix the timetable for the panel process, taking into account the provisions of paragraph 9 of Article 4, if relevant.
4. In determining the timetable for the panel process, the panel shall provide sufficient time for the parties to the dispute to prepare their submissions.
5. Panels should set precise deadlines for written submissions by the parties and the parties should respect those deadlines.
6. Each party to the dispute shall deposit its written submissions with the Secretariat for immediate transmission to the panel and to the other party or parties to the dispute. The complaining party shall submit its first submission in advance of the responding party's first submission unless the panel decides, in fixing the timetable referred to in paragraph 3 and after consultations with the parties to the dispute, that the parties should submit their first submissions simultaneously. When there are sequential arrangements for the deposit of first submissions, the panel shall establish a firm time-period for receipt of the responding party's submission. Any subsequent written submissions shall be submitted simultaneously.
7. Where the parties to the dispute have failed to develop a mutually satisfactory solution, the panel shall submit its findings in the form of a written report to the DSB. In such cases, the report of a panel shall set out the findings of fact, the applicability of relevant provisions and the basic rationale behind any findings and recommendations that it makes. Where a settlement of the matter among the parties to the dispute has been found, the report of the panel shall be confined to a brief description of the case and to reporting that a solution has been reached.
8. In order to make the procedures more efficient, the period in which the panel shall conduct its examination, from the date that the composition and terms of

reference of the panel have been agreed upon until the date the final report is issued to the parties to the dispute, shall, as a general rule, not exceed six months. In cases of urgency, including those relating to perishable goods, the panel shall aim to issue its report to the parties to the dispute within three months.

9. When the panel considers that it cannot issue its report within six months, or within three months in cases of urgency, it shall inform the DSB in writing of the reasons for the delay together with an estimate of the period within which it will issue its report. In no case should the period from the establishment of the panel to the circulation of the report to the Members exceed nine months.

10. In the context of consultations involving a measure taken by a developing country Member, the parties may agree to extend the periods established in paragraphs 7 and 8 of Article 4. If, after the relevant period has elapsed, the consulting parties cannot agree that the consultations have concluded, the Chairman of the DSB shall decide, after consultation with the parties, whether to extend the relevant period and, if so, for how long. In addition, in examining a complaint against a developing country Member, the panel shall accord sufficient time for the developing country Member to prepare and present its argumentation. The provisions of paragraph 1 of Article 20 and paragraph 4 of Article 21 are not affected by any action pursuant to this paragraph.

11. Where one or more of the parties is a developing country Member, the panel's report shall explicitly indicate the form in which account has been taken of relevant provisions on differential and more-favourable treatment for developing country Members that form part of the covered agreements which have been raised by the developing country Member in the course of the dispute settlement procedures.

12. The panel may suspend its work at any time at the request of the complaining party for a period not to exceed 12 months. In the event of such a suspension, the time-frames set out in paragraphs 8 and 9 of this Article, paragraph 1 of Article 20, and paragraph 4 of Article 21 shall be extended by the amount of time that the work was suspended. If the work of the panel has been suspended for more than 12 months, the authority for establishment of the panel shall lapse.

### Article 13
### Right to Seek Information

1. Each panel shall have the right to seek information and technical advice from any individual or body which it deems appropriate. However, before a panel seeks such information or advice from any individual or body within the jurisdiction of a Member it shall inform the authorities of that Member. A Member should respond promptly and fully to any request by a panel for such information as the panel considers necessary and appropriate. Confidential information which is provided shall not be revealed without formal authorization from the individual, body, or authorities of the Member providing the information.

2. Panels may seek information from any relevant source and may consult experts to obtain their opinion on certain aspects of the matter. With respect to a factual

issue concerning a scientific or other technical matter raised by a party to a dispute, a panel may request an advisory report in writing from an expert review group. Rules for the establishment of such a group and its procedures are set forth in Appendix 4.

## Article 14
### Confidentiality

1. Panel deliberations shall be confidential.
2. The reports of panels shall be drafted without the presence of the parties to the dispute in the light of the information provided and the statements made.
3. Opinions expressed in the panel report by individual panelists shall be anonymous.

## Article 15
### Interim Review Stage

1. Following the consideration of rebuttal submissions and oral arguments, the panel shall issue the descriptive (factual and argument) sections of its draft report to the parties to the dispute. Within a period of time set by the panel, the parties shall submit their comments in writing.
2. Following the expiration of the set period of time for receipt of comments from the parties to the dispute, the panel shall issue an interim report to the parties, including both the descriptive sections and the panel's findings and conclusions. Within a period of time set by the panel, a party may submit a written request for the panel to review precise aspects of the interim report prior to circulation of the final report to the Members. At the request of a party, the panel shall hold a further meeting with the parties on the issues identified in the written comments. If no comments are received from any party within the comment period, the interim report shall be considered the final panel report and circulated promptly to the Members.
3. The findings of the final panel report shall include a discussion of the arguments made at the interim review stage. The interim review stage shall be conducted within the time-period set out in paragraph 8 of Article 12.

## Article 16
### Adoption of Panel Reports

1. In order to provide sufficient time for the Members to consider panel reports, the reports shall not be considered for adoption by the DSB until 20 days after the date they have been circulated to the Members.
2. Members having objections to a panel report shall give written reasons to explain their objections for circulation at least 10 days prior to the DSB meeting at which the panel report will be considered.
3. The parties to a dispute shall have the right to participate fully in the consideration of the panel report by the DSB, and their views shall be fully recorded.
4. Within 60 days after the date of circulation of a panel report to the Members, the report shall be adopted at a DSB meeting[7] unless a party to the dispute

formally notifies the DSB of its decision to appeal or the DSB decides by consensus not to adopt the report. If a party has notified its decision to appeal, the report by the panel shall not be considered for adoption by the DSB until after completion of the appeal. This adoption procedure is without prejudice to the right of Members to express their views on a panel report.

### Article 17
### Appellate Review

*Standing Appellate Body*

1. A standing Appellate Body shall be established by the DSB. The Appellate Body shall hear appeals from panel cases. It shall be composed of seven persons, three of whom shall serve on any one case. Persons serving on the Appellate Body shall serve in rotation. Such rotation shall be determined in the working procedures of the Appellate Body.

2. The DSB shall appoint persons to serve on the Appellate Body for a four-year term, and each person may be reappointed once. However, the terms of three of the seven persons appointed immediately after the entry into force of the WTO Agreement shall expire at the end of two years, to be determined by lot. Vacancies shall be filled as they arise. A person appointed to replace a person whose term of office has not expired shall hold office for the remainder of the predecessor's term.

3. The Appellate Body shall comprise persons of recognized authority, with demonstrated expertise in law, international trade and the subject matter of the covered agreements generally. They shall be unaffiliated with any government. The Appellate Body membership shall be broadly representative of membership in the WTO. All persons serving on the Appellate Body shall be available at all times and on short notice, and shall stay abreast of dispute settlement activities and other relevant activities of the WTO. They shall not participate in the consideration of any disputes that would create a direct or indirect conflict of interest.

4. Only parties to the dispute, not third parties, may appeal a panel report. Third parties which have notified the DSB of a substantial interest in the matter pursuant to paragraph 2 of Article 10 may make written submissions to, and be given an opportunity to be heard by, the Appellate Body.

5. As a general rule, the proceedings shall not exceed 60 days from the date a party to the dispute formally notifies its decision to appeal to the date the Appellate Body circulates its report. In fixing its timetable the Appellate Body shall take into account the provisions of paragraph 9 of Article 4, if relevant. When the Appellate Body considers that it cannot provide its report within 60 days, it shall inform the DSB in writing of the reasons for the delay together with an estimate of the period within which it will submit its report. In no case shall the proceedings exceed 90 days.

6. An appeal shall be limited to issues of law covered in the panel report and legal interpretations developed by the panel.

7. The Appellate Body shall be provided with appropriate administrative and legal support as it requires.

8. The expenses of persons serving on the Appellate Body, including travel and subsistence allowance, shall be met from the WTO budget in accordance with criteria to be adopted by the General Council, based on recommendations of the Committee on Budget, Finance and Administration.

*Procedures for Appellate Review*

9. Working procedures shall be drawn up by the Appellate Body in consultation with the Chairman of the DSB and the Director-General, and communicated to the Members for their information.

10. The proceedings of the Appellate Body shall be confidential. The reports of the Appellate Body shall be drafted without the presence of the parties to the dispute and in the light of the information provided and the statements made.

11. Opinions expressed in the Appellate Body report by individuals serving on the Appellate Body shall be anonymous.

12. The Appellate Body shall address each of the issues raised in accordance with paragraph 6 during the appellate proceeding.

13. The Appellate Body may uphold, modify or reverse the legal findings and conclusions of the panel.

*Adoption of Appellate Body Reports*

14. An Appellate Body report shall be adopted by the DSB and unconditionally accepted by the parties to the dispute unless the DSB decides by consensus not to adopt the Appellate Body report within 30 days following its circulation to the Members.[8] This adoption procedure is without prejudice to the right of Members to express their views on an Appellate Body report.

## Article 18
### Communications with the Panel or Appellate Body

1. There shall be no *ex parte* communications with the panel or Appellate Body concerning matters under consideration by the panel or Appellate Body.

2. Written submissions to the panel or the Appellate Body shall be treated as confidential, but shall be made available to the parties to the dispute. Nothing in this Understanding shall preclude a party to a dispute from disclosing statements of its own positions to the public. Members shall treat as confidential information submitted by another Member to the panel or the Appellate Body which that Member has designated as confidential. A party to a dispute shall also, upon request of a Member, provide a non-confidential summary of the information contained in its written submissions that could be disclosed to the public.

## Article 19
### Panel and Appellate Body Recommendations

1. Where a panel or the Appellate Body concludes that a measure is inconsistent with a covered agreement, it shall recommend that the Member concerned[9] bring the measure into conformity with that agreement.[10] In addition to its recommendations, the panel or Appellate Body may suggest ways in which the Member concerned could implement the recommendations.

2. In accordance with paragraph 2 of Article 3, in their findings and recommendations, the panel and Appellate Body cannot add to or diminish the rights and obligations provided in the covered agreements.

## Article 20
### Time-frame for DSB Decisions

Unless otherwise agreed to by the parties to the dispute, the period from the date of establishment of the panel by the DSB until the date the DSB considers the panel or appellate report for adoption shall as a general rule not exceed nine months where the panel report is not appealed or 12 months where the report is appealed. Where either the panel or the Appellate Body has acted, pursuant to paragraph 9 of Article 12 or paragraph 5 of Article 17, to extend the time for providing its report, the additional time taken shall be added to the above periods.

## Article 21
### Surveillance of Implementation of Recommendations and Rulings

1. Prompt compliance with recommendations or rulings of the DSB is essential in order to ensure effective resolution of disputes to the benefit of all Members.

2. Particular attention should be paid to matters affecting the interests of developing country Members with respect to measures which have been subject to dispute settlement.

3. At a DSB meeting held within 30 days[11] after the date of adoption of the panel or Appellate Body report, the Member concerned shall inform the DSB of its intentions in respect of implementation of the recommendations and rulings of the DSB. If it is impracticable to comply immediately with the recommendations and rulings, the Member concerned shall have a reasonable period of time in which to do so. The reasonable period of time shall be:

    (a) the period of time proposed by the Member concerned, provided that such period is approved by the DSB; or, in the absence of such approval,

    (b) a period of time mutually agreed by the parties to the dispute within 45 days after the date of adoption of the recommendations and rulings; or, in the absence of such agreement,

    (c) a period of time determined through binding arbitration within 90 days after the date of adoption of the recommendations and rulings.[12] In such arbitration, a guideline for the arbitrator[13] should be that the reasonable period of time to implement panel or Appellate Body recommendations should not exceed 15 months from the date of adoption of a panel or Appellate Body report. However, that time may be shorter or longer, depending upon the particular circumstances.

4. Except where the panel or the Appellate Body has extended, pursuant to paragraph 9 of Article 12 or paragraph 5 of Article 17, the time of providing its report, the period from the date of establishment of the panel by the DSB until the date of determination of the reasonable period of time shall not exceed 15 months unless the parties to the dispute agree otherwise. Where either the panel or the Appellate Body has acted to extend the time of providing its report, the additional time taken shall be added to the 15-month period; provided that unless the parties to the dispute agree that there are exceptional circumstances, the total time shall not exceed 18 months.

5. Where there is disagreement as to the existence or consistency with a covered agreement of measures taken to comply with the recommendations and rulings such dispute shall be decided through recourse to these dispute settlement procedures, including wherever possible resort to the original panel. The panel shall circulate its report within 90 days after the date of referral of the matter to it. When the panel considers that it cannot provide its report within this time frame, it shall inform the DSB in writing of the reasons for the delay together with an estimate of the period within which it will submit its report.

6. The DSB shall keep under surveillance the implementation of adopted recommendations or rulings. The issue of implementation of the recommendations or rulings may be raised at the DSB by any Member at any time following their adoption. Unless the DSB decides otherwise, the issue of implementation of the recommendations or rulings shall be placed on the agenda of the DSB meeting after six months following the date of establishment of the reasonable period of time pursuant to paragraph 3 and shall remain on the DSB's agenda until the issue is resolved. At least 10 days prior to each such DSB meeting, the Member concerned shall provide the DSB with a status report in writing of its progress in the implementation of the recommendations or rulings.

7. If the matter is one which has been raised by a developing country Member, the DSB shall consider what further action it might take which would be appropriate to the circumstances.

8. If the case is one brought by a developing country Member, in considering what appropriate action might be taken, the DSB shall take into account not only the trade coverage of measures complained of, but also their impact on the economy of developing country Members concerned.

### Article 22
### Compensation and the Suspension of Concessions

1. Compensation and the suspension of concessions or other obligations are temporary measures available in the event that the recommendations and rulings are not implemented within a reasonable period of time. However, neither compensation nor the suspension of concessions or other obligations is preferred to full implementation of a recommendation to bring a measure into conformity

with the covered agreements. Compensation is voluntary and, if granted, shall be consistent with the covered agreements.

2. If the Member concerned fails to bring the measure found to be inconsistent with a covered agreement into compliance therewith or otherwise comply with the recommendations and rulings within the reasonable period of time determined pursuant to paragraph 3 of Article 21, such Member shall, if so requested, and no later than the expiry of the reasonable period of time, enter into negotiations with any party having invoked the dispute settlement procedures, with a view to developing mutually acceptable compensation. If no satisfactory compensation has been agreed within 20 days after the date of expiry of the reasonable period of time, any party having invoked the dispute settlement procedures may request authorization from the DSB to suspend the application to the Member concerned of concessions or other obligations under the covered agreements.

3. In considering what concessions or other obligations to suspend, the complaining party shall apply the following principles and procedures:

(a) the general principle is that the complaining party should first seek to suspend concessions or other obligations with respect to the same sector(s) as that in which the panel or Appellate Body has found a violation or other nullification or impairment;

(b) if that party considers that it is not practicable or effective to suspend concessions or other obligations with respect to the same sector(s), it may seek to suspend concessions or other obligations in other sectors under the same agreement;

(c) if that party considers that it is not practicable or effective to suspend concessions or other obligations with respect to other sectors under the same agreement, and that the circumstances are serious enough, it may seek to suspend concessions or other obligations under another covered agreement;

(d) in applying the above principles, that party shall take into account:

(i) the trade in the sector or under the agreement under which the panel or Appellate Body has found a violation or other nullification or impairment, and the importance of such trade to that party;

(ii) the broader economic elements related to the nullification or impairment and the broader economic consequences of the suspension of concessions or other obligations;

(e) if that party decides to request authorization to suspend concessions or other obligations pursuant to subparagraphs (b) or (c), it shall state the reasons therefor in its request. At the same time as the request is forwarded to the DSB, it also shall be forwarded to the relevant Councils and also, in the case of a request pursuant to subparagraph (b), the relevant sectoral bodies;

(f) for purposes of this paragraph, 'sector' means:

(i) with respect to goods, all goods;

(ii) with respect to services, a principal sector as identified in the current 'Services Sectoral Classification List' which identifies such sectors;[14]

(iii) with respect to trade-related intellectual property rights, each of the categories of intellectual property rights covered in Section 1, or Section 2, or Section 3, or Section 4, or Section 5, or Section 6, or Section 7 of Part II, or the obligations under Part III, or Part IV of the Agreement on TRIPS;

(g) for purposes of this paragraph, 'agreement' means:

(i) with respect to goods, the agreements listed in Annex 1A of the WTO Agreement, taken as a whole as well as the Plurilateral Trade Agreements in so far as the relevant parties to the dispute are parties to these agreements;

(ii) with respect to services, the GATS;

(iii) with respect to intellectual property rights, the Agreement on TRIPS.

4. The level of the suspension of concessions or other obligations authorized by the DSB shall be equivalent to the level of the nullification or impairment.

5. The DSB shall not authorize suspension of concessions or other obligations if a covered agreement prohibits such suspension.

6. When the situation described in paragraph 2 occurs, the DSB, upon request, shall grant authorization to suspend concessions or other obligations within 30 days of the expiry of the reasonable period of time unless the DSB decides by consensus to reject the request. However, if the Member concerned objects to the level of suspension proposed, or claims that the principles and procedures set forth in paragraph 3 have not been followed where a complaining party has requested authorization to suspend concessions or other obligations pursuant to paragraph 3(b) or (c), the matter shall be referred to arbitration. Such arbitration shall be carried out by the original panel, if members are available, or by an arbitrator[15] appointed by the Director-General and shall be completed within 60 days after the date of expiry of the reasonable period of time. Concessions or other obligations shall not be suspended during the course of the arbitration.

7. The arbitrator[16] acting pursuant to paragraph 6 shall not examine the nature of the concessions or other obligations to be suspended but shall determine whether the level of such suspension is equivalent to the level of nullification or impairment. The arbitrator may also determine if the proposed suspension of concessions or other obligations is allowed under the covered agreement. However, if the matter referred to arbitration includes a claim that the principles and procedures set forth in paragraph 3 have not been followed, the arbitrator shall examine that claim. In the event the arbitrator determines that those principles and procedures have not been followed, the complaining party shall apply them consistent with paragraph 3. The parties shall accept the arbitrator's decision as final and the parties concerned shall not seek a second arbitration. The DSB shall be informed promptly of the decision of the arbitrator and shall upon request, grant authorization to suspend concessions or other obligations where the request is consistent with the decision of the arbitrator, unless the DSB decides by consensus to reject the request.

8. The suspension of concessions or other obligations shall be temporary and

shall only be applied until such time as the measure found to be inconsistent with a covered agreement has been removed, or the Member that must implement recommendations or rulings provides a solution to the nullification or impairment of benefits, or a mutually satisfactory solution is reached. In accordance with paragraph 6 of Article 21, the DSB shall continue to keep under surveillance the implementation of adopted recommendations or rulings, including those cases where compensation has been provided or concessions or other obligations have been suspended but the recommendations to bring a measure into conformity with the covered agreements have not been implemented.

9. The dispute settlement provisions of the covered agreements may be invoked in respect of measures affecting their observance taken by regional or local governments or authorities within the territory of a Member. When the DSB has ruled that a provision of a covered agreement has not been observed, the responsible Member shall take such reasonable measures as may be available to it to ensure its observance. The provisions of the covered agreements and this Understanding relating to compensation and suspension of concessions or other obligations apply in cases where it has not been possible to secure such observance.[17]

### Article 23
### Strengthening of the Multilateral System

1. When Members seek the redress of a violation of obligations or other nullification or impairment of benefits under the covered agreements or an impediment to the attainment of any objective of the covered agreements, they shall have recourse to, and abide by, the rules and procedures of this Understanding.

2. In such cases, Members shall:

(a) not make a determination to the effect that a violation has occurred, that benefits have been nullified or impaired or that the attainment of any objective of the covered agreements has been impeded, except through recourse to dispute settlement in accordance with the rules and procedures of this Understanding, and shall make any such determination consistent with the findings contained in the panel or Appellate Body report adopted by the DSB or an arbitration award rendered under this Understanding;

(b) follow the procedures set forth in Article 21 to determine the reasonable period of time for the Member concerned to implement the recommendations and rulings; and

(c) follow the procedures set forth in Article 22 to determine the level of suspension of concessions or other obligations and obtain DSB authorization in accordance with those procedures before suspending concessions or other obligations under the covered agreements in response to the failure of the Member concerned to implement the recommendations and rulings within that reasonable period of time.

## Article 24
### Special Procedures Involving Least-Developed Country Members

1. At all stages of the determination of the causes of a dispute and of dispute settlement procedures involving a least-developed country Member, particular consideration shall be given to the special situation of least-developed country Members. In this regard, Members shall exercise due restraint in raising matters under these procedures involving a least-developed country Member. If nullification or impairment is found to result from a measure taken by a least-developed country Member, complaining parties shall exercise due restraint in asking for compensation or seeking authorization to suspend the application of concessions or other obligations pursuant to these procedures.

2. In dispute settlement cases involving a least-developed country Member, where a satisfactory solution has not been found in the course of consultations the Director-General or the Chairman of the DSB shall, upon request by a least-developed country Member offer their good offices, conciliation and mediation with a view to assisting the parties to settle the dispute, before a request for a panel is made. The Director-General or the Chairman of the DSB, in providing the above assistance, may consult any source which either deems appropriate.

## Article 25
### Arbitration

1. Expeditious arbitration within the WTO as an alternative means of dispute settlement can facilitate the solution of certain disputes that concern issues that are clearly defined by both parties.

2. Except as otherwise provided in this Understanding, resort to arbitration shall be subject to mutual agreement of the parties which shall agree on the procedures to be followed. Agreements to resort to arbitration shall be notified to all Members sufficiently in advance of the actual commencement of the arbitration process.

3. Other Members may become party to an arbitration proceeding only upon the agreement of the parties which have agreed to have recourse to arbitration. The parties to the proceeding shall agree to abide by the arbitration award. Arbitration awards shall be notified to the DSB and the Council or Committee of any relevant agreement where any Member may raise any point relating thereto.

4. Articles 21 and 22 of this Understanding shall apply *mutatis mutandis* to arbitration awards.

## Article 26

### 1. Non-Violation Complaints of the Type Described in Paragraph 1(b) of Article XXIII of GATT 1994

Where the provisions of paragraph 1(b) of Article XXIII of GATT 1994 are applicable to a covered agreement, a panel or the Appellate Body may only make rulings and recommendations where a party to the dispute considers that any benefit accruing to it directly or indirectly under the relevant covered agreement is being nullified or impaired or the attainment of any objective of that

Agreement is being impeded as a result of the application by a Member of any measure, whether or not it conflicts with the provisions of that Agreement. Where and to the extent that such party considers and a panel or the Appellate Body determines that a case concerns a measure that does not conflict with the provisions of a covered agreement to which the provisions of paragraph 1(b) of Article XXIII of GATT 1994 are applicable, the procedures in this Understanding shall apply, subject to the following:

(a) the complaining party shall present a detailed justification in support of any complaint relating to a measure which does not conflict with the relevant covered agreement;

(b) where a measure has been found to nullify or impair benefits under, or impede the attainment of objectives, of the relevant covered agreement without violation thereof, there is no obligation to withdraw the measure. However, in such cases, the panel or the Appellate Body shall recommend that the Member concerned make a mutually satisfactory adjustment;

(c) notwithstanding the provisions of Article 21, the arbitration provided for in paragraph 3 of Article 21, upon request of either party, may include a determination of the level of benefits which have been nullified or impaired, and may also suggest ways and means of reaching a mutually satisfactory adjustment; such suggestions shall not be binding upon the parties to the dispute;

(d) notwithstanding the provisions of paragraph 1 of Article 22, compensation may be part of a mutually satisfactory adjustment as final settlement of the dispute.

## 2. Complaints of the Type Described in Paragraph 1(c) of Article XXIII of GATT 1994

Where the provisions of paragraph 1(c) of Article XXIII of GATT 1994 are applicable to a covered agreement, a panel may only make rulings and recommendations where a party considers that any benefit accruing to it directly or indirectly under the relevant covered agreement is being nullified or impaired or the attainment of any objective of that Agreement is being impeded as a result of the existence of any situation other than those to which the provisions of paragraphs 1(a) and 1(b) of Article XXIII of GATT 1994 are applicable. Where and to the extent that such party considers and a panel determines that the matter is covered by this paragraph, the procedures of this Understanding shall apply only up to and including the point in the proceedings where the panel report has been circulated to the Members. The dispute settlement rules and procedures contained in the Decision of 12 April 1989 (BISD 36S/61-67) shall apply to consideration for adoption, and surveillance and implementation of recommendations and rulings. The following shall also apply:

(a) the complaining party shall present a detailed justification in support of any argument made with respect to issues covered under this paragraph;

(b) in cases involving matters covered by this paragraph, if a panel finds that cases also involve dispute settlement matters other than those covered by this paragraph, the panel shall circulate a report to the DSB addressing any such matters and a separate report on matters falling under this paragraph.

### Article 27
### Responsibilities of the Secretariat

1. The Secretariat shall have the responsibility of assisting panels, especially on the legal, historical and procedural aspects of the matters dealt with, and of providing secretarial and technical support.

2. While the Secretariat assists Members in respect of dispute settlement at their request, there may also be a need to provide additional legal advice and assistance in respect of dispute settlement to developing country Members. To this end, the Secretariat shall make available a qualified legal expert from the WTO technical cooperation services to any developing country Member which so requests. This expert shall assist the developing country Member in a manner ensuring the continued impartiality of the Secretariat.

3. The Secretariat shall conduct special training courses for interested Members concerning these dispute settlement procedures and practices so as to enable Members' experts to be better informed in this regard.

*Appendix 1*
*Agreements Covered by the Understanding*

(A) Agreement Establishing the World Trade Organization
(B) Multilateral Trade Agreements
    Annex 1A: Multilateral Agreements on Trade in Goods
    Annex 1B: General Agreement on Trade in Services
    Annex 1C: Agreement on Trade-Related Aspects of Intellectual Property Rights
    Annex 2: Understanding on Rules and Procedures Governing the Settlement of Disputes
(C) Plurilateral Trade Agreements
    Annex 4:   Agreement on Trade in Civil Aircraft
              Agreement on Government Procurement
              International Dairy Agreement
              International Bovine Meat Agreement

The applicability of this Understanding to the Plurilateral Trade Agreements shall be subject to the adoption of a decision by the parties to each agreement setting out the terms for the application of the Understanding to the individual agreement, including any special or additional rules or procedures for inclusion in Appendix 2, as notified to the DSB.

# Appendix B

### Appendix 2
### Special or Additional Rules and Procedures
### Contained in the Covered Agreements

| Agreement | Rules and Procedures |
|---|---|
| Agreement on the Application of Sanitary and Phytosanitary Measures | 11.2 |
| Agreement on Textiles and Clothing | 2.14, 2.21, 4.4, 5.2, 5.4, 5.6, 6.9, |
| 6.10, 6.11, 8.1 through 8.12 | |
| Agreement on Technical Barriers to Trade | 14.2 through 14.4, Annex 2 |
| Agreement on Implementation of Article VI of GATT 1994 | 17.4 through 17.7 |
| Agreement on Implementation of Article VII of GATT 1994 | 19.3 through 19.5, Annex II.2(f), |
| 3, 9, 21 | |
| Agreement on Subsidies and Countervailing | 4.2 through 4.12, 6.6, 7.2 through |
| Measures  footnote 35, 24.4, 27.7, Annex V | 7.10, 8.5, |
| General Agreement on Trade in Services | XXII:3, XXIII:3 |
| Annex on Financial Services | 4 |
| Annex on Air Transport Services | 4 |
| Decision on Certain Dispute Settlement Procedures for the GATS | 1 through 5 |

The list of rules and procedures in this Appendix includes provisions where only a part of the provision may be relevant in this context.

Any special or additional rules or procedures in the Plurilateral Trade Agreements as determined by the competent bodies of each agreement and as notified to the DSB.

### Appendix 3
### Working Procedures

1. In its proceedings the panel shall follow the relevant provisions of this Understanding. In addition, the following working procedures shall apply.
2. The panel shall meet in closed session. The parties to the dispute, and interested parties, shall be present at the meetings only when invited by the panel to appear before it.
3. The deliberations of the panel and the documents submitted to it shall be kept confidential. Nothing in this Understanding shall preclude a party to a dispute from disclosing statements of its own positions to the public. Members shall treat as confidential information submitted by another Member to the panel which that Member has designated as confidential. Where a party to a dispute submits a confidential version of its written submissions to the panel, it shall also, upon request of a Member, provide a non-confidential summary of the information contained in its submissions that could be disclosed to the public.
4. Before the first substantive meeting of the panel with the parties, the parties to the dispute shall transmit to the panel written submissions in which they present the facts of the case and their arguments.
5. At its first substantive meeting with the parties, the panel shall ask the party which has brought the complaint to present its case. Subsequently, and still at the same meeting, the

party against which the complaint has been brought shall be asked to present its point of view.
6. All third parties which have notified their interest in the dispute to the DSB shall be invited in writing to present their views during a session of the first substantive meeting of the panel set aside for that purpose. All such third parties may be present during the entirety of this session.
7. Formal rebuttals shall be made at a second substantive meeting of the panel. The party complained against shall have the right to take the floor first to be followed by the complaining party. The parties shall submit, prior to that meeting, written rebuttals to the panel.
8. The panel may at any time put questions to the parties and ask them for explanations either in the course of a meeting with the parties or in writing.
9. The parties to the dispute and any third party invited to present its views in accordance with Article 10 shall make available to the panel a written version of their oral statements.
10. In the interest of full transparency, the presentations, rebuttals and statements referred to in paragraphs 5 to 9 shall be made in the presence of the parties. Moreover, each party's written submissions, including any comments on the descriptive part of the report and responses to questions put by the panel, shall be made available to the other party or parties.
11. Any additional procedures specific to the panel.
12. Proposed timetable for panel work:

|  |  |  |
|---|---|---|
| (a) | Receipt of first written submissions of the parties: | |
| | (1) complaining Party: | 3-6 weeks |
| | (2) Party complained against: | 2-3 weeks |
| (b) | Date, time and place of first substantive meeting with the parties; third party session: | 1-2 weeks |
| (c) | Receipt of written rebuttals of the parties: | 2-3 weeks |
| (d) | Date, time and place of second substantive meeting with the parties: | 1-2 weeks |
| (e) | Issuance of descriptive part of the report to the parties: | 2-4 weeks |
| (f) | Receipt of comments by the parties on the descriptive part of the report: | 2 weeks |
| (g) | Issuance of the interim report, including the findings and conclusions, to the parties: | 2-4 weeks |
| (h) | Deadline for party to request review of part(s) of report: | 1 week |
| (i) | Period of review by panel, including possible additional meeting with parties: | 2 weeks |
| (j) | Issuance of final report to parties to dispute: | 2 weeks |
| (k) | Circulation of the final report to the Members: | 3 weeks |

The above calendar may be changed in the light of unforeseen developments. Additional meetings with the parties shall be scheduled if required.

### Appendix 4
### Expert Review Groups

The following rules and procedures shall apply to expert review groups established in accordance with the provisions of paragraph 2 of Article 13.
1. Expert review groups are under the panel's authority. Their terms of reference and detailed working procedures shall be decided by the panel, and they shall report to the panel.

2. Participation in expert review groups shall be restricted to persons of professional standing and experience in the field in question.

3. Citizens of parties to the dispute shall not serve on an expert review group without the joint agreement of the parties to the dispute, except in exceptional circumstances when the panel considers that the need for specialized scientific expertise cannot be fulfilled otherwise. Government officials of parties to the dispute shall not serve on an expert review group. Members of expert review groups shall serve in their individual capacities and not as government representatives, nor as representatives of any organization. Governments or organizations shall therefore not give them instructions with regard to matters before an expert review group.

4. Expert review groups may consult and seek information and technical advice from any source they deem appropriate. Before an expert review group seeks such information or advice from a source within the jurisdiction of a Member, it shall inform the government of that Member. Any Member shall respond promptly and fully to any request by an expert review group for such information as the expert review group considers necessary and appropriate.

5. The parties to a dispute shall have access to all relevant information provided to an expert review group, unless it is of a confidential nature. Confidential information provided to the expert review group shall not be released without formal authorization from the government, organization or person providing the information. Where such information is requested from the expert review group but release of such information by the expert review group is not authorized, a non-confidential summary of the information will be provided by the government, organization or person supplying the information.

6. The expert review group shall submit a draft report to the parties to the dispute with a view to obtaining their comments, and taking them into account, as appro-priate, in the final report, which shall also be issued to the parties to the dispute when it is submitted to the panel. The final report of the expert review group shall be advisory only.

## Notes

1. The DSB shall be deemed to have decided by consensus on a matter submitted for its consideration, if no Member, present at the meeting of the DSB when the decision is taken, formally objects to the proposed decision.

2. This paragraph shall also be applied to disputes on which panel reports have not been adopted or fully implemented.

3. Where the provisions of any other covered agreement concerning measures taken by regional or local governments or authorities within the territory of a Member contain provisions different from the provisions of this paragraph, the provisions of such other covered agreement shall prevail.

4. The corresponding consultation provisions in the covered agreements are listed hereunder: Agreement on Agriculture, Article 19; Agreement on the Application of Sanitary and Phytosanitary Measures, paragraph 1 of Article 11; Agreement on Textiles and Clothing, paragraph 4 of Article 8; Agreement on Technical Barriers to Trade, paragraph 1 of Article 14; Agreement on Trade-Related Investment Measures, Article 8; Agreement on Implementation of Article VI of GATT 1994, paragraph 2 of Article 17; Agreement on Implementation of Article VII of GATT 1994, paragraph 2 of Article 19; Agreement on Preshipment Inspection, Article 7; Agreement on Rules of Origin, Article 7; Agreement on Import Licensing

Procedures, Article 6; Agreement on Subsidies and Countervailing Measures, Article 30; Agreement on Safeguards, Article 14; Agreement on Trade-Related Aspects of Intellectual Property Rights, Article 64.1; and any corresponding consultation provisions in Plurilateral Trade Agreements as determined by the competent bodies of each Agreement and as notified to the DSB.

5. If the complaining party so requests, a meeting of the DSB shall be convened for this purpose within 15 days of the request, provided that at least 10 days' advance notice of the meeting is given.

6. In the case where customs unions or common markets are parties to a dispute, this provision applies to citizens of all member countries of the customs unions or common markets.

7. If a meeting of the DSB is not scheduled within this period at a time that enables the requirements of paragraphs 1 and 4 of Article 16 to be met, a meeting of the DSB shall be held for this purpose.

8. If a meeting of the DSB is not scheduled during this period, such a meeting of the DSB shall be held for this purpose.

9. The 'Member concerned' is the party to the dispute to which the panel or Appellate Body recommendations are directed.

10. With respect to recommendations in cases not involving a violation of GATT 1994 or any other covered agreement, see Article 26.

11. If a meeting of the DSB is not scheduled during this period, such a meeting of the DSB shall be held for this purpose.

12. If the parties cannot agree on an arbitrator within ten days after referring the matter to arbitration, the arbitrator shall be appointed by the Director-General within ten days, after consulting the parties.

13. The expression 'arbitrator' shall be interpreted as referring either to an individual or a group.

14. The list in document MTN.GNS/W/120 identifies eleven sectors.

15. The expression 'arbitrator' shall be interpreted as referring either to an individual or a group.

16. The expression 'arbitrator' shall be interpreted as referring either to an individual or a group or to the members of the original panel when serving in the capacity of arbitrator.

17. Where the provisions of any covered agreement concerning measures taken by regional or local governments or authorities within the territory of a Member contain provisions different from the provisions of this paragraph, the provisions of such covered agreement shall prevail.

# Appendix C
# The Organization: Members and Observers

*Members (132) as of May 1998*

| | |
|---|---|
| Antigua and Barbuda | 1 January 1995 |
| Angola | 1 December 1996 |
| Argentina | 1 January 1995 |
| Australia | 1 January 1995 |
| Austria | 1 January 1995 |
| Bahrain | 1 January 1995 |
| Bangladesh | 1 January 1995 |
| Barbados | 1 January 1995 |
| Belgium | 1 January 1995 |
| Belize | 1 January 1995 |
| Benin | 22 February 1996 |
| Bolivia | 13 September 1995 |
| Botswana | 31 May 1995 |
| Brazil | 1 January 1995 |
| Brunei Darussalam | 1 January 1995 |
| Bulgaria | 1 December 1996 |
| Burkina Faso | 3 June 1995 |
| Burundi | 23 July 1995 |
| Cameroon | 13 December 1995 |
| Canada | 1 January 1995 |
| Central African Republic | 31 May 1995 |
| Chad | 19 October 1996 |
| Chile | 1 January 1995 |
| Colombia | 30 April 1995 |
| Congo | 27 March 1997 |
| Costa Rica | 1 January 1995 |
| Côte d'Ivoire | 1 January 1995 |
| Cuba | 20 April 1995 |
| Cyprus | 30 July 1995 |
| Czech Republic | 1 January 1995 |
| Democratic Republic of the Congo | 1 January 1997 |
| Denmark | 1 January 1995 |
| Djibouti | 31 May 1995 |
| Dominica | 1 January 1995 |
| Dominican Republic | 9 March 1995 |
| Ecuador | 21 January 1996 |
| Egypt | 30 June 1995 |

| | |
|---|---|
| El Salvador | 7 May 1995 |
| European Communities | 1 January 1995 |
| Fiji | 14 January 1996 |
| Finland | 1 January 1995 |
| France | 1 January 1995 |
| Gabon | 1 January 1995 |
| Gambia | 23 October 1996 |
| Germany | 1 January 1995 |
| Ghana | 1 January 1995 |
| Greece | 1 January 1995 |
| Grenada | 22 February 1996 |
| Guatemala | 21 July 1995 |
| Guinea Bissau | 31 May 1995 |
| Guinea | 25 October 1995 |
| Guyana | 1 January 1995 |
| Haiti | 30 January 1996 |
| Honduras | 1 January 1995 |
| Hong Kong, China | 1 January 1995 |
| Hungary | 1 January 1995 |
| Iceland | 1 January 1995 |
| India | 1 January 1995 |
| Indonesia | 1 January 1995 |
| Ireland | 1 January 1995 |
| Israel | 21 April 1995 |
| Italy | 1 January 1995 |
| Jamaica | 9 March 1995 |
| Japan | 1 January 1995 |
| Kenya | 1 January 1995 |
| Korea | 1 January 1995 |
| Kuwait | 1 January 1995 |
| Lesotho | 31 May 1995 |
| Liechtenstein | 1 September 1995 |
| Luxembourg | 1 January 1995 |
| Macau | 1 January 1995 |
| Madagascar | 17 November 1995 |
| Malawi | 31 May 1995 |
| Malaysia | 1 January 1995 |
| Maldives | 31 May 1995 |
| Mali | 31 May 1995 |
| Malta | 1 January 1995 |
| Mauritania | 31 May 1995 |
| Mauritius | 1 January 1995 |
| Mexico | 1 January 1995 |
| Mongolia | 29 January 1997 |

| | |
|---|---|
| Morocco | 1 January 1995 |
| Mozambique | 26 August 1995 |
| Myanmar | 1 January 1995 |
| Namibia | 1 January 1995 |
| Netherlands – For the Kingdom in Europe and for the Netherlands Antilles | 1 January 1995 |
| New Zealand | 1 January 1995 |
| Nicaragua | 3 September 1995 |
| Niger | 13 December 1996 |
| Nigeria | 1 January 1995 |
| Norway | 1 January 1995 |
| Pakistan | 1 January 1995 |
| Panama | 6 September 1997 |
| Papua New Guinea | 9 June 1996 |
| Paraguay | 1 January 1995 |
| Peru | 1 January 1995 |
| Philippines | 1 January 1995 |
| Poland | 1 July 1995 |
| Portugal | 1 January 1995 |
| Qatar | 13 January 1996 |
| Romania | 1 January 1995 |
| Rwanda | 22 May 1996 |
| Saint Kitts and Nevis | 21 February 1996 |
| Saint Lucia | 1 January 1995 |
| Saint Vincent & the Grenadines | 1 January 1995 |
| Senegal | 1 January 1995 |
| Sierra Leone | 23 July 1995 |
| Singapore | 1 January 1995 |
| Slovak Republic | 1 January 1995 |
| Slovenia | 30 July 1995 |
| Solomon Islands | 26 July 1996 |
| South Africa | 1 January 1995 |
| Spain | 1 January 1995 |
| Sri Lanka | 1 January 1995 |
| Suriname | 1 January 1995 |
| Swaziland | 1 January 1995 |
| Sweden | 1 January 1995 |
| Switzerland | 1 July 1995 |
| Tanzania | 1 January 1995 |
| Thailand | 1 January 1995 |
| Togo | 31 May 1995 |
| Trinidad and Tobago | 1 March 1995 |
| Tunisia | 29 March 1995 |
| Turkey | 26 March 1995 |

| | |
|---|---|
| Uganda | 1 January 1995 |
| United Arab Emirates | 10 April 1996 |
| United Kingdom | 1 January 1995 |
| United States | 1 January 1995 |
| Uruguay | 1 January 1995 |
| Venezuela | 1 January 1995 |
| Zambia | 1 January 1995 |
| Zimbabwe | 3 March 1995 |

*Observer governments (32)*

| | |
|---|---|
| Albania | Lithuania |
| Algeria | former Yugoslav Republic of |
| Andorra | Macedonia |
| Armenia | Moldova |
| Azerbaijan | Nepal |
| Belarus | Oman |
| Cambodia | Russian Federation |
| China | Saudi Arabia |
| Croatia | Seychelles |
| Estonia | Sudan |
| Ethiopia | Chinese Taipei |
| Georgia | Tonga |
| Holy See (Vatican) | Ukraine |
| Jordan | Uzbekistan |
| Kazakstan | Vanuatu |
| Kyrgyz Republic | Vietnam |
| Latvia | |

*Note: All observer countries have applied to join the WTO.*

*Observers for General Council only (observers in other councils and committees differ)*

United Nations (UN)
United Nations Conference on Trade and Development (UNCTAD)
International Monetary Fund (IMF)
World Bank
Food and Agricultural Organization (FAO)
World Intellectual Property Organization (WIPO)
Organization for Economic Cooperation and Development (OECD)

# Appendix D  WTO Structure: Organization Chart

## WTO structure

All WTO members may participate in all councils, committees, etc., except Appellate Body, Dispute Settlement panels, Textiles Monitoring Body, and plurilateral committees

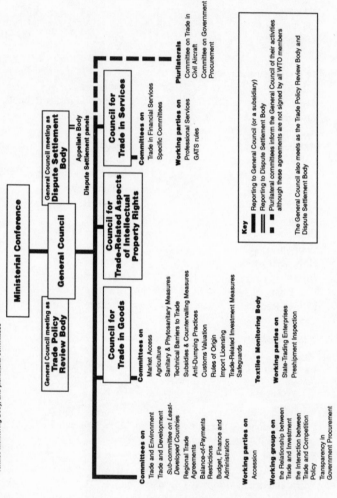

**Ministerial Conference**

**General Council meeting as Trade Policy Review Body**

**General Council meeting as Dispute Settlement Body**

**General Council**

Appellate Body
Dispute Settlement panels

**Council for Trade in Goods**

**Council for Trade-Related Aspects of Intellectual Property Rights**

**Council for Trade in Services**

**Committees on**
Market Access
Agriculture
Sanitary & Phytosanitary Measures
Technical Barriers to Trade
Subsidies & Countervailing Measures
Anti-Dumping Practices
Customs Valuation
Rules of Origin
Import Licensing
Trade-Related Investment Measures
Safeguards

**Textiles Monitoring Body**

**Working parties on**
State-Trading Enterprises
Preshipment Inspection

**Committees on**
Trade in Financial Services
Specific Committees

**Working parties on**
Professional Services
GATS rules

**Plurilaterals**
Committee on Trade in Civil Aircraft
Committee on Government Procurement

**Committees on**
Trade and Environment
Trade and Development
*Sub-committee on Least-Developed Countries*
Regional Trade Agreements
Balance-of-Payments Restrictions
Budget, Finance and Administration

**Working parties on**
Accession

**Working groups on**
the Relationship between Trade and Investment
the Interaction between Trade and Competition Policy
Transparency in Government Procurement

**Key**
━━━ Reporting to General Council (or a subsidiary)
━━━ Reporting to Dispute Settlement Body
■■■ Plurilateral committees inform the General Council of their activities although these agreements are not signed by all WTO members

The General Council also meets as the Trade Policy Review Body and Dispute Settlement Body

# Appendix E
# Outline of Uruguay Round Texts[1]

## Agreement Establishing the World Trade Organization

ANNEX 1
    ANNEX 1A: Multilateral Agreements on Trade in Goods
        General Agreement on Tariffs and Trade 1947, as amended
        General Agreement on Tariffs and Trade 1994
        Understanding on Article II:1(b)
        Understanding on Article XVII
        Understanding on Balance-of-Payments Provisions
        (including 1979 Declaration)
        Understanding on Article XXIV
        Understanding in Respect of Waivers
        Understanding on Article XXVIII
        Marrakesh Protocol
        Agreement on Agriculture
        Agreement on the Application of Sanitary and Phytosanitary Measures
        Agreement on Textiles and Clothing
        Agreement on Technical Barriers to Trade
        Agreement on Trade-Related Investment Measures
        Agreement on Implementation of Article VI
        Agreement on Implementation of Article VII
        Agreement on Preshipment Inspection
        Agreement on Rules of Origin
        Agreement on Import Licensing Procedures
        Agreement on Subsidies and Countervailing Measures
        Agreement on Safeguards
    ANNEX 1B: General Agreement on Trade in Services
    ANNEX 1C: Agreement on Trade-Related Aspects of Intellectual Property
    Rights

ANNEX 2: Understanding on Rules and Procedures Governing the Settlement
of Disputes

ANNEX 3: Trade Policy Review Mechanism

ANNEX 4: Plurilateral Trade Agreements
        Agreement on Trade in Civil Aircraft
        Agreement on Government Procurement
        International Dairy Agreement
        International Bovine Meat Agreement

## Ministerial Decisions and Declarations

Decision on Measures in Favour of Least-Developed Countries

Declaration on the Contribution of the World Trade Organization to Achieving Greater Coherence in Global Economic Policymaking

Decision on Notification Procedures

Declaration on the Relationship of the World Trade Organization with the International Monetary Fund

Decision on Measures Concerning the Possible Negative Effects of the Reform Programme on Least-Developed and Net Food-Importing Developing Countries

Decision and Declaration Relating to the Agreement on Implementation of Article VI of the General Agreement on Tariffs and Trade 1994

Decision Relating to the General Agreement on Trade in Services

Decision on Certain Dispute Settlement Procedures for the General Agreement on Trade in Services

Decision on Accession to the Agreement on Government Procurement

Decision on the Application and Review of the Understanding on Rules and Procedures Governing the Settlement of Disputes

Understanding on Commitments in Financial Services

**Note**

1. Taken from J. H. Jackson, W. J. Davey and A. O. Sykes, *Legal Problems of International Economic Relations* (St Paul, MN.: West Publishing 1995), Document Supplement.

# Appendix F
# General Agreement on Tariffs and Trade 1994[1]

1. The General Agreement on Tariffs and Trade 1994 ('GATT 1994') shall consist of:

(a) the provisions in the General Agreement on Tariffs and Trade, dated 30 October 1947, annexed to the Final Act Adopted at the Conclusion of the Second Session of the Preparatory Committee of the United Nations Conference on Trade and Employment (excluding the Protocol of Provisional Application), as rectified, amended or modified by the terms of legal instruments which have entered into force before the date of entry into force of the WTO agreement;

(b) The provisions of the legal instruments set forth below that have entered into force under the GATT 1947 before the date of entry into force of the WTO Agreement:

    (i) protocols and certifications relating to tariff concessions;

    (ii) protocols of accession (excluding the provisions (a) concerning provisional application and withdrawal of provisional application and (b) providing that Part II of GATT 1947 shall be applied provisionally to the fullest extent not inconsistent with legislation existing on the date of the Protocol);

    (iii) decisions on waivers granted under Article XXV of GATT 1947 and still in force on the date of entry into force of the WTO Agreement;

    (iv) other decisions of the CONTRACTING PARTIES to GATT 1947;

(c) the Understandings set forth below:

    (i) Understanding on the Interpretation of Article II:1(b) of the General Agreement on Tariffs and Trade 1994;

    (ii) Understanding on the Interpretation of Article XVII of the General Agreement on Tariffs and Trade 1994;

    (iii) Understanding on Balance-of-Payments Provisions of the General Agreement on Tariffs and Trade 1994;

    (iv) Understanding on the Interpretation of Article XXIV of the General Agreement on Tariffs and Trade 1994;

    (v) Understanding the Respect of Waivers of Obligations under the General Agreement on Tariffs and Trade 1994;

    (vi) Understanding on the Interpretation of Article XXVII of the General Agreement on Tariffs and Trade 1994; and

(d) the Marrakesh Protocol to GATT 1994.

2. Explanatory Notes

(a) The references to 'contracting party' in the provisions of GATT 1994 shall be deemed to read 'Member'. The references to 'less-developed contracting party' and 'developed contracting party' shall be deemed to read 'developing country Member' and 'developed country Member'. The references to 'Executive Secretary' shall be deemed to read 'Director-General of the WTO'.

(b) The references to the CONTRACTING PARTIES acting jointly in Articles XV:1, XV:2, XV:8, XXXVIII and the Notes Ad Article XII and XVIII; and in the provisions on special exchange agreements in Articles XV:2, XV:3, XV:6, XV:7, and XV:9 of GATT 1994 shall be deemed to be references to the WTO. The other functions that the provisions of GATT 1994 assign to the CONTRACTING PARTIES acting jointly shall be allocated by the Ministerial Conference.

(c) (i) The text of GATT 1994 shall be authentic in English, French and Spanish.

> (ii) The text of GATT 1994 in the French language shall be subject to the rectifications of terms indicated in Annex A to document MTN.TNC/41.

> (iii) The authentic text of GATT 1994 in the Spanish language shall be text in Volume IV of the Basic Instruments and Selected Documents series, subject to the rectifications of terms indicated in Annex B to document MTN.TNC/41

3. (a) The provisions of Part II of GATT 1994 shall not apply to measures taken by a Member under specific mandatory legislation, enacted by that Member before it became a contracting party to GATT 1947, that prohibits the use, sale or lease of foreign-built or foreign-reconstructed vessels in commercial applications between points in national waters or the waters of an exclusive economic zone. This exemption applied to: (a) the continuation or prompt renewal of a non-conforming provision of such legislation; and (b) the amendment to a non-conforming provision of such legislation to the extent that the amendment does not decrease the conformity to the provision with Part II of GATT 1947. This exemption is limited to measures taken under legislation described above that is notified and specified prior to the date of entry into force of the WTO Agreement. If such legislation is subsequently modified to decrease its conformity with Part II of GATT 1994, it will no longer qualify for coverage under this paragraph.

(b) The Ministerial Conference shall review this exemption not later than five years after the date of entry into force of the WTO Agreement and thereafter every two years for as long as the exemption is in force for the purpose of examining whether the conditions which created the need for the exemption still prevail.

(c) A Member whose measures are covered by this exemption shall annually submit a detailed statistical notification consisting of a five-year moving average of actual and expected deliveries of relevant vessels as well as additional information on the use, sale, lease or repair of relevant vessels covered by this exemption.

(d) A Member that considered that this exemption operates in such a manner as to justify a reciprocal and proportionate limitation on the use, sale, the exemption shall be free to introduce such a limitation subject to prior notification to the Ministerial Conference.

(e) This exemption is without prejudice to solutions concerning specific aspects of the legislation covered by this exemption negotiated in sectoral agreements or in other fora.

**Note**

1. Taken from J. H. Jackson, W. J. Davey and A. O. Sykes, *Legal Problems of International Economic Relations* (St Paul, MN.: West Publishing 1995), Document Supplement.

# Appendix G
# Ministerial Declaration on the Uruguay Round

## DECLARATION OF 20 SEPTEMBER 1986

Ministers, meeting on the occasion of the Special Session of the Contracting Parties at Punta del Este, have decided to launch Multilateral Trade Negotiations (The Uruguay Round). To this end, they have adopted the following Declaration. The Multilateral Trade Negotiations will be open to the participation of countries as indicated in Parts I and II of this Declaration. A Trade Negotiations committee is established to carry out the negotiations. The Trade Negotiations Committee shall hold its first meeting not later than 31 October 1986 It shall meet as appropriate at Ministerial level. The Multilateral Trade Negotiations will be concluded within four years.

## PART I
### Negotiations on Trade in Goods

The Contracting Parties meeting at Ministerial level

Determined to halt and reverse protectionism and to remove distortions to trade

Determined also to preserve the basic principles and to further the objectives of the GATT

Determined also to develop a more open, viable and durable multilateral trading system

Convinced that such action would promote growth and development

Mindful of the negative effects of prolonged financial and monetary instability in the world economy, the indebtedness of a large number of less developed contracting parties, and considering the linkage between trade, money, finance and development

Decide to enter into Multilateral Trade Negotiations on trade in goods within the framework and under the aegis of the General Agreement on Tariff and Trade.

## A. Objectives
Negotiations shall aim to:
(i)  bring about further liberalization and expansion of world trade to the benefit of all countries, especially less developed contracting parties, including the improvement of access to markets by the reduction and elimination of tariffs, quantitative restrictions and other non-tariff measures and obstacles;
(ii) strengthen the role of GATT, improve the multilateral trading system based on the principles and rules of the GATT and bring about a wider coverage of world trade under agreed, effective and enforceable multilateral disciplines;

180

(iii) increase the responsiveness of the GATT system to the evolving international economic environment, through facilitating necessary structural adjustment, enhancing the relationship of the GATT with the relevant international organizations and taking account of changes in trade patterns and prospects, including the growing importance of trade in high technology products, serious difficulties in commodity markets and the importance of an improved trading environment providing, inter alia, for the ability of indebted countries to meet their financial obligations;

(iv) foster concurrent cooperative action at the national and international levels to strengthen the interrelationship between trade policies and other economic policies affecting growth and development, and to contribute towards continued, effective and determined efforts to improve the functioning of the international monetary system and the flow of financial and real investment resources to developing countries.

## B. General Principles Governing Negotiations

(i) Negotiations shall be conducted in a transparent manner, and consistent with the objectives and commitments agreed in this Declaration and with the principles of the General Agreement in order to ensure mutual advantage and increased benefits to all participants.

(ii) The launching, the conduct and the implementation of the outcome of the negotiations shall be treated as parts of a single undertaking. However, agreements reached at an early stage may be implemented on a provisional or a definitive basis by agreement prior to the formal conclusion of the negotiations. Early agreements shall be taken into account in assessing the overall balance of the negotiations.

(iii) Balanced concessions should be sought within broad trading areas and subjects to be negotiated in order to avoid unwarranted cross-sectoral demands.

(iv) The Contracting Parties agree that the principle of differential and more favourable treatment embodied in Part IV and other relevant provisions of the General Agreement and in the Decision of the Contracting Parties of 28 November 1979 on Differential and More Favourable Treatment, Reciprocity and Fuller Participation of Developing Countries applies to the negotiations. In the implementation of standstill and rollback, particular care should be given to avoiding disruptive effects on the trade of less-developed contracting parties.

(v) The developed countries do not expect reciprocity for commitments made by them in trade negotiations to reduce or remove tariffs and other barriers to the trade of developing countries, i.e. the developed countries do not expect the developing countries, in the course of trade negotiations, to make contributions which are inconsistent with their individual development, financial and trade needs. Developed contracting parties shall therefore not seek, neither shall less-developed contracting parties be required to make, concessions that are inconsistent with the latter's development, financial and trade needs.

(vi) Less-developed contracting parties expect that their capacity to make contributions or negotiated concessions or take other mutually agreed action under the provisions and procedures of the General Agreement would improve with the progressive development of their economies and improvement in their trade situation and they would accordingly expect to participate more fully in the framework of rights and obligations under the General Agreement.

(vii) Special attention shall be given to the particular situation and problems of the least-developed countries and to the need to encourage positive measures to facilitate expansion of their trading opportunities. Expeditious implementa-tion of the relevant provisions of the 1982 Ministerial Declaration concerning the least developed countries shall also be given appropriate attention.

## C. Standstill and Rollback

Commencing immediately and continuing until the formal completion of the negotiations, each participant agrees to apply the following commitments:

*Standstill*

(i) not to take any trade restrictive or distorting measure inconsistent with the provisions of the General Agreement or the Instruments negotiated within the framework of GATT or under its auspices;

(ii) not to take any trade restrictive or distorting measure in the legitimate exercise of its GATT rights, that would go beyond that which is necessary to remedy specific situations, as provided for in the General Agreement and the Instruments referred to in (i) above;

(iii) not to take any trade measures in such a manner as to improve its negotiating positions.

*Rollback*

(i) that all trade restrictive or distorting measures inconsistent with the provisions of the General Agreement or Instruments negotiated within the framework of GATT or under its auspices, shall be phased out or brought into conformity within an agreed time frame not later than by the date of the formal completion of the negotiations, taking into account multilateral agreements, undertakings and understandings, including strengthened rules and disciplines, reached in pursuance of the Objectives of the Negotiations;

(ii) there shall be progressive implementation of this commitment on an equitable basis in consultations among participants concerned, including all affected participants. This commitment shall take account of the concerns expressed by any participant about measures directly affecting its trade interests;

(iii) there shall be no GATT concessions requested for the elimination of these measures.

*Surveillance of standstill and rollback*
Each participant agrees that the implementation of these commitments on stand-still and rollback shall be subject to multilateral surveillance so as to ensure that these commitments are being met. The Trade Negotiations Committee will decide on the appropriate mechanisms to carry the surveillance, including periodic reviews and evaluations. Any participant may bring to the attention of the appropriate surveillance mechanism any actions or omissions it believes to be relevant to the fulfillment of these commitments. These notifications should be addressed to the GATT secretariat which may also provide further relevant information.

## D. Subjects for Negotiation
*Tariffs*
Negotiations shall aim, by appropriate methods, to reduce or, as appropriate, eliminate tariffs including the reduction or elimination of high tariffs and tariff escalation. Emphasis shall be given to the expansion of the scope of tariff concessions among all participants.

*Non-tariff measures*
Negotiations shall aim to reduce or eliminate non-tariff measures, including quantitative restrictions, without prejudice to any action to be taken in fulfillment of the rollback commitments.

*Tropical products*
Negotiations shall aim at the fullest liberalization of trade in tropical products, including in their processed and semi-processed forms, and shall cover both tariff and all non-tariff measures affecting trade in these products.

The CONTRACTING PARTIES recognize the importance of trade in tropical products to a large number of less developed contracting parties and agree that negotiations in this area shall receive special attention, including the timing of the negotiations and the implementation of the results as provided for in B(ii).

*Natural resource-based products*
Negotiations shall aim to achieve the fullest liberalization of trade in natural resource-based products, including in their processed and semi-processed forms. The negotiations shall aim to reduce or eliminate tariff and non-tariff measures, including tariff escalation.

*Textiles and clothing*
Negotiations in the area of textiles and clothing shall aim to formulate modalities that would permit the eventual integration of this sector into GATT on the basis of strengthened GATT rules and disciplines, thereby also contributing to the objective of further liberalization of trade.

## Appendix G

### Agriculture

The CONTRACTING PARTIES agree that there is an urgent need to bring more discipline and predictability to world agricultural trade by correcting and preventing restrictions and distortions including those related to structural surpluses so as to reduce the uncertainty, imbalances and instability in world agricultural markets.

Negotiations shall aim to achieve greater liberalization of trade in agriculture and bring all measures affecting import access and export competition under strengthened and more operationally effective GATT rules and disciplines, taking into account the general principles governing the negotiations, by:

(i)  improving market access through, inter alia, the reduction of import barriers;

(ii)  improving the competitive environment by increasing discipline on the use of all direct and indirect subsidies and other measures affecting directly or indirectly agricultural trade, including the phased reduction of their negative effects and dealing with their causes;

(iii)  minimizing the adverse effects that sanitary and phytosanitary regulations and barriers can have on trade in agriculture, taking into account the relevant international agreements.

In order to achieve the above objectives, the negotiating group having primary responsibility for all aspects of agriculture will use the Recommendations adopted by the CONTRACTING PARTIES at their Fortieth Session which were developed in accordance with the GATT 1982 Ministerial Work Programme, and take account of the approaches suggested in the work of the Committee on Trade in Agriculture without prejudice to other alternatives that might achieve the objectives of the negotiations.

### GATT Articles

Participants shall review existing GATT Articles,, provisions and disciplines as requested by interested contracting parties, and as appropriate, undertake negotiations.

### Safeguards

(i)  A comprehensive agreement on safeguards is of particular importance to the strengthening of the GATT system and to progress in the Multilateral Trade Negotiations.

(ii)  The agreement on safeguards:
  –  shall be based on the basic principles of the General Agreement;
  –  shall contain, inter alia, the following elements: transparency, coverage, objective criteria for action including the concept of serious injury or

184

threat thereof, temporary nature, degressivity and structural adjustment, compensation and retaliation, notification, consultation, multilateral surveillance and dispute settlement; and

- shall clarify and reinforce the disciplines of the General Agreement and should apply to all contracting parties.

## MTN Agreements and Arrangements

Negotiations shall aim to improve, clarify, or expand, as appropriate, Agreements and Arrangements negotiated in the Tokyo Round of Multilateral Negotiations.

## Subsidies and countervailing measures

Negotiations on subsidies and countervailing measures shall be based on a review of Articles VI and XVI and the MTN agreement on subsidies and countervailing measures with the objective of improving GATT disciplines relating to all subsidies and countervailing measures that affect international trade. A negotiating group will be established to deal with these issues.

## Dispute settlement

In order to ensure prompt and effective resolution of disputes to the benefit of all contracting parties, negotiations shall aim to improve and strengthen the rules and the procedures of the dispute settlement process, while recognizing the contribution that would be made by more effective and enforceable GATT rules and disciplines. Negotiations shall include the development of adequate arrangements for overseeing and monitoring of the procedures that would facilitate compliance with adopted recommendations.

## Trade-related aspects of intellectual property rights, including trade in counterfeit goods

In order to reduce the distortions and impediments to international trade, and taking into account the need to promote effective and adequate protection of intellectual property rights, and to ensure that measures and procedures to enforce intellectual property rights do not themselves become barriers to legitimate trade, the negotiations shall aim to clarify GATT provisions and elaborate as appropriate new rules and disciplines.

Negotiations shall aim to develop a multilateral framework of principles, rules and disciplines dealing with international trade in counterfeit goods, taking into account work already undertaken in the GATT.

These negotiations shall be without prejudice to other complementary initiatives that may be taken in the World Intellectual Property Organization and elsewhere to deal with these matters.

## Trade-related investment measures

Following an examination of the operation of GATT Articles related to the trade restrictive and distorting effects of investment measures, negotiations should elaborate, as appropriate, further provisions that may be necessary to avoid such adverse effects on trade.

### E. Functioning of the GATT System
Negotiations shall aim to develop understandings and arrangements:
(i) to enhance the surveillance in the GATT to enable regular monitoring of trade policies and practices of contracting parties and their impact on the functioning of the multilateral trading system;
(ii) to improve the overall effectiveness and decision-making of the GATT as an institution, including, inter alia, through involvement of Ministers;
(iii) to increase the contribution of the GATT to achieving greater coherence in global economic policy-making through strengthening its relationship with other international organizations responsible for monetary and financial matters.

### F. Participation
(a) Negotiations will be open to:
    (i) all contracting parties,
    (ii) countries having acceded provisionally,
    (iii) countries applying the GATT on a de facto basis having announced, not later than 30 April 1987, their intention to accede to the GATT and to participate in the negotiations,
    (iv) countries that have already informed the CONTRACTING PARTIES, at a regular meeting of the Council of Representatives, of their intention to negotiate the terms of their membership as a contracting party, and
    (v) developing countries that have, by 30 April 1987, initiated procedures for accession to the GATT, with the intention of negotiating the terms of their accession during the course of the negotiations.
(b) Participation in negotiations relating to the amendment or application of GATT provisions or the negotiation of new provisions will, however, be open only to contracting parties.

### G. Organization of the Negotiations
A Group of Negotiations on Goods (GNG) is established to carry out the programme of negotiations contained in this Part of the Declaration. The GNG shall, inter alia:
(i) elaborate and put into effect detailed trade negotiating plans prior to 19 December 1986;
(ii) designate the appropriate mechanism for surveillance of commitments to standstill and rollback;
(iii) establish negotiating groups as required. Because of the interrelationship of some issues and taking fully into account the general principles governing the negotiations as stated in B(ii) above it is recognized that aspects of one issue may be discussed in more than one negotiating group. Therefore each

negotiating group should as required take into account relevant aspects emerging in other groups;

(iv) also decide upon inclusion of additional subject matters in the negotiation;

(v) co-ordinate the work of the negotiating groups and supervise the progress of the negotiations. As a guideline not more than two negotiating groups should meet at the same time;

(vi) the GNG shall report to the Trade Negotiations Committee.

In order to ensure effective application of differential and more favourable treatment the GNG shall, before the formal completion of the negotiations, conduct an evaluation of the results attained therein in terms of the objectives and the General Principles Governing Negotiations as set out in the Declaration, taking into account all issues of interest to less-developed contracting parties.

## PART II
### Negotiations on Trade in Services

Ministers also decide, as part of the Multilateral Trade Negotiations, to launch negotiations on trade in services.

Negotiations in this area shall aim to establish a multilateral framework of principles and rules for trade in services, including elaboration of possible disciplines for individual sectors, with a view to expansion of such trade under conditions of transparency and progressive liberalization and as a means of promoting economic growth of all trading partners and the development of developing countries. Such framework shall respect the policy objectives of national laws and regulations applying to services and shall take into account the work of relevant international organizations.

GATT procedures and practices shall apply to these negotiations. A Group of Negotiations on Services is established to deal with these matters. Participation in the negotiations under this Part of the Declaration will be open to the same countries as under this Part I. GATT secretariat support will be provided, with technical support from other organizations as decided by the Group of Negotiations on Services.

The Group of Negotiations on Services shall report to the Trade Negotiations Committee

## IMPLEMENTATION OF RESULTS UNDER PARTS I AND II

When the results of the Multilateral Trade Negotiations in all areas have been established, Ministers meeting also on the occasion of a Special Session CONTRACTING PARTIES shall decide regarding the international implementation of the respective results.

187

## Statement by the Chairman
## of the Ministerial Meeting

Before proposing adoption of the Ministerial Declaration on the Uruguay Round, the CHAIRMAN noted that the purpose of the Declaration was to launch multilateral trade negotiations on goods and services. This involved taking three decisions: the first would be to adopt, as the CONTRACTING PARTIES, Part I of the Declaration, relating to negotiations on trade in goods; the second would be to adopt Part II, on trade in services, as representatives of Governments meeting on the occasion of the Special Session of the CONTRACTING PARTIES at Punta del Este; thirdly, again as representatives of Governments meeting on the occasion of the Special Session of the CONTRACTING PARTIES at Punta del Este, to adopt the Declaration as a whole.

He then made the following specific points:

Representatives of certain governments had expressed concern regarding a number of problems relating, in particular, to commodities, natural resource-based products and tropical products. Those governments were concerned that solutions to their problems be found and implemented quickly. Specific proposals had been put forward by certain African governments in MIN(86)/W/18. While he was sure that this conference attached great importance to those concerns, it had not been possible to complete consideration of the proposals at the conference. It had, therefore, been agreed that the proposals would be considered by the Trade Negotiations Committee foreseen in the Declaration.

In order to participate fully in the negotiations, developing countries would require technical support. There was agreement that technical support by the Secretariat, adequately strengthened, should be available to developing countries participating in the negotiations.

Some governments had expressed concern over trade measures applied for non-economic reasons.

He then summarized discussions that had taken place on the objectives of the negotiations:

- There had been a proposal to include, among the objectives of the negotiations, that of redressing growing disequilibria in world trade and of achieving, in the spirit of the Preamble to the General Agreement, a greater mutuality of interests.
- However, it had been represented that the foregoing proposal might lead to a trading system incompatible with the basic objectives and principles of GATT, the guarantor of the open and non-discriminatory trading system.
- Nevertheless, it was common ground that growing disequilibria in world trade constituted a serious problem and would need to be tackled by the countries concerned by various policy means including macro-economic policy, exchange rates, structural reform and trade policy.
- It was furthermore agreed that in the negotiations every contracting party should make genuine efforts to ensure mutual advantages and increased

benefits to all participants, in accordance with the principles of the GATT.

Some proposals had been received regarding the setting up of negotiating groups for the negotiations. These proposals would be formally circulated after the Session.

He noted that there were certain issues raised by delegations on which a consensus to negotiate could not be reached at this time. These issues included the export of hazardous substances, commodity arrangements, restrictive business practices and workers' rights.

He then clarified that it was understood that paragraph F(b) was interpreted as meaning that (a) all participants in the multilateral trade negotiations have the right to participate in all negotiations on all issues and that (b) non-contracting parties shall only be precluded from participation in decisions of contracting parties relating to the results of these negotiations.

The conference had noted requests by certain governments, not at present covered by the provisions in the Declaration on participation, to take part in the multilateral trade negotiations. The Director-General was authorized, upon request by such governments, to keep them informed of progress in the negotiations..

The CONTRACTING PARTIES adopted Part 1 of the Declaration.

Delegations made statements.[1]

The CHAIRMAN then addressed participants as representatives of Governments meeting on the occasion of the Special Session of the CONTRACTING PARTIES at Punta del Este.

He stated that a number of the agreed points that he had read out before the adoption of Part I of the Declaration also applied to Part II.

The representatives of Governments meeting on the occasion of the Special Session of the CONTRACTING PARTIES at Punta del Este adopted Part II of the Declaration.

These representatives then adopted the Declaration as a whole as a single political undertaking launching the Uruguay Round.

**Note**

1. Reflected in the Summary Records.

# Appendix H
# Document List

John H. Jackson, William J. Davey and Alan O. Sykes, 1995 Documents Supplement to *Legal Problems of International Economic Relations* (3rd edn) (St Paul, MN: West Publishing, 1995).

*Analytical Index: Guide to GATT Law and Practice* (Geneva: World Trade Organization, 1995).

Frances Williams, 'WTO: Sets Up Panel to Probe US Shrimp Row', *The Financial Times*, 26 February 1997.

Uruguay Round Agreements Act, Public Law no. 103-465; 108 Stat. 4809 (1994).

Final Act Embodying the Results of the Uruguay Round of Multilateral Trade Negotiations, 15 April 1994, *Legal Instruments – Results of the Uruguay Round* Vol. 1 (1994), 33 I.L.M. 1125 (1994).

General Agreement on Tariffs and Trade, 30 October 1947, 61 Stat. A-11, T.I.A.S. 1700, 55 U.N.T.S. 194.

Montreal/Geneva Mid-Term Review. Decisions adopted at the Mid-Term Review of the Uruguay Round, 28 I.L.M. 1025 (1989).

*Singapore Ministerial Declaration*, Adopted 13 December 1996, WTO Doc. WT/MIN(96)/DEC 18 December 1996.

*US Standards for Reformulated and Conventional Gasoline*, Appellate Body Report and Panel Report, World Trade Organization, WT/DS2/9, 20 May 1996.

*US Taxes on Automobiles*, DS31/R. Geneva, 1994.

*US Restrictions on Imports of Cotton & Man-Made Fibre: Underwear*, Complaint by Costa Rica. WT/DS24. Geneva, 1997 (adopted by the Dispute Settlement Body on 25 February 1997).

*Japan – Taxes on Alcoholic Beverages*, Report of the Appellate Body, World Trade Organization, WT/DS8,10,11/AB/R, 4 October 1996.

*Overview of the State-of-Play of WTO Disputes* >http://www.wto.org/wto/dispute/bulletin.html<

*GATT Focus* and *WTO Focus*. Under GATT, and now under the WTO, the organization published a brief newsletter with developments outlined and some documents included. These are public and quite useful. The new series, *WTO Focus*, started in January/February 1995 with issue no. 1, and, as of March 1998, had reached issue no. 28. See especially: *GATT Focus*, no. 104, December 1993: 'The Final Act of the Uruguay Round: A Summary'; *GATT Focus*, no. 107, Special Issue, May 1994: 'Marrakesh Ministerial Meeting. The WTO Is Born'; *GATT Focus*, no. 113, Final Issue, December 1994: 'Implementation Conference, The WTO Enters Into Force'; *WTO Focus*, no. 1 (January 1995): 'Appellate Body Established'.

BISD. The most significant set of GATT documents is the BISD, *Basic*

*Instruments and Selected Documents*, which have been published annually over virtually all of the history of the GATT. They are usually cited by 'supplement number', but virtually all of the issues are so-called 'supplements'. Supplement 40 contains documents of 1992 and 1993. There are projections to complete the set with an additional one or two supplements, but as of May 1998 it is unclear when these will be published. The BISD generally contains most of the panel reports that were adopted under the GATT. The WTO is developing a programme of publishing all the panel reports as they are made public (much faster than under the GATT), but publishing details have not yet been announced. Most of the GATT dispute settlement panel reports, and so far all of the published WTO panel and appellate body reports, can be found in the Web pages of the WTO Web site, http://www.wto.org.

### Documents for the 1990 Brussels Ministerial Conference
There are numerous official documents for the preparation and conduct of this meeting. Preparatory work can be found at:

GATT Fiche:
> 89-1133 MF: 'TNC Agrees on Final Ministerial Meeting in Brussels in Period 26 November–8 December 1990'.
> 90-0029 MF: 'Many New Proposals Tabled as Year Ends – TNC Decides Dates for Brussels Ministerial Meeting'.

Other documents can be found at:
> 90-1758 MF: 'Uruguay Round: Closing Statement by Dr Hector Gros Espiell, Chairman of the Ministerial Meeting of the Trade Negotiations Committee, Brussels 7 December 1990'.
> MTN.TNC/W/35: 'Draft Text of the Final Act as issued 26 November 1990 for the Ministerial Meeting held at Brussels in December 1990'.
> MTN.TNC/MIN(90): 'Trade Negotiations Committee – Meeting at Ministerial Level, Brussels, 1990: Documents'.

The best sources for GATT information apart from official documents are the publications *GATT Focus* and *Inside US Trade*. These have detailed coverage of the Brussels Ministerial, its preparatory work, and coverage of the impasse that resulted.

### Documents for the 1996 Singapore Ministerial Conference
The *Singapore Ministerial Declaration* can be found at 36 I.L.M. 218 (1997). Coverage of the preparatory work can be found in the *WTO Focus* (successor to *GATT Focus*) and *Inside US Trade*. The *Information Technology Agree-ment*, which was agreed to at the Singapore Conference but was formally concluded in early 1997, appears at 36 I.L.M. 375 (1997).

# Appendix I
## Select Bibliography

Aaronson, S.A., *Trade and the American Dream: A Social History of Postwar Trade Policy* (Lexington, KY: University of Kentucky Press, 1996).

Bhagwati, J. and Hudec, R.E. (eds), *Fair Trade and Harmonization: Prerequisites for Free Trade?* (Cambridge, MA: MIT Press, 1996).

Bourgeois, J.H.J., Berrod, F., and Fournier, E.G. (eds), *The Uruguay Round Results: A European Lawyers' Perspective* (Brussels: European Interuniversity Press, 1995).

Croley, S. and. Jackson, J.H., 'WTO Dispute Procedures, Standard of Review, and Deference to National Governments', *American Journal of International Law*, 90 (1997): 2.

Croome, J., *Reshaping the World Trading System: A History of the Uruguay Round* (Geneva: WTO, 1995).

Davey, W.J., *Pine and Swine: Canada–United States Trade Dispute Settlement – the FTA Experience and NAFTA Prospects* (Ottawa: Centre for Trade Policy and Law, 1996).

Fretillet, J.-P., and Veglio, C., *Le GATT démystifié* (Paris: Syros, 1994).

Hart, M., *Canadian Economic Development and the International Trading System: Constraints and Opportunities* (Toronto: University of Toronto Press, 1985).

Hart, M., *Decision at Midnight: Inside the Canada–U.S. Free Trade Negotiations* (Vancouver: UBC Press, 1994).

Hoekman, B.M., and Kostecki, M.M., *The Political Economy of the World Trading System: From GATT to the WTO* (Oxford and New York: Oxford University Press, 1995).

Hudec, R.E., *The GATT Legal System and World Trade Diplomacy,* 2nd edn (Salem, MA: Butterworth Legal Publishers, 1990).

Hudec, M.E., *Enforcing International Trade Law, The Evolution of the Modern GATT Legal System* (Salem, MA: Butterworth Legal Publishers, 1993).

Iwasawa, Y., *WTO No Funso Shori* (The Dispute Settlement of the World Trade Organization) (in Japanese) (Tokyo: Sanseido, 1995).

Jackson, J.H., 'The Legal Meaning of a GATT Dispute Settlement Report: Some Reflections', in N. Blokker and S. Muller (eds), *Towards More Effective Supervision by International Organizations, Essays in Honor of Henry G. Schermers*, Vol. 1 (Boston, MA: Kluwer Academic, 1994).

Jackson, J.H., *Restructuring the GATT System* (London: Royal Institute of International Affairs/Pinter, 1990).

Jackson, J.H., *World Trade and the Law of GATT: Treaties on a Legal Analysis of the General Agreement on Tariffs and Trade* (Indianapolis, IN: Bobbs-Merrill, 1969).

Jackson, J.H., *The World Trading System: Law and Policy of International Economic Relations* (Cambridge, MA: MIT Press, 1989; 2nd edn 1997).

Jackson, J.H., 'The World Trade Organization: Watershed Innovation or Cautious Small Step Forward?', *World Economics,* 11 (1995): pp. 11-31.

Jackson, J.H., 'The WTO Dispute Settlement Understanding – Misunderstandings on the Nature of Legal Obligation', *American Journal of International Law,* 90 (1997): 60.

Jackson, J.H., Davey, W.J., and Sykes, A.O., *Legal Problems of International Economic Relations: Cases, Materials and Text on the National and International Regulation of Transnational Economic Relations* (St Paul, MN: West Publishing, 1995).

Jackson, J.H., and Sykes, A.O., *Implementing the Uruguay Round* (Oxford: Clarendon Press, 1997).

Kenen, P.B. (ed.), *Managing the World Economy: Fifty Years after Bretton Woods* (Washington, DC: Institute for International Economics, 1994).

Organization for Economic Cooperation and Development, *Assessing the Effects of the Uruguay Round* (Paris: OECD, 1993).

Paemen, H., and Bensch, A., *From GATT to the WTO: The European Community in the Uruguay Round* (Leuven: Leuven University Press, 1995).

Pescatore, P., Davey, W.J., and Lowenfeld, A., *Handbook of GATT Dispute Settlement* (Irvington-on-Hudson, NY: Kluwer Law International, 1995).

Petersmann, E.-U., 'How to Promote the International Rule of Law? Contributions by the World Trade Organization Appellate Review System', *Journal of International Economic Law,* 1 (1998): 25.

Preeg, E., *Traders in a Brave New World: The Uruguay Round and the Future of the International Trading System* (Chicago, IL: University of Chicago Press, 1995).

Qureshi, A.H., *The World Trade Organization: Implementing International Trade Norms* (Manchester and New York: Manchester University Press, 1996).

Schott, J.J., *The Uruguay Round: An Assessment* (Washington, DC: Institute for International Economics, 1994).

Schott, J.J. (ed.), *The World Trading System: Challenges Ahead* (Washington, DC: Institute for International Economics, 1996).

Stewart, T. (ed.), *The World Trade Organization: the Multilateral Trade Framework for the 21st Century and US Implementing Legislation* (Washington DC: American Bar Association, 1996).

Swacker, F.W., Redden, K., and Wenger, L., *World Trade without Barriers: The World Trade Organization (WTO) and Dispute Resolution* (Charlottesville, VA: Michie Co./Butterworth, 1995).